This book is a must-read if…

- you find yourself swallowing words to keep the peace, yet long for deeper, more honest relationships

- your childhood taught you to be quiet, to be "good", or to hide how you truly felt – and now you are ready to reclaim your voice

- anxiety creeps into your conversations, leaving you either silent or saying things you later regret

- you are navigating a divorce, separation, or major relationship change, and want to speak your truth with clarity, not chaos

- you are a parent wanting to guide your child through emotional storms with calm, attuned communication rather than control

- your relationships feel strained, stuck, or surface-level – and you are ready to repair, reset, or release what no longer serves you

- you have been the "strong one" for too long, and now you want tools that support both courage and gentleness

- you are curious about the hidden emotional maps we all carry – and how understanding yours can bring relief and renewal

- you want a guide that speaks not only to your mind but to your heart – with stories, science, poetry, and soul

# Praise for *Conversations at the Shoreline*

"Eve has written an immensely powerful book because she writes from the perspective of a fellow learner, someone who has faced significant challenges of her own and overcome them through difficult conversations."

Suzanne Heywood<br>
Author of *Wavewalker*

"A calming and yet empowering read, packed full of practical advice. Eve uses a wonderful blend of therapy, coaching, and real-life experiences. This book takes you on a healing journey which I know will help many people."

Sara Davison<br>
The Divorce Coach, author, coach,<br>
trainer and podcast host

"Eve Stanway is a fountain of essential knowledge when it comes to relationships, communication, boundaries, and break-ups. The world would be a better place if more of us knew how to advocate for our needs with skill and kindness. The tools, wisdom, and stories Eve shares in this book will change the way you think about difficult conversations forever.

I recommend reading if you want to learn how to hold your own, and hold the people around you with care."

Anna Herber<br>
Writer, witch, creator of Message Alignment

"Everyone needs a sprinkle of Eve's wisdom in their lives. Her thoughtful and beautifully crafted *Conversations at the Shoreline* is a gift to us all.

With courage, grace and relatability, Eve offers a glimpse into her extraordinary story and learnings – while gently inviting us to explore and express our own inner truths and voices in a way that brings meaning and connection. Compassion, curiosity and a sense of calm flow through Eve's words; hope and inspiration float from the pages.

This is a truly special book that I will read and learn from over and over – tender, insightful, and empowering."

GL<br/>Client

"We all struggle with having difficult conversations. What makes this book so powerful is Eve's vivid use of storytelling, which gently guides you to understand how to communicate more effectively. In showing that she understands, you no longer feel alone. Everyone needs to read this book – the world will be a much better place when we all become more adept at having difficult conversations."

Nicola J Rowley<br/>Author, speaker and The Power of Storytelling Podcast host

"As someone who teaches the power of storytelling for connection, this book cut right to the core of me.

*Conversations at the Shoreline* isn't just a guide, it's a lifeline for anyone who's ever struggled to find the words, or feared what might happen if they finally spoke them out loud. Eve writes with such intimacy, clarity, and quiet strength that I felt held from the very first page. Her storytelling is tender, courageous, and precise. She doesn't just tell stories – she teaches us how to listen to our own.

I found myself pausing again and again, not because I was lost, but because I was found. Seen. There's a kind of emotional truth in these pages that makes you sit up straighter and breathe deeper. The Magic Three framework is practical, but it's the emotional invitation behind it – the call to reclaim your voice. That truly stays with you.

For anyone who speaks, teaches, writes, or holds space for others, this book is a reminder that vulnerability isn't a crack in the foundation, it *is* the foundation. I'll be recommending this to every client, every friend, and keeping it close for myself, too."

Arif Isikgun<br>
Founder of Ai Beauty Consultancy

*Conversations at the Shoreline* is a courageous project showing how its readers can likewise be courageous and find, as the author did, a path from the shadows to the light of self-discovery and meaningful communications. With unflinching honesty and emotional depth, the author invites readers into her world, not to dwell on the pain, but to witness the resilience that bloomed from it.

This book is a lifeline. A guide. A powerful reminder that no matter what, living a fulfilling life is possible, and our voices, long silenced by fear or shame, can rise again, stronger than ever.

I wholeheartedly recommend this book to anyone who has endured, to those on their own healing journey, and to anyone seeking to better understand how to speak up and speak out. It is a testament to human resilience and the power of reclaiming one's narrative.

Prepare to be inspired, to cry, and ultimately, to feel a quiet kind of hope settle in your heart."

Fiona Biddle<br>Author and host of Therapy Natters Podcast

"Empowering, insightful, and above all, personal. Eve writes with such skill and warmth, it feels less like a book and more like a warm hug."

JB<br>Client

# Conversations at the Shoreline

### Dare to Speak

Navigate Life's Toughest Conversations
with Confidence and Clarity

Eve Stanway

First published in Great Britain in 2025
by Book Brilliance Publishing
265A Fir Tree Road, Epsom, Surrey, KT17 3LF
+44 (0)20 8641 5090
www.bookbrilliancepublishing.com
admin@bookbrilliancepublishing.com

© Copyright Eve Stanway 2025
Back cover photo: Vicki Head Photography

The moral right of Eve Stanway to be identified as
the author of this work has been asserted in accordance
with the Copyright, Designs and Patents Acts 1988.

All rights reserved. No part of this publication may be reproduced, stored in a retrieval system, or transmitted, in any form or by any means without the prior written permission of the publisher, nor be otherwise circulated in any form of binding or cover than that in which it is published and without similar condition being imposed on the subsequent purchaser.

A CIP catalogue record for this book
is available at the British Library.

ISBN 978-1-917534-02-4

Some names and identifying details have been
changed to protect the privacy of individuals.

Although the author and publisher have made every effort to ensure that the information in this book was correct at press time, the author and publisher do not assume and hereby disclaim any liability to any party for any loss, damage, or disruption caused by errors or omissions, whether such errors or omissions result from negligence, accident, or any other cause.

For my children, Lucy and Michael.
Through you, I have rediscovered the world –
its wonder, its lessons, its truths.
You are my greatest teachers,
and my truest anchors,
holding me steady as I grew alongside you.

And for all my clients
who have shared their stories,
daring to speak the words that matter most,
and which are so often the hardest to say.

# Contents

Author's Note ................................................................. 1
Prologue: Casting Spoons into the Deep ........................... 3
Your Compass: Steering Through the Chapters ................ 7
Introduction: Setting Sail on Difficult Conversations ........ 7

## Setting Sail: Understanding the Waters     21

**Part 1: Lost at Sea:**
**The Challenge of Finding Your Own Voice** ................ 23

   Introduction: Becalmed in Silence:
   Finding Your Own Voice ............................................. 23

   The Hidden World of Childhood Emotions ............... 27

   The Magic Three: A Framework for Speaking and
   Being Heard ................................................................. 33

   The Three Steps: Clarify, Communicate, and Correct .... 36

   The Magic Three Framework:
   A Steady Approach to Difficult Conversations ........... 38

   Eve's Anchor ................................................................ 40

   A Poem for Those Who Dare to Speak ..................... 43

**Part 2: Holding the Storm Within:**
**The Silent Impact of Suppression** ............................... 45

   Introduction: The Lingering Effects of Silence ........... 45

   The Roots of Silence in Mental Health Issues ............ 52

   The Physical Impact of Suppression and Repression .... 55

   Breaking the Silence: The Power of
   Difficult Conversations ................................................ 58

   The Magic Three Framework for Breaking Silence .... 62

   The Benefits of Breaking Silence ................................ 64

The Role of Grounding for Managing Overwhelming
Emotions .................................................................................. 66

**Part 3: Mapping the Currents:
Understanding What Lies Beneath** ................................... **71**
Facing the Challenge of Difficult Conversations ................. 71
The Benefits of Undertaking Difficult Conversations .......... 73
The Two Conversations in Every Difficult Conversation ..... 75
The Brain's Role in High-Stakes Conversations .................. 78
Quick Calm Strategies for Difficult Conversations .............. 81
Preparing for a Positive Conversation ................................. 84

# Charting the Course:
# Preparing for the Journey     91

**Part 4: Camouflaged Sailors:
Disguises We Use to Navigate Emotional Seas** ................. **93**
Eve's Reflections by the Shoreline ....................................... 93
The Origins of Our Masks .................................................... 98
The Costs of Covering Up .................................................. 105
Creating Safe Spaces for Vulnerability .............................. 107
Practical Strategies for Reclaiming Authenticity ............... 109
Embracing Authenticity in Different Relationships ........... 114
Curiosity and Play in Rediscovering Authenticity ............. 117

**Part 5: Finding a Safe Harbour: Tools to Anchor
Emotional Security** ........................................................... **123**
Introduction: Preparing for Meaningful Communication ... 123
Cultivating Curiosity as a Foundation for Difficult
Conversations Is Essential ................................................. 127
Embracing Self-Affirmation as a Tool for Confidence ........ 129
The Concept of Healthy Masks as Boundaries .................. 131
Reframing "No" as Self-Care .............................................. 133
Practising Authenticity Through Role-Play and Exercises .. 134

Self-Care After the Conversation ............................................. 138

**Part 6: Plotting Your Course:**
**How to Navigate Stormy Seas** ............................................**143**

Introduction: The Power of Preparation .............................. 143

Self-Reflection: Preparing for Difficult Conversations ......... 152

Staying Open: A Path to Connection ................................... 155

Emotional Data: Recognising Feelings as
Essential Information ............................................................ 158

Dealing with Emotional Overwhelm in Real Time ............... 160

Preparing for a Collaborative Conversation ......................... 163

Setting the Stage: Timing and Setting for the
Conversation ......................................................................... 165

# Navigating the Waves:
# Facing the Conversation    171

**Part 7: Raising the Flags:**
**Setting Signals for Clear Communication** ......................... **173**

Clarify: The First Step in Defining Boundaries .................... 177

Communicate: Expressing Boundaries Openly
and Respectfully .................................................................... 180

Correct: The Role of Correction in Boundary Setting ......... 185

Overcoming Resistance When Setting Boundaries .............. 187

Managing Boundaries in the Heat of the Moment .............. 189

Practical Applications of The Magic Three in
Boundary Setting ................................................................... 194

**Part 8: Keeping the Helm Steady:**
**Strategies for Emotional Stability** ..................................... **203**

Building Emotional Resilience ............................................. 205

Managing Real-Time Anxiety:
Finding Calm in the Moment ............................................... 207

Setting Realistic Expectations for High-Stakes
Conversations ....................................................................... 209

Remaining Calm Under Accusations or
Misinterpretations .......................................................................211
Taking Breaks During High-Stakes Conversations ...............212
Listening Is Your Superpower! ...................................................214

## Part 9: Strategies for Different Relationships: Adjusting the Sails – Navigating Varying Winds of Relationships ...219

Introduction: Appreciating the Value of Tailored
Communication............................................................................220
Communicating with Partners ..................................................222
Communicating with Family Members ...................................224
Communicating with Colleagues ..............................................225
Communicating with Children..................................................227
Navigating Co-Parenting Challenges ........................................229

# Reaching the Shore: Growth Through Dialogue  235

## Part 10: Navigating Relationship Changes: Changing Tides: Adapting to New Horizons ................... 237

Introduction: Embracing Change in Relationships ..............237
Recognising the Impact of Honest Conversations ................238
Practising Healthy Detachment .................................................239
Recognising When Relationships Need to End.....................240
When Relationships Strengthen Through Change ...............241
Embracing Acceptance and Moving Forward........................242

## Part 11: Anchoring Your True North: Living with Integrity....................................................................... 247

Introduction: Sailing True............................................................247
Why Core Values Matter in Communication ........................249
Practising Values-Based Communication:
A New Perspective........................................................................250
Future Conversations Aligned with Values.............................254

Conclusion: Reflecting on the Journey:
    Logbook Reflections: Charting Growth and Wisdom .........259
    Eve's Final Moment of Reflection ..........................................260
    Next Steps: Continuing the Practice ......................................262

Appendices..................................................................................................265
    Glossary of Terms.....................................................................267
    References ................................................................................281
    Postscript: Continue Your Journey:
    The Conversations at the Shoreline Course..........................293
Acknowledgements.....................................................................................297
About Eve...................................................................................................301

# Author's Note

This book is for you. The tools and lessons I share come from 35 years of studying philosophy and psychology, and 25 years' experience as a practising therapist and coach. They are techniques and insights I have used in my life and shared with countless others. My hope is that they will help you navigate tough conversations and create more honest and meaningful connections. These conversations can be isolating, but you are not alone on this journey.

I share my experiences to show that change is possible. I understand how hard these exchanges can be because I have faced them too. The stories I share reflect my perspective, and I acknowledge that others may have experienced these moments differently. Even so, they connect the ideas in this book to real life – your life – and demonstrate how these tools can make a difference.

The client stories included are based on real occurrences but have been carefully adapted to protect privacy. Names, details, and contexts have been changed, while the lessons and insights remain faithful to the essence of their experiences. These stories, like mine, show what is possible and offer guidance as you navigate your challenges.

This book is here for YOU – to encourage and guide you, providing practical tools to help you listen with understanding and speak to be heard.

QR Code to access the online resources that go alongside *Conversations at the Shoreline.*

www.evestanway.co.uk/shoreline

# PROLOGUE

## Casting Spoons into the Deep

Sunlight pours across the undulating waves of the South Atlantic, turning the sea into a shifting canvas of silver and grey. I sit in the cockpit of our 30ft catamaran, cradled in my orange safety harness, the straps snug against my small frame. The harness tethered me to the vessel, a constant reminder of the delicate balance between safety and freedom in my daily life. The bright orange webbing stood out against the soft, worn whites and blues of the boat, a contrast to the endless expanse of shifting sea and sky around me. Being secured to the boat was second nature for me – a lifeline that kept me connected to my floating home while the ocean heaved and whispered its eternal song.

The boat crests and dips with the rhythm of the water, a lullaby of motion that lures my small hands into action. One by one, I let silver teaspoons slip from my grasp. They glitter and tumble, tracing arcs of light before vanishing into the shadowed depths. I remember the strange thrill in letting go – casting something familiar into the unknown and watching it disappear.

The sound of my father's voice rumbles from the cabin, sharp and loud, clashing with the serene rhythm of the waves. I glance up at my mother, her eyes fixed on the distant line where sky meets sea, her blonde hair caught in the wind. She grips the wheel with the steadiness of someone who has learned to weather storms. I yearn for her gaze, for her to notice the quiet joy in my minor rebellion. A tremble dances within me as I think of his anger, a storm that will shake the fragile sanctuary of my world. Despite this, I cannot regret the release – the silver arc of freedom, the silent plunge into the unknown.

There was something shipwrecked about those moments. My small defiance like casting fragments of hope into the waves from a sinking vessel. Even at that young age, I sensed that my actions – much like the ocean – carried the weight of hidden truths, unspoken words, and deep, unseen wounds. Rising from silence is like salvaging something precious from ruin. It demands courage – a willingness to sift through what is broken, bring it to the surface, and allow it to be seen, understood, and healed.

## Poem: Flying Spoons

*She sat, tossing the family silver into the rolling depths of the Southern Ocean,*
*Each teaspoon spinning through the salty air, catching sunlight like the flying fish*
*That once landed in her bed, flashing and shining, before becoming breakfast –*
*Crisp and golden, and delicious!*

I was raised on the sea and later found myself washed ashore. Life can often feel like that, can't it? We are carried by the waves, only to be left standing on unfamiliar ground, clutching the broken pieces of what once was. The shoreline becomes a space in between – where the past meets the present, and being lost can transform into an opportunity to rediscover ourselves.

Some of us are born into storms, others into calm waters, but no matter where we begin, we all search for belonging. We long for a place where our voices can rise – unafraid, unmuted, and understood. Like casting spoons into the deep, there are moments when we must let go – of fear, of silence, or of the safety of the familiar – and take a step into the unknown. Courage is born in these moments.

If you feel adrift, caught between the tides of misunderstanding and a longing for connection, this book is for you. It is for those yearning to speak with truth, to find their voice, and to build bridges of understanding. At the shoreline, where we meet the fragments of our past, we begin the work of sifting through the wreckage – using clarity, courage, and connection as tools to rebuild.

Together, we will walk this shoreline, where conversations begin. Here, in the ebb and flow of release and discovery, we will dare to speak to be heard, listen to understand. Let us begin.

# YOUR COMPASS: STEERING THROUGH THE CHAPTERS

*"I am not afraid of storms,
for I am learning how to sail my ship."*

Louisa May Alcott
American author and campaigner

## Introduction:
## Setting Sail on Difficult Conversations

We all face challenges, don't we? For me, the hardest one has always been asking for help. When I decided to write this book, I remember sitting, staring at a blank page, the faint smell of coffee cooling beside me, my dog curled at my feet and the weight of silence pressing down. Self-doubt rolling in like a grey fog – thick, stifling, impossible to ignore. Could I really do this? My mind spun with sharp, biting questions that only made the emptiness feel heavier.

It felt like I had two choices: give up or ask for help. The thought of asking sent a sharp pang of fear through my stomach. I told myself

I had to manage alone, convinced that asking for help would reveal a weakness I was not ready to face.

Surrounded by my library of well-loved books, I reached for inspiration, flipping through pages that had guided me before. One book spoke to me: *Daring Greatly* by Brené Brown. Her words about vulnerability resonated deeply. She describes vulnerability as the courage to show up even when the outcome is uncertain – it is a powerful idea. For many of us, however, vulnerability feels more like a risk – a doorway to judgement or shame. At the same time, it is through vulnerability that we form the connections we crave.

When I asked for help, I felt a deeper truth: reaching out is not a sign of weakness. It is an act of profound strength and self-compassion. Knowing this changes everything. As a philosopher, coach and therapist specialising in communication, I have spent years peeling back the layers of vulnerability, like unwrapping something fragile and precious. Still, that inner voice – the one that told me asking for help meant failure – held me back for far too long, convincing me that needing support made me unworthy.

When I finally reached out, I was surprised by how willingly people offered their help. Their kindness felt like warm sunlight breaking through the clouds of limiting beliefs I had carried for years. It clashed with everything I had learned growing up. I was raised to see asking for help as a weakness, something to avoid. On the rare occasions I did ask, the outcome was often teasing or humiliation. Silence became my safety net, and I became good – too good – at solving problems on my own.

I believed the rules were different for me. When others asked for help, I admired their strength. When I considered asking, I saw only failure. All my life I have been shifting this perspective. Accepting help, like offering it, is a fundamental part of being human. It is not easy, but it is necessary. Dropping the shame I felt was liberating; suddenly, real connections were possible.

For years, I avoided the very conversations I encouraged others to have – those raw, vulnerable exchanges with themselves and the people they loved. The thought of expressing my true feelings filled me with dread, a cold weight tightening in my chest. I was dedicated to helping others face their struggles, yet I treated my own truths as if they were too sharp to touch.

I still remember being eight years old, standing on the quay by a neighbour's boat, trembling with outrage as I defended a child I thought had been unfairly scolded. My voice shook, but I stood firm, insisting they deserved to be heard. Looking back, I cannot remember anyone ever standing up for me in the same way.

This is why I write to you now. The daring to speak, to ask for help, to face the silence – this is where connection begins. It is not easy, but it is possible. And it is worth it.

I often felt frustrated when others could not see solutions as quickly as I could. I now realise that my perceived cleverness stemmed from the trauma of constantly needing to predict and avoid conflict to survive, leaving me emotionally detached. As Pete Walker explores in *The Tao of Fully Feeling*, emotional repression can develop as a survival response, teaching us to shut down feelings that might overwhelm or threaten us. I had unknowingly mastered the art of compartmentalising my emotions, pushing them aside in favour of appearing strong and capable. While emotional numbness protected me as a child, it left me ill-equipped to manage my emotions as an adult.

This disconnection revealed an almost unbearable truth. How could I dedicate myself to championing courage and honesty in others while avoiding the truths in my own life? Perhaps you have felt this too – trying to lead with confidence in one area of life while staying silent in another, shrinking from your own shadows. For me, it felt as though I was living two parallel lives. In one, I stood boldly, guiding others to find their voice. In the other, I stayed quiet, trapped by fear and self-doubt. The contradiction became impossible to ignore, and I knew the time had come to confront it.

Why is it that the conversations we fear most – the ones with the power to change everything – feel so far out of reach? Why does it seem hardest to speak honestly with the people we expect to hold us, protect us, and keep us safe? These questions stayed with me, pressing me to begin peeling back the layers of my own silence. Perhaps they linger for you too, waiting to be answered.

The answer lies, at least in part, in how our bodies and minds are wired. As Daniel Goleman explains in *Emotional Intelligence*, our emotional brain, the amygdala, reacts faster than our rational brain. In moments of high tension, this emotional centre triggers a fight, flight, or freeze response. It is a survival mechanism; one that helped our ancestors escape predators but now works against us in emotionally charged situations. The very conversations we most need to have – those that demand honesty and vulnerability – can feel like a threat, setting off a cascade of physical and emotional reactions. A lump forms in the throat, the chest tightens, and the words we planned so carefully vanish like smoke.

> *"In a very real sense we have two minds, one that thinks and one that feels."*
>
> Daniel Goleman

This physiological reaction often intertwines with the emotional landscapes of our childhoods. Perhaps you recognise this too – how vulnerability, instead of being met with safety, was met with dismissal, ridicule, or rejection. Over time, we learn to equate honesty with danger. As a child, admitting fear or sadness felt to me like stepping into quicksand, with no guarantee that someone would reach out to pull me free. These early experiences leave their mark, shaping a roadmap of avoidance that we carry with us into adulthood.

The people closest to us – our parents, partners, friends – should be the ones we trust the most. Yet they also hold the greatest power to hurt us. The stakes feel higher, the fear of rejection sharper. The risk of being misunderstood or dismissed can make us hesitate, stumble, or retreat entirely.

Here is the paradox: the very act of leaning into these difficult conversations, of sharing what we are most afraid to say, is what creates the connection we long for. It is through vulnerability that we build bridges – not only with others but within ourselves. This truth, though profoundly simple, is not easy to embrace. It requires unlearning the reflex to silence ourselves and rewiring the patterns that have kept us stuck for so long.

These are the questions this book explores. Why do we hold back when we most need to speak? How can we move beyond fear, the physiological response, and the conditioning of the past to find our voice? Most importantly, how can we transform moments of uncomfortable conversation into opportunities for growth, connection, and change?

There are no quick fixes here, but rather steps along a journey – a journey I invite you to take with me. Together, we will face the silence, uncover its roots, and learn to navigate the raw and uncharted terrain of difficult conversations.

## Therapy on Zoom

During the Covid pandemic, like many others, I had to reimagine my work and how I connected with others. The uncertainty was palpable – none of us truly knew what it would mean to speak through the cold lens of a screen day after day, or whether the intimacy of therapy could survive without the warmth of face-to-face meetings. Yet, as I stumbled through IT updates, and navigating Zoom and Teams, something remarkable happened. The very tool I feared might hinder connection – technology – became an unexpected window into myself as a therapist.

For the first time, I saw myself through my clients' eyes: the subtle movements of my face, the tilt of my head, the way my posture softened to mirror their emotions. Micro-expressions I had noted unconsciously became vivid. It was as though I had rediscovered an invisible layer of language – my body's unspoken dialogue crafted over years of listening, observing, and responding.

Connection, it seems, transcends words; it lives in the spaces between. It is a symphony of gestures, expressions, and presence. Our thoughts, emotions, and posture weave a constant, silent conversation that shapes how we relate to ourselves and to others. Daniel Goleman captures this beautifully in *Emotional Intelligence*, explaining that *"empathy is the bridge that connects us to another's emotional world"* (Goleman, 1996). Trust and understanding are built not just through spoken words, but through a flicker in the eyes, a loosening of the shoulders, or a quiet, shared moment of recognition.

This delicate interplay lies at the heart of this book. *Conversations at the Shoreline* is a guide to discovering and empowering your voice by tuning into these layers of connection – both verbal and non-verbal – and learning to navigate the silent currents of emotion and dialogue. The pandemic journey, filled with isolation and uncertainty, unexpectedly illuminated the profound impact of our relationships on navigating difficult conversations.

## Why Do Conversations Feel So Hard?

> *"You are never too old to set a new goal or dream a new dream."*
>
> attributed to C.S. Lewis

For many of us, the roots of silence can be traced back to childhood. Think back for a moment – were you ever told you were *"too sensitive,"* or told you *"don't be a baby,"* or *"you will need to toughen up"*? Perhaps someone suggested your feelings were *"too much."* These words, sharp as razors, sliced through our defences, wounding the parts of us that needed the most love. These messages, over time, insidiously silence the most vulnerable and authentic aspects of our being.

Brené Brown's research on shame captures this dynamic with striking clarity. She explains that early experiences of being labelled as *"too much"* or *"too sensitive"* can create an inner narrative of unworthiness. Vulnerability becomes tangled with shame, teaching us to hide the very parts of ourselves that most need to be seen (*Daring Greatly*, Brown, 2012). And while shame may silence us in the moment, it lingers into adulthood, leaving us feeling unseen, disconnected, and unsure why we feel so adrift.

This silence comes at a cost. When we suppress our emotions, we lose touch with who we are. We carry the weight of isolation without understanding its source, and our relationships – both with others and with ourselves – begin to suffer. As Esther Perel, renowned for her work on relationships, writes, *"The quality of our relationships determines the quality of our lives"* (*The State of Affairs*, Perel, 2017).

What if we could break this silence? What if we could choose honesty and compassionate communication, not as a quick fix, but as a path toward self-awareness, clarity, and connection? It is possible. This book invites you to join me on that journey – to face the silence, embrace your voice, and open the doors to a deeper understanding of yourself and others.

## How To Make the Most of This Book

This book is designed to support you wherever you are on your journey. You can read it cover to cover for a complete understanding of the ideas, tools, and strategies, or dip into the sections that feel most relevant to your current challenges. It has been created with flexibility and depth in mind, giving you the freedom to engage with it in the way that works best for you.

## Find Your Path

You can follow the chapters in order, immersing yourself in the ideas step by step, or start with the parts that resonate most with your needs. Tailor your reading experience to suit your unique situation.

## Pause and Reflect

Keeping a notebook nearby can help you capture thoughts, reflections, and insights as they arise. Writing down your responses deepens your understanding and creates a record of your progress. These small moments of reflection will add up over time.

## Take Small Steps

Transformation does not happen overnight. Start by applying the tools in simple, everyday situations. Taking small, deliberate steps will build your confidence and prepare you for navigating more complex conversations.

## Go At Your Own Pace

Growth takes time. If a section feels overwhelming, it is okay to pause, take a breath, and return when you feel ready. There is no rush, and no fixed timeline. This journey is yours to explore at your own pace.

## Resources To Support You Further

To help you bring the ideas in this book to life, I have created additional resources designed to provide practical guidance and deeper understanding:

- Free downloadable workbooks: Each workbook is filled with examples, exercises, and reflective prompts to help you apply what you learn to your own life.

- Guided meditations: Audio recordings are available to help you stay grounded, cultivate calm, and find clarity as you prepare for or reflect on difficult conversations.

- Expanded case studies: Real-life scenarios with additional details and reflections offer practical insights you can adapt to your own circumstances.

- Further reading lists: Each chapter comes with curated recommendations to help you dive deeper into key themes and topics.

You can access these resources through the QR code in the Introduction or by visiting my website (www.evestanway.co.uk/shoreline). They are there to guide you step by step, offering support whenever you need it.

## A Shared Journey

Whether you choose to follow the chapters sequentially or focus on specific sections, this book is here to meet you where you are. Every tool, every idea, and every resource is designed to help you turn insights into action, one step at a time.

This journey is about more than just understanding – it is about change. With these tools and resources as your companions, you will discover the confidence to navigate even the most challenging conversations. Take your time, start small, and know that every step forward is meaningful.

Let's set out together. You have everything you need to begin.

> *"Perhaps the biggest tragedy of our lives is that freedom is possible, yet we can pass our years trapped in the same old patterns... We may want to love other people without holding back, to feel authentic, to breathe in the beauty around us, to dance and sing. Yet each day we listen to inner voices that keep our life small."*
>
> Tara Brach<br>*Radical Acceptance*, 2003

*"Patience is not passive;
on the contrary, it is concentrated strength."*

Bruce Lee (1940–1973)
Hong-Kong American martial artist

## Eve's Opening Epiphany

My journey in coaching and therapy began with many of the techniques explored in this book. At the time, they felt like stepping stones – simple yet essential foundations for helping others navigate their most difficult emotions.

Over the years, people have often asked whether working with those in distress is overwhelming or draining. The truth is, it is not. These techniques provide structure and clarity, allowing me to support others without becoming entangled in their pain. By helping clients hold space for their emotions – rather than absorbing them – I can guide them toward growth while maintaining my own emotional balance. Each day, I witness the quiet courage of those I work with – their willingness to sit with their emotions, challenge old patterns, and take meaningful steps forward. It is a privilege I treasure, a reminder that healing is not just about finding the right words, but about daring to speak them.

Therapy and coaching are not about one person holding all the answers. They are a collaboration in partnership, where coach and client work together to create change. Knowledge is shared rather than imposed, and through this shared process, insight emerges, actions are taken, and transformation is revealed. This dynamic, rooted in mutual respect and the belief in every individual's capacity for growth, is at the very heart of this work.

It was this collaborative approach that inspired me to write this book. The tools and techniques we use in therapy – methods that bring clarity and calm to emotional challenges – can be just as valuable for anyone navigating life's difficult conversations. These strategies are not reserved for professionals; they are practical tools you can use to feel more confident and capable in the moments that matter most. My hope for you is that by exploring these techniques, you will feel empowered to approach challenging conversations with a sense of ease, clarity, and purpose.

## A Gentle Word of Caution

While these tools can be transformative, they are not intended to make you a therapist or to place the burden of always being the *"strong one"* on your shoulders. Being the person everyone turns to can feel overwhelming, and no one should have to carry that weight alone. These strategies are designed to help you manage overwhelming moments, not to place the responsibility of everyone else's emotional well-being solely on you.

Therapists and coaches work within specific boundaries to protect both themselves and those they work with. We have support systems in place to ensure we stay grounded, and we share only what is needed to build trust – never so much that it becomes a burden to the client. In the same way, these tools are not a substitute for professional support when it is needed, for yourself or for others.

## Practical Tools and Resources

To help you build your confidence in applying these techniques, I have included additional resources in the accompanying workbook, which is designed to complement this book. The workbook provides practical exercises and reflective prompts, allowing you to explore these strategies in your own time and at your own pace. You can also find further resources on my website (www.evestanway.co.uk), where you can deepen your understanding and practice in a way that suits you.

## Poems and Illustrations

As I wrote this book, I found that some ideas and emotions could not be fully captured in structured prose. Instead, they emerged in different forms – some as poems, some as drawings – both offering another way of expressing what I was thinking and feeling. Just as we navigate the world with three brains – the survival brain, the rational brain, and the emotional brain – we also process our experiences differently. The survival brain urges us to react, the rational brain tries to make sense of things, and the emotional brain feels. When we face difficult conversations, all three are at play. We feel the urge to retreat or defend, we try to find the right words, and, beneath it all, we experience emotions that tell us how we engage with the world.

Both poetry and imagery surfaced naturally during this process, arriving in moments where words alone felt insufficient. Some poems took shape as I reflected on my own experiences; some drawings appeared as I explored the themes of this book, offering me new ways to see and understand. Neither are interruptions but invitations – ways of accessing emotion beyond logic, beyond analysis. As difficult conversations are not only about what we say but also about what we feel, these creative expressions speak in a language beyond explanation, allowing meaning to surface in its own way.

I have included these poems and illustrations because they felt necessary, both to my own process and, I hope, to yours. I intend that they will help you connect with your own emotions, your own sensations, and your own ways of experiencing the world. Perhaps they will offer a different kind of language that moves beyond thinking into feeling, creating space for reflection, recognition, and, ultimately, understanding.

## Poem: Time

*There was a time when I carried my silence
like a balm for wounds unspoken,
always a steady pulse in my chest
where words might have lived.*

*In a mask, I moved through the world unseen,
letting others decide the shape of things,
fitting myself into spaces
where my voice dissolved, quiet, safe.*

*Then, one day, a child looked at me,
green eyes wide with a question too heavy to hold.
"Why do we hurt?" she asked,
and in that moment, my silence cracked.*

*Words gathered, uneven, stumbling, hesitant, hopeful —
not answers, but fragments of truth,
rough as coarse stones turned in the dark, grinding, screeching,
breaking through the years I had pressed them down.
I traced the old boundaries, fingers running,
feeling each scar as it lay beneath my skin.
These were not walls to hold me,
but the lifelines that told me who I was.*

*Now, silence sits sipping tea beside me, in peaceful contentment,
no longer a place to disappear,
but a refuge, a long breath before I speak,
a sure reminder that I have a choice.*

# SETTING SAIL: UNDERSTANDING THE WATERS

*"Do not let your fire go out, spark by irreplaceable spark, in the hopeless swamps of the not-quite, the not-yet, and the not-at-all."*

Ayn Rand (1905–1982)
Russian-American novelist and philosopher

Let us begin with the truth: expressing yourself can feel like standing at the edge of a storm, with the wind tugging at your resolve. Silence may seem like the safest shelter, yet as Thomas Moore writes in *The Eloquence of Silence*, it comes at a cost – creating distance between us and those we love, tethering us to relationships that no longer serve us. The choice before you is clear: remain hidden, or step forward and reclaim your voice.

Blame and regret have no place here. This is about breaking free from the fear of judgement, the longing for approval, and the armour that has kept you silent for too long. Within these pages, you will uncover the roots of that silence and begin to dismantle it, discovering strength with every step forward.

At the core of this journey is the **Magic Three Framework: Clarify, Communicate, and Correct**. This simple yet transformative tool will help you navigate even the hardest conversations, giving you the confidence to speak with purpose, even when fear lingers.

Your voice holds power, waiting to be released. Together, we will break through the barriers that silence you and find the courage to speak your truth – with grace, wisdom, and compassion.

## Poem: A Path Begins

*The silence we carry – a shield, a cage,*
*holding untold stories in its shadowed grip.*
*With courage, words begin to rise,*
*and as silence loosens, the heart finds its peace.*

The journey begins now.

# Part 1

# LOST AT SEA: THE CHALLENGE OF FINDING YOUR OWN VOICE

*"The power of a single word can shape our inner world, yet finding that word can feel like unearthing a hidden treasure."*

Eve Stanway

### Introduction: Becalmed in Silence: Finding Your Voice

I was gripping a paper map in my hands, my fingers pressing into the creases as the miles slipped by. My father was driving, trusting my directions, and for a while, I believed we were on the right road. But then, a cold wave of realisation crashed over me. We were going the wrong way.

My stomach knotted. My throat tightened. I stared at the map as if I could will the ink to shift, to rewrite my mistake. Stafford. Stratford. They looked similar at a glance – but we were miles off course.

I should have said something immediately. But I didn't.

Fear wrapped around me like a fog, thick and paralysing. I had been wrong before, and mistakes often came with teasing, with criticism. What if I spoke up and was met with anger? What if I looked foolish? The weight of unspoken words pressed against my ribs.

So, I stayed silent.

Mile after mile, I let the mistake grow heavier. The wrong road stretched before us, the moment to correct it slipping further away.

Eventually, I forced the words out – hesitant, small. "I think we are going the wrong way."

I braced for disappointment, for frustration.

Instead, my father smiled. "Well, then, let's make an adventure of it."

I had spent all that time dreading his reaction, believing my silence would keep me safe. Instead, it had only kept me trapped in fear.

It was not the last time I stayed quiet when I should have spoken. Not the last time I swallowed my voice, believing silence was protection. That moment in the car was small, but the pattern was deep. Silence became my shield. It became my survival. Over time, it did not just protect me – it separated me from connection, from opportunity, from myself.

## What Has Silence Cost You?

Has fear ever held your tongue? Have you ever felt something so deeply, yet struggled to find the words? Maybe you wanted to say *"I am struggling,"* or *"I need something to change."* Maybe you swallowed the words instead, afraid of what might happen if you spoke.

You are not alone. For many of us, silence feels safer – a shield against judgement, rejection, or conflict.

Here is what I have learned: silence does not keep us safe. It keeps us stuck.

I know this because I lived it.

For years, I let silence take up space where my voice should have been. It was easier to pretend I knew the way, even when I didn't. Easier to stay quiet than to risk looking foolish. Easier to hold my breath than to ask for what I needed.

However, silence comes at a cost. It steals connection. It builds walls. It makes us feel alone, even in a crowded room.

## The First Step Toward Speaking Up

This chapter is about breaking that silence – not in a reckless rush, but with intention, courage, and clarity. It is about finding your voice, one step at a time, in places where it once faltered.

Together, we will begin to loosen the grip of silence. I will share tools to help you take small, deliberate steps forward. The **Magic Three Framework: Clarify, Communicate, and Correct** has guided countless difficult conversations for me and my clients. This chapter also introduces the "anchor word", a grounding technique to help you stay steady when emotions surge.

Breaking silence is not about speaking for the sake of speaking. It is about choosing when and how to use your voice so that your words carry meaning, strength, and truth.

> *"The attempt to escape from pain creates more pain."*
>
> Gabor Maté<br>*The Myth of Normal*, 2022

## The Silence We Learn

I was eleven years old, standing in yet another unfamiliar classroom, clutching a pencil as if it were an anchor. The faces around me blurred into a sea of newness – different accents, different rules, different expectations. By then, I had learned a single, unspoken lesson: stay quiet, stay unnoticed, and you will survive.

For many of us, this lesson begins early.

Perhaps you heard it in phrases like *"Don't make a fuss"* or *"Be nice!"* – instructions that taught you to push your feelings down, to smooth over discomfort, to be agreeable at all costs. Maybe you were told to be seen and not heard, as though your voice mattered less than your obedience.

Even the stories we were raised on carried hidden warnings. *The Boy Who Cried Wolf* taught children to doubt their own needs, to fear asking for help too often. Bruno Bettelheim, in *The Uses of Enchantment*, observed that fairy tales are not just stories – they are coded lessons that shape a child's sense of self. *"The child intuitively comprehends that although these stories are unreal, they are not untrue"* (Bettelheim, 1976, p. 25).

A quiet child is often praised, but what does that quietness cost?

Katherine May captures this vividly in *Wintering: The Power of Rest and Retreat in Difficult Times*:

> *"As children, we tolerate working conditions that we'd find intolerable as adults: the constant interrogation of our attainment to a hostile audience, the motivation by threat instead of encouragement (and big threats too: if you don't do this, you'll ruin your whole future life...), the social world in which you are mocked and teased, your most embarrassing desires exposed, your new-formed body held up for the kind of scrutiny that would destroy an adult."*

Children adapt. They learn that emotions – especially the difficult ones – are disruptive. That anger is unacceptable, sadness is inconvenient, and frustration is ungrateful. If tears were met with *"Calm down,"* or *"Stop bothering me,"* you may have absorbed the idea that your feelings were too much, too messy, or simply unwelcome.

Silence becomes a shield. It protects, but it also isolates.

## The Hidden World of Childhood Emotions

Emotions do not disappear when we push them aside. They resurface as a tightness in the chest, an ache in the shoulders, a restless anxiety that has no name.

For years, psychologists, doctors, and writers have explored how childhood experiences shape the people we become. What happens beneath the surface – the feelings we suppress, the needs we silence – leaves an imprint that lingers long after childhood.

Gabor Maté explains that trauma is not just what happens to us, but what happens inside us when we suppress our emotions to survive. The body remembers what the mind tries to forget. Bessel van der Kolk describes this vividly in *The Body Keeps the Score*:

> *"Trauma is not just an event that took place sometime in the past; it is also the imprint left by that experience on mind, brain, and body."*

As children, many of us learned to shrink, to make ourselves smaller so we could fit into the spaces others expected of us. Over time, that shrinking becomes so familiar, we mistake it for our true size.

Reclaiming your voice is not about forcing yourself to speak before you are ready. It is about recognising that your silence has a story – one that deserves to be heard.

## My Story: A Childhood of Silence

I spent my childhood moving – eleven schools in eleven years, scattered across different countries. On paper, it sounds adventurous. The reality was anything but.

Each new place meant new rules to navigate, new social codes to decipher, and an overwhelming awareness that I was always the outsider. Friendships were temporary. Home was a shifting concept. The safest strategy? Stay quiet, observe, adapt.

At fourteen, my schooling stopped entirely. My father, the son of a grammar school headmaster and an English teacher, believed he could educate me better than any institution. His vision was built on self-reliance, but in practice, it meant isolation. My classroom was an empty room. My teachers were books I had to teach myself to understand.

Determined not to be left behind, I took matters into my own hands. I found an Oxford and Cambridge exam syllabus, cycled fifteen miles to Penrith Library, and spent hours poring over textbooks. There were no classmates to compare notes with, no guidance, no safety net. Just me, the books, and the cold certainty that if I failed, no one would catch me.

From a distance, I watched other children laughing, sharing secrets, touching a world that felt out of reach. Their lives seemed like a distant land, glittering on the horizon – one I did not belong to.

Adolescence, I later learned, is a time when our brains crave connection. Instead, I was alone. At home, my father's authority was absolute. To challenge him was dangerous. I learned to swallow my emotions, lock away my thoughts, and wrap myself in compliance. Not to create peace – there was no peace – but to survive.

By the time I re-entered formal education at sixteen, silence had settled into me like a second skin. I stood at the edges of conversations, watching as laughter rippled through the air while my own words felt trapped behind a wall I did not know how to break.

Six months passed before I finally spoke.

Even then, each word felt like chiselling through stone – chipping away at the fortress I had built to keep myself safe.

## The Echoes of Silence

The fear did not vanish with time. Even in my thirties, I found myself avoiding groups of teenagers – ghosts of my younger self. I would cross the street to avoid passing them, afraid of being seen, of being reminded of who I once was.

One day, walking home from work in a tailored suit, I spotted a group near the school gates. Instinct told me to turn away.

Instead, I kept going.

As I passed, they stepped aside. No jeering, no judgement – just a polite acknowledgment. My heart pounded. My palms were damp. Yet something shifted.

That moment showed me a truth I carry into my work as a therapist and coach:

> *People see the swan gliding across the water,*
> *not the frantic paddling beneath the surface.*

For years, I had believed silence kept me safe. The truth was, silence was not the same as peace.

I have learned to share my voice in many areas of my life. Yet one conversation still evades me – a meaningful dialogue with my father.

Perhaps, one day, I will find the words.

Perhaps, one day, we all will.

> *"We all have an unsuspected reserve of strength inside that emerges when life puts us to the test."*
>
> Isabel Allende (1942–)<br>Chilean-American author

Patterns of hiding and avoiding can take root so deeply that they become second nature. For many of us, they begin in childhood, shaped by lessons in compliance, perfectionism, or relentless self-reliance. These habits often become part of our identity, even a source of pride. Yet, when they harden too much, they can stop us from being fully ourselves when we most need to be.

## Jane's Journey: Letting Go of the Superwoman Mask

Jane walked into my office with an air of effortless control. Her tailored blazer sat perfectly on her shoulders, her heels clicked with quiet precision against the floor, and her smile – warm yet distant – never wavered. She moved like a woman who had mastered the art of composure, each gesture deliberate, each breath measured.

Her handshake was firm, her posture upright, her voice even. If you did not look closely, you might miss the tightness in her jaw, the flicker of hesitation in her eyes, the way her fingers twisted together in her lap when she thought no one was watching.

"I have a perfectly balanced life," she said, smoothing an imaginary crease from her trousers. "I manage a team of thirty, I keep my house in order, I make sure my parents are looked after, I plan my children's schedules. I know how to handle things."

She was impeccable, polished, in control. Yet her words, so carefully arranged, carried a weight that did not match the script she was presenting. The tiredness in her voice betrayed a truth she was unwilling to admit: she was drowning in the very life she had built.

A pause. A glance away. A breath held just a second too long.

"I am the one everyone depends on," she said finally, her voice steady but laced with something raw. "Sometimes, it feels like I am disappearing under it all."

### The Mask of Strength

Jane's story is one I have heard many times, though the details shift from one person to another. The relentless competence. The dismissal of exhaustion as just another thing to manage. The belief that admitting struggle would unravel everything.

She had worn her strength like armour for so long that she could not imagine a world where she put it down. To be seen as vulnerable, even for a moment, was unthinkable. Her mask – composure, capability, control – had become a part of her, so much so that she did not know where it ended and she began.

Yet masks, no matter how seamlessly they fit, have a price.

### Where It Began

We traced the roots of her belief back to a moment that had once felt small but had shaped her world.

She was fourteen. It had been a difficult day at school. The girls in her class had closed ranks, whispering behind cupped hands, leaving her standing on the outside. The sting of rejection sat heavy in her chest as she walked home.

That evening, while her mother stirred a pot on the stove, Jane hovered, hoping for comfort, for a moment of reassurance. She found the courage to speak.

"They left me out today," she admitted, her voice small. "I don't know why."

Her mother, without looking up, kept stirring. "You are strong," she said. "You'll figure it out."

The words were not cruel. They were not meant to wound. But they landed with a finality that left no room for anything else.

In that moment, Jane made a decision.

She would not need. She would not ask. She would be the kind of person who held things together, no matter what.

She had spent a lifetime honouring that unspoken vow.

### The Realisation

In our coaching sessions, Jane began to notice the contradiction between the "balanced" life she described and the reality of the exhaustion she was living. She was not failing. She was not weak. Her exhaustion was a message – one she had spent years ignoring.

She started small. Saying no to requests that stretched her too thin. Admitting, even if only to herself at first, that she was tired. Taking ten quiet minutes with a cup of tea, not as a luxury but as a necessity.

The first time she admitted to a friend, "I am struggling," she expected the world to shift beneath her feet. Instead, her friend simply nodded. "I know," she said. "You do not always have to be the strong one."

It was a startling thought.

"It feels strange," Jane admitted one day, "but freeing – like I am finally figuring out who I really am without the mask."

### Redefining Strength

Letting go of the roles we create to protect ourselves is never easy. They become so deeply woven into our identity that the thought of change feels unsettling.

But for Jane, it was not about abandoning her strength. It was about reshaping it.

She learned that true strength was not about enduring everything alone. It was about allowing space for herself within the life she had built. It was about trusting that she was worthy of rest, of support, of love that did not have to be earned through sacrifice.

"It's freeing," she said, a small, quiet smile replacing the tight, distant one she had first walked in with. And that freedom – no matter how tentative – became the foundation for something new.

### The Power of Small Shifts

When perfectionism or relentless self-reliance loosens its grip, transformation begins – not in grand, sweeping changes, but in the smallest acts of self-compassion.

A pause. A breath. A choice.

One moment at a time, Jane was learning to step out from behind the mask.

And in doing so, she was finally learning what it meant to be seen.

> *"A problem shared really is a problem halved."*

## The Magic Three: A Framework for Speaking and Being Heard

Silence may feel safe, but it keeps us stuck. If staying quiet has held you back, what helps you move forward?

Many of us were never taught how to navigate difficult conversations, yet communication is at the heart of every relationship. Whether with a partner, a friend, a family member, or a colleague, these exchanges shape our connections, defining whether relationships deepen or fracture.

Avoiding difficult conversations does not make the discomfort disappear. It lingers in unspoken resentment, unresolved misunderstandings, and quiet distances that grow wider over time. If relationships matter, then the way we communicate matters.

This is why I developed the **Magic Three Framework** – a simple but powerful approach designed to make difficult conversations not just possible, but repeatable in a way that is calm, assertive, and compassionate.

## Introducing the Magic Three:
## Clarify, Communicate, and Correct

This is a pivotal moment. Whether through reflection, frustration, or necessity, you have recognised that a conversation needs to happen.

It might be a conversation you have avoided, one you have rehearsed in your head but never voiced aloud. It could be a discussion that has gone badly before, where emotions flared or words were misheard. Perhaps you have stayed silent, waiting for the right moment, only to realise there may never be a perfect time.

These are not just conversations. They are crossroads.

The right approach can lead to understanding, repair, and deeper trust. The wrong approach can lead to defensiveness, distance, and conflict. The difference is not just in what you say – it is in how you say it.

Psychologist and relationship expert John Gottman has spent decades studying how communication strengthens or erodes relationships. His research identified 'The Four Horsemen of the Apocalypse' – criticism, defensiveness, contempt, and stonewalling – which are the four behaviours most destructive to meaningful connection. In high-stakes conversations, these instincts take over, creating barriers instead of bridges (Gottman and Silver, 1999).

Difficult conversations are often derailed by these unconscious patterns. If we want to communicate in a way that builds trust rather than destroys it, we need a clear, structured approach – one that allows us to express what matters, listen with openness, and navigate difficult moments without blame or avoidance.

This is what the **Magic Three Framework** is designed to do.

It is not about winning an argument. It is not about forcing a resolution. It is about finding a way through – a way to speak with clarity and purpose, to listen without shutting down, and to create space for understanding, even when emotions run high.

## Why This Framework Matters

Think of a time when you felt unheard. When you spoke, but your words landed badly. When frustration took over, or when silence seemed safer than the risk of conflict.

Perhaps you have walked away from a conversation wishing you had said something different. Maybe you have been on the receiving end of someone else's anger or disappointment, unsure of how to respond.

**The Magic Three is for these moments.**

- It is for the conversations you dread.
- It is for the times when you need to ask for something important but worry about how it will be received.
- It is for when someone else needs to be heard, and you are unsure how to hold space for them.
- It is for anyone who has ever struggled to find the right words.

Experts such as John Gottman, Douglas Stone, and Brené Brown have spent years researching what makes communication effective.

- Gottman's work reveals how criticism, defensiveness, and avoidance erode relationships over time.
- Stone's research in *Difficult Conversations* (1999) highlights how unspoken emotions drive conflict just as much as words do.
- Brown's insights into vulnerability and courage remind us that real connection is built on honesty – not perfection, not agreement, but the willingness to be seen and heard.

The **Magic Three Framework** brings these insights together into a repeatable, structured approach – one that allows you to navigate difficult conversations without losing yourself in defensiveness, overwhelm, or avoidance.

# The Three Steps:
# Clarify, Communicate, and Correct

The framework is built around three essential steps:

1. **Clarify: Before you speak, get clear on what matters most.**
   - What do you want to express?
   - What emotions are shaping your response?
   - What outcome are you hoping for?

2. **Communicate: Speak in a way that invites understanding, not defensiveness.**
   - How can you frame your words so they are heard?
   - Are you speaking from emotion or from clarity?
   - Are you ready to listen as much as you speak?

3. **Correct: If a conversation goes wrong, how can you repair and realign?**
   - What needs adjusting if you or the other person react badly?
   - How can you acknowledge hurt without shifting into blame?
   - How do you ensure that what was said leads to change rather than further distance?

This approach is not about rigid rules; it is about creating a repeatable method that helps you approach difficult conversations with intention, emotional steadiness, and clarity.

## Where in Your Life Do You Need This?

Right now, think about the conversations in your own life – the ones you have postponed, the ones you replay in your mind, the ones that feel impossible.

- The conversations that carry unsaid things – resentments, confessions, boundaries left unspoken.

- The conversations that feel too delicate, too painful, or too overwhelming to approach.

- The conversations that could change everything – if only they were handled well.

Imagine if, instead of fearing these moments, you had a framework to guide you through them with confidence and purpose.

This is what the **Magic Three** offers – a path through uncertainty, a way to communicate that strengthens rather than divides.

It is not about saying everything perfectly. It is about building trust, understanding, and connection – one conversation at a time.

## You Will See It in Action

This framework is woven throughout this book.

You will see it in real-life examples, in case studies of people who have used it to:

- Find their voice in long-silenced friendships.

- Communicate more clearly in strained relationships.

- Become better listeners in everyday life.

This is not just a theory. It is a practical tool that works.

Are you ready to step into it?

Are you ready to find your voice?

> *"In the end, the goals of conflict are really not about winning or losing. They are about reaching understanding and letting go of our need to control."*
>
> John Gottman
> *The Seven Principles for Making Marriage Work*, 1999

# The Magic Three Framework:
# A Steady Approach to Difficult Conversations

Let's bring this to life with real-world examples. Whether you are parenting, managing workplace challenges, or addressing personal relationships, the **Magic Three** can be applied in many situations. Here's how it works in action:

## The Magic Three Framework

- **Clarify**: Identify what you need or try to understand what is driving the other person's behaviour.

- **Communicate**: Express yourself calmly and constructively, avoiding blame or escalation.

- **Correct**: If things do not go as planned, revisit the issue with patience and respect, reinforcing your needs or seeking further clarity.

### Example 1: Kids – Balancing screen time and homework

Your child is glued to a screen instead of doing their homework. You have reminded them multiple times, but they keep saying, *"Just five more minutes."* Nothing changes.

- **Clarify:** Before reacting, get to the core of what you need: *"I need them to complete their homework before screen time."*

- **Communicate:** Speak calmly and be specific. Instead of saying, *"You never listen!"* try: *"I understand you want to finish your game, but homework comes first. Let's set a timer – twenty minutes of focus, and then you can have screen time."*

- **Correct:** If they still do not follow through, stay calm and reinforce the boundary: *"The timer went off, but your homework is not done yet. Let's pause the game now and finish up so you can have your screen time later."*

The key here is **consistency** – staying calm while reinforcing expectations.

## Example 2: Work – A colleague who is always late to meetings

A colleague regularly arrives late to team meetings, disrupting discussions and slowing everyone down.

- **Clarify:** Focus on the real impact: *"Our meetings need to start on time so we can plan efficiently."*

- **Communicate:** Keep it direct but collaborative: *"I have noticed that when meetings start late, it affects the whole team. Can we find a way to make sure everyone is on time?"*

- **Correct:** If the issue continues, revisit it without frustration: *"I know mornings can be hectic, but starting on time is important. Is there something we can adjust to make it easier for you to be on time?"*

This keeps the conversation solution-focused rather than critical.

## Why the Magic Three Works

Conversations rarely go perfectly the first time. People need time to process, adjust, and respond. That is why the **Magic Three** is designed to be revisited. If a conversation does not go as planned, you return to it with patience and clarity.

Throughout this book, we will explore how to apply the **Magic Three** in different real-life situations – from navigating difficult conversations with family to handling workplace conflicts.

If you want extra support, my website offers a workbook with journal prompts, exercises, and deeper insights to help you practice these strategies. (www.evestanway.co.uk/shoreline)

The **Magic Three Framework** is not about perfect conversations – it is about building trust, adapting when needed, and creating meaningful connections – one step at a time.

## Anchoring Yourself in Conversation

If expressing yourself feels difficult, choose one word that captures your intention: honesty, calm, courage, or clarity. A single word can act as a guide, keeping you focused when emotions rise or doubts creep in.

Write it down. Keep it somewhere visible – a note on your phone, a slip of paper in your wallet, or even written on your hand. Before a challenging conversation, take a slow breath, read your word, and let it settle in your mind.

Psychologists call this a grounding technique – a way to keep your brain engaged in the present rather than slipping into automatic reactions. By focusing on your word, you create a mental anchor, helping you stay steady, intentional, and true to yourself.

## Eve's Anchor

### Finding My Voice: The Journey From Silence to Freedom

For much of my life, I swallowed my words. I told myself it was easier that way – easier to keep the peace, easier to avoid conflict, easier to stay in the background. Daring to speak felt risky, like stepping onto unsteady ground. What if my words were ignored? What if they made things worse?

At first, silence felt like control. If I did not speak, I could not be wrong. If I held my emotions in check, no one could use them against me. Yet, staying quiet did not make things easier. It only made me disappear. I felt trapped in roles I never chose, disconnected from the people I loved, and, most painfully, disconnected from myself.

Breaking that silence was not just about speaking. It was about learning to move again, to trust my voice and step forward, even when my words felt fragile. Speaking is not about perfection. Every time we express our truth, no matter how uncertain it feels, we reclaim a part of ourselves.

It did not happen all at once. The first time I tried to speak my truth, my voice felt thin, uncertain. I hesitated, expecting resistance. My body tensed, bracing for rejection. Something remarkable happened. The world did not collapse. No one turned away in disgust. My words, imperfect as they were, did not ruin everything.

I had always thought of vulnerability as weakness. Years of avoiding it had left me hiding behind competence, control, and the quiet certainty that I could handle things on my own. Allowing my real thoughts and emotions to surface felt like a risk. With time, I realised that vulnerability was not a sign of failure. It was strength in its rawest form.

This journey is what led me to create the **Magic Three Framework**. I needed a way to navigate difficult conversations – a way to say what mattered without shutting down or pushing people away. The **Magic Three** is not just a method. It is a lifeline for those moments when speaking feels impossible, when emotions rise, when the fear of being unheard makes silence seem safer.

Some conversations come easily. Others take everything we have. Asking for what we need, setting boundaries, telling the truth about how we feel – these are not just words. They are acts of courage. They are moments that shape our relationships and, more importantly, shape how we see ourselves.

For anyone who has spent years feeling unheard, stepping into that courage can feel like a battle. If emotions have been dismissed, if needs have been ignored, saying *"This matters to me"* can feel like standing on the edge of a cliff. The fear of not being heard is real.

Speaking your truth is never wasted. Even if your voice shakes, even if the words come out messy.

As we move forward together, exploring the space between silence and speech, past and future, connection and difficulty, I invite you to reflect:

- **What part of yourself has remained quiet for too long?**
- **What might change if that voice was finally heard?**

These are not easy questions, but they are powerful ones. Salvaging your voice is not just about speaking. It is about reclaiming your truth. It is about stepping into the freedom of being fully seen, fully heard, and fully you.

---

### Lost at Sea: Key Takeaways

**Silence Feels Safe, But It Traps You:** What starts as protection can become a prison, shutting down connection, self-expression, and growth.

**What You Bury, You Carry:** Suppressed emotions do not disappear; they show up as stress, tension, and strained relationships.

**The Magic Three is Your Compass:** Clarify, Communicate, and Correct – three steps to navigate tough conversations with confidence and empathy.

**Anchor Your Voice:** A single word like courage or clarity can steady you when emotions rise, keeping you focused and present.

## A Poem for Those Who Dare to Speak

*We stand at the edge of silence, where fear holds its weight,
our hearts steady, yet our voices waver, tangled in the quiet.*

*There is fire in the unspoken, a truth beneath the mask,
where courage stirs gently, waiting in the hush of our thoughts.*

*A single word can cut through shadow, a whisper can shift the tide,
for the world does not change in silence, but in the echo of truth set free.*

*So stand firm, seeker – let your voice rise, let your words take flight,
for each truth spoken is a ripple, reshaping the shore.*

## Next Step

In this chapter, we explored how silence shapes our lives and limits growth, introducing the **Magic Three Framework** to approach difficult conversations with clarity and compassion. Beyond relationships, silence impacts our physical and mental health, manifesting as stress, fatigue, and anxiety. In the chapters ahead, we will uncover the hidden costs of silence and how breaking it can free your voice and lead to a more authentic, connected life.

*"Listen to the wind, it talks.
Listen to the silence, it speaks.
Listen to your heart, it knows."*

Native American Proverb

A Poem for Those Who Think in Space

# Part 2

# HOLDING THE STORM WITHIN: THE SILENT IMPACT OF SUPPRESSION

*"Silence often stems from a child's natural curiosity being stifled by an environment that feels unsafe, suppressing their instincts to question, explore, and express themselves."*

Eve Stanway

## Introduction:
### The Lingering Effects of Silence

Children are endlessly fascinating. They absorb as much from what is left unspoken as from what is taught outright. They pick up on the tone of a conversation, the pauses between words, the way emotions are handled – or ignored.

In families where parents have split up or in high-pressure households, the desire to maximise quality time can sometimes overshadow a child's need for quiet reflection. Rushing schedules, competing priorities, and adult responsibilities can hurry them along, leaving little space for them to explore their thoughts and emotions. From an early age, we learn what is acceptable to express and what must remain hidden. Silence begins in childhood – sometimes encouraged by well-meaning parents, sometimes as a survival mechanism. The effects are profound. This chapter explores how silence shapes us, the toll it takes, and how we can reclaim our voices.

Alice Miller observed, *"What is less well understood is that repression of our true feelings is not a survival tool at all, but a burden that can cause great suffering in adulthood"* (*The Drama of the Gifted Child*). A child who swallows their tears to avoid a scolding, or a teenager who holds back frustration to keep the peace, is not simply being well-behaved – they are learning, deeply and silently, that their emotions are unwelcome.

These moments leave lasting marks, especially when reinforced by phrases like, *"Stop bothering me," "Can't you see I'm busy?"* or *"Why can't you work it out for yourself?"* When parents are overwhelmed, these words can accumulate, chipping away at a child's sense of self-worth. Teaching self-restraint is important, but it must be balanced with giving children the confidence to express their emotions and needs without fear of rejection.

The words we hear as children shape us in ways we may struggle to understand as adults. Rebecca's story is a poignant example. A polished, accomplished lawyer, she questioned why a person like her needed therapy at each and every appointment, even as she explained that she was anxious, unable to sleep, and that even sleeping pills had failed to help. *"I just want to know why I'm struggling when I should be fine,"* she said. *"And I want you to tell me what I am not doing right."*

As she spoke, a pattern emerged. As a teenager, Rebecca had not stopped crying because her pain had disappeared – she had stopped because she learned her tears made others uncomfortable. Her parents spoke about her within earshot, calling her *"difficult"* and *"hard to please."* She learned to swallow her anger, dismissing it as *"dramatic."* Over time, she withdrew from her emotions, using silence as a shield against rejection.

Yet her voice was not wholly lost. She channelled it into her career, becoming a fierce advocate for others. But silence, even when repurposed, is rarely sustainable. Eventually, she sought help – not to fight for someone else's cause, but to reclaim her own voice.

Tanya Byron captures this beautifully: *"Children are not small adults. They are works in progress, shaped by their experiences"* (*Your Child Your Way*). Many of us grew up in environments where emotions felt unwelcome or overwhelming. A quiet child might appear well-behaved, but beneath that calm exterior often lies a wealth of unspoken feelings, waiting to be understood.

**Now take a moment for yourself.** It is not always easy to look back, but understanding where our patterns come from can help us move forward.

- What did you learn about expressing emotions as a child, and how does it shape your communication today?
- When do you hold back from speaking up, and what might change if you allowed those feelings to be heard?

There are no right or wrong answers – just an opportunity to listen to yourself with curiosity and compassion.

## Eve's Course Correction

Children who grow up in difficult circumstances often learn to be invisible. I certainly did. Hypervigilant and acutely aware of my surroundings, I had learned to fit in, to take up as little space as possible. Silence and self-sufficiency became second nature.

That summer, my invisibility began to unravel.

My Godmother Diana's home was a sanctuary. Warm. Safe. Magical.

The air carried the scent of fresh flowers and home cooking. Kittens padded across the wooden floor, their tiny paws tapping like whispers. We baked cakes for her church, our hands dusted with flour, laughter filling the kitchen. The market brimmed with bursts of colour – stalls piled high with fruit, the chatter of vendors, the weight of coins exchanged for something sweet. Riding lessons became moments of pure freedom, the wind in my hair, the world wide open. For a while, my life outside this idyllic bubble faded away.

Diana made me feel something unfamiliar: the sensation of being cherished.

Then, one night, that bubble burst.

I woke to the cold, damp realisation that I had wet the bed. Shame hit like a wave – sharp, unrelenting. My heart pounded as I stripped the sheets in silence, desperate to erase any trace of what had happened. I scrubbed the mattress with trembling hands, convinced that if I could hide it, I could undo it.

The next morning, I carried my secret like a heavy weight. Diana, perceptive as always, seemed to notice something was wrong. As we drove through Axminster in her Morris Traveller, she pointed to the odometer just as it rolled from 99,999 to zero. "A fresh start," she said with a warm smile.

Her kindness should have eased my guilt. Instead, it only deepened the ache of my secret.

On the train home, guilt consumed me. The rhythmic clatter of the tracks echoed the dread rising in my chest. Outside, the coastline slipped past in a blur, but inside, my thoughts were fixed on what Diana might think when she discovered the stain.

At nine years old, I did not know that love could survive mistakes. I had been taught to be invisible, to avoid causing trouble, to hold myself together no matter what. The weight of breaking those rules was suffocating.

By the time we reached Southampton, I had made two decisions.

First, I would not tell my father. His anger frightened me, but more than that, I could not bear the shame of admitting my failure. To him, I was supposed to be grown-up, responsible. Upsetting him was unthinkable. Even though I knew I would not tell him, my stomach churned at the thought that he might somehow *know*. I would have to act as if nothing had happened.

Second, I decided to write to Diana. A thank-you note was expected, but disguising the truth with polite words felt impossible. Instead, I confessed everything – what had happened, how I had tried to clean up, and how ashamed I was. I admitted I was not only ashamed of the accident but of my cowardice in not telling her in person.

Writing that letter was agony. Each word dragged feelings to the surface that I wanted to bury.

What happened next will be revealed later in this chapter as we explore the cost of silence and the power of finding our voice in challenging moments.

For now, consider this: Has silence ever kept you isolated? What might happen if you allowed yourself to speak? Sometimes, breaking the silence is the first step toward dissolving the distance it creates.

## Two Foundations That Shape This Book

Over the years, two core ideas have emerged – principles that shape this book and the foundation of the **Magic Three Framework**. They come from both research and lived experience:

1. **Mental health struggles often stem from silence.** Suppressed emotions and unresolved experiences do not disappear; they take root. Left unspoken, they can fuel anxiety,

depression, and inner turmoil. Over time, what begins as self-protection can become a cycle of disconnection, making it harder to reach out when help is needed.

2. **Breaking silence is the first step toward healing.** Speaking your truth – even when it feels uncomfortable – can be profoundly transformative. Naming what has been hidden releases its hold, easing both emotional and physical distress.

These principles shape every tool and technique in this book, including the **Magic Three Framework: Clarify, Communicate, and Correct.**

Silence is not passive. It shapes our experiences, our relationships, and our sense of self. Learning to break that silence is not just about speaking – it is about reclaiming who we are.

## The Impact of Silence: Mind and Body

Silence is not just the absence of words. It is the quiet accumulation of unspoken emotions, the weight of feelings left unheard. When we push our emotions down, they do not disappear – they settle into our bodies, shaping how we experience life.

In the first volume of her autobiography, Maya Angelou wrote, *"There is no greater agony than bearing an untold story inside you,"* (*I Know Why the Caged Bird Sings*, 1981). This is not just a metaphor. Suppressed emotions affect us physically, just as surely as they do mentally. The tension in your shoulders after a hard day, the knot in your stomach before a difficult conversation, the persistent headaches when stress builds – these are not random discomforts. They are your body's way of speaking when words feel unsafe.

Gabor Maté explains, *"Trauma is not what happens to you; it is what happens inside you."* When emotions remain unexpressed, they do not fade. They manifest as stress, anxiety, chronic tension, and even physical illness. In *The Body Keeps the Score*, Bessel van der Kolk highlights how long-term emotional suppression changes the way our nervous system functions, keeping us in a state of heightened stress.

As children, many of us were subtly taught that certain emotions were unacceptable. We learned to hide sadness to avoid making others uncomfortable, to suppress anger to prevent conflict, and to pretend happiness even when we felt anything but. Over time, we internalised a dangerous lesson: that silence is safer than expression.

Yet silence is not neutral. It is a barrier between us and those we love. It is a slow erosion of self-worth, an invisible wound that deepens each time we swallow our words.

But if silence shapes our experience, breaking that silence can transform it. The act of expressing our emotions – whether through words, movement, or creative outlets – releases the emotional pressure we carry. It allows us to process, to heal, to reclaim the parts of ourselves that have been buried.

Take a moment to reflect:

- What emotions have you been silencing?
- Where in your body do you feel that tension?
- What would it be like to let those feelings have a voice?

Silence may feel protective, but true connection – both with ourselves and others – comes when we dare to speak.

## Moving Forward: Finding Your Voice

There is hope. By recognising these patterns and understanding their origins, we can begin to break free. Psychologist John Bradshaw wrote, *"In reclaiming our inner child, we heal our emotional wounds and unlock the power of authenticity"* (*Homecoming*). Taking back your voice is not about changing the past; it is about embracing a future where open emotion is a positive quality.

What could change if you began to speak clearly and calmly, not with anger or fear?

As we look ahead, we will explore how the **Magic Three** can help you clarify your needs, communicate openly, and mend the gaps silence has created. Reflection, centring exercises, and practical steps will help you release the emotional weight of silence.

**Remember – your voice matters.**

## The Roots of Silence in Mental Health Issues

*"The opposite of courage in our society is not cowardice; it is conformity"*

Rollo May (1909–1994)
American psychologist and author

### Theory One: Silence: The Weight We Carry

When it comes to mental health, silence is not merely the absence of sound. It is the weight of unspoken emotions, the truths we sidestep, the pain we bury because facing it feels unbearable. It settles into the body like a stone in deep water – out of sight but ever-present, its pull shaping our movements, our choices, the way we breathe.

Perhaps you know this kind of silence. The kind that begins as protection but slowly grows heavy, pressing down in ways you do not even realise.

*The Shape of Silence*

For Lawrence, silence had been his first language. As a child, he learned quickly that expressing emotions led to rejection. Disappointment earned a dismissive shake of the head. Hurt was met with an eye-roll. Frustration was labelled overreaction. The lesson was clear: emotions made people uncomfortable. They were messy, inconvenient, best kept to yourself.

So, he buried them.

For years, it worked. He became the person others relied on – the steady one, the problem-solver, the calm in the storm. But silence is not the absence of feeling; it is the compression of it. And what is pushed down will always find a way back up.

Sleepless nights. A tight band of tension across his forehead. A gnawing restlessness that no amount of work, exercise, or scrolling through his phone could quiet. His emotions had not disappeared. They had simply changed form, demanding attention in ways he could no longer ignore.

In *The Secret of the Ages*, Robert Collier wrote, *"Any thought that is passed on to the subconscious often enough and convincingly enough is finally accepted."*

Silence works much the same way.

## The Cost of Silence

We do not wake up one day and decide to suppress parts of ourselves. It happens gradually, shaped by the messages we receive as children. Maybe you were told to *"cheer up"* when you were sad or to *"calm down"* when you were angry. Maybe you learned that certain emotions made people pull away, that love came more easily when you were easy, agreeable, undemanding.

Lawrence had learned that lesson well.

His parents had always told him, *"We just want you to be happy."* He understood what they meant: happiness was acceptable. Anything else was not.

So, he became fine. Fine was safe. Fine was expected.

But fine had a cost.

Decades of swallowing his emotions had worn him down. The body does not forget what the mind tries to ignore. The tension in his shoulders. The dull ache in his chest. The feeling, not quite pain, but not quite right either, like something pressing against the edges of his ribs.

He had spent so long keeping things inside that he was no longer sure who he was without the silence.

### Finding His Voice

Starting therapeutic coaching felt like breaking an unspoken rule. Talking about his feelings seemed risky. What if sharing them made him seem weak? Ungrateful?

He hesitated at first, choosing his words with the same caution he had always used. But little by little, the silence cracked.

He started by writing things down. Words that had long remained unspoken, even in his own mind. Frustration. Sadness. Longing. At first, they felt foreign, as though they belonged to someone else. But the more he wrote, the more he recognised them as his own.

It was not weakness. It was recognition.

He was becoming visible to himself again.

### A New Beginning

As Lawrence grew more comfortable expressing his emotions, his relationships began to shift.

When he told a friend he was struggling, they did not turn away. They listened.

When he admitted to his partner that he felt overwhelmed, she did not accuse him of being dramatic. She held his hand.

Speaking did not weaken his connections; it strengthened them.

But the most profound change came in his role as a father. He wanted his children to grow up knowing their emotions were valid, that their sadness, anger, and uncertainty were not things to be fixed but to be felt. So he did something unfamiliar: he listened.

When his daughter came to him, upset about a falling out with a friend, he resisted the urge to tell her it would be fine. Instead, he sat beside her. "That sounds really hard," he said. "Tell me more."

For the first time, he was giving his children what he had always needed.

In Stephen Daldry's 2002 film *The Hours*, Virginia Woolf's character says, *"You cannot find peace by avoiding life."*

Lawrence had spent years avoiding his emotions, convinced that silence was safety. But real safety – the kind he longed for – came not from pushing feelings down, but from making space for them.

### Reclaiming Your Voice

The journey back to yourself does not happen in grand gestures. It begins in small, quiet moments. A pause before dismissing your own emotions. A breath before brushing past your pain. A choice to let yourself be seen, little by little, in safe spaces.

Each step chips away at the silence.

Each step is a return.

Each step makes room for something new.

## The Physical Impact of Suppression and Repression

Your body holds on to unspoken emotions, often in ways you may not consciously recognise. The weight of what is unsaid does not simply vanish – it settles into muscles, breath, heartbeat, and tension.

While suppression and repression have similar effects, they work differently. Suppression is deliberate – the choice to push aside frustration, sadness, or fear so you can focus on the moment. Repression, however, happens beneath awareness, burying emotions so deeply that you may not even realise they are there.

*"When the Body Says No,"* explains Gabor Maté, *"suppressed emotions keep the body on high alert, constantly releasing stress hormones like cortisol."* Over time, this wears on the body, leading to chronic muscle tension, headaches, digestive issues, and fatigue. These discomforts are not random – they are your body's way of speaking when words have been withheld.

In *The Body Keeps the Score,* Bessel van der Kolk describes how unresolved emotions alter the body's natural balance. The immune system weakens, stress hormones remain elevated, and the nervous system stays on high alert. The body does not forget what the mind pushes away.

Perhaps you have felt it – tight shoulders that never seem to relax, a heaviness in your chest, a stomach that churns when emotions rise. These are not just physical sensations; they are signs of emotions that have been held in for too long.

Breaking the silence is not only about speaking. It is also about allowing the body to release what it has carried. At first, this can feel unsettling, like removing armour you have worn for years. Yet, consider what might happen if you allowed those feelings to surface – if instead of resisting them, you let them have space. This is where emotional freedom begins.

## The Brain's Response to Emotional Suppression

The mind and body are not separate. Emotional suppression rewires the brain, making it harder to manage stress and process emotions.

The amygdala, which processes fear and emotional responses, becomes overactive, making even small stressors feel like threats. Bessel van der Kolk describes this as being *"stuck in alarm mode,"* constantly scanning for danger. At the same time, the prefrontal cortex, responsible for decision-making and emotional regulation, becomes overworked, struggling to hold back suppressed feelings. The result? Mental fatigue, difficulty concentrating, and a growing sense of emotional numbness.

Neurochemicals also shift. When emotions are suppressed, the brain produces less serotonin and dopamine, the chemicals that regulate mood, motivation, and connection. Over time, this can lead to irritability, exhaustion, and a sense of detachment – from yourself and others.

Gabor Maté reminds us that unprocessed emotions do not disappear – they manifest in the body. Suppression does not just silence feelings; it builds tension, creating a cycle of stress that spills into everyday life.

Think about the moments you avoid. The conversations that feel too overwhelming to have. The way stress lingers in your shoulders or chest after a difficult day. Suppressed emotions turn ordinary interactions into sources of discomfort, leaving you feeling out of sync with yourself.

Recognising the toll of suppression is the first step to breaking free. By facing the emotions you have pushed aside, you begin to reconnect with yourself, allowing space for deeper emotional awareness.

**Quick Practice: Release Tension with a Body Scan**

Take a moment to pause. Find a quiet spot where you feel at ease.

- Close your eyes and take three slow, deep breaths.
- Gently scan your body from head to toe. Notice where tension lingers – perhaps in your jaw, shoulders, or lower back.
- As you exhale, imagine that tension softening. Let your shoulders drop, your jaw relax, your breath deepen.
- After finishing, take a final deep breath. Notice how your body feels now.

This simple practice helps tune into the physical impact of suppressed emotions. Over time, it creates a space where emotions can be acknowledged instead of held in, making room for more honest conversations – with yourself and with others.

## Breaking the Silence: The Power of Difficult Conversations

*"In the end, we will remember not the words of our enemies, but the silence of our friends."*

Martin Luther King, Jr., (1929–1968)
American Baptist minister, activist and philosopher

### Theory Two: Conversations as a Key to Mental Wellness

For many of us, sharing emotions feels like stepping into uncharted territory, especially if we grew up in homes where feelings were brushed aside. Maybe you learnt to hold things in to keep the peace or were met with responses such as, *"Don't cry, it's not a big deal,"* or *"We don't talk about that here."* These messages, however well-intended, often lead to emotional bottlenecks.

Emotions do not disappear when unspoken – they settle in, creating tension and unease. Processing them is much like untangling a knot. Left unattended, the knot tightens, becoming harder to manage. Speaking aloud – whether to a trusted friend, therapist, or loved one – loosens those threads, making space for understanding and healing.

John Bradshaw's work on family dynamics highlights how silence acts as a barrier to mental health. When emotional expression is discouraged, children often internalise their pain. These unspoken feelings may later manifest as chronic stress, physical symptoms, or difficulty forming trusting relationships. Without conversation, emotions remain trapped, leaving individuals feeling isolated and unheard.

Yet talking about our struggles does more than release tension – it invites new perspectives. It reminds us we are not alone.

## The Power of Speaking Aloud

Elizabeth, a teacher, carried the weight of her father's criticism long into adulthood. *"What happened to the other 3%?"* he would say whenever she scored 97% on a test. For years, this voice echoed in her mind, shaping how she saw herself. In therapy, she repeated those words aloud for the first time. I asked her what she would say to someone else in her position. Her response was immediate: *"That must have been so hard."*

At last, she heard the kindness she had needed all along – this time, from her own mouth.

Zain, an estate agent in a high-pressure job, had a different experience. He bottled up stress to maintain professionalism, believing that admitting difficulty meant weakness. The first sign that something was wrong came unexpectedly – an outburst in traffic so uncharacteristic, it startled even him.

Realising something had to change, he confided in a trusted colleague, who admitted to feeling the same way. That single conversation shifted everything. He was not failing – he was human. From there, small changes followed: he asked for time off, returned to running, and slowly rebuilt balance.

These stories reveal a universal truth: conversations help us process emotions in ways silence never can. Speaking aloud transforms confusion into clarity, pain into understanding, and isolation into connection.

Starting to speak is not just about being heard – it is about realising you are not alone and that solutions are possible.

## Navigating Difficult Conversations

Of course, not every conversation leads to understanding. Some people use gaslighting and stonewalling (see glossary) to deflect, leaving you doubting your own feelings.

If you have ever been met with *"You're imagining things"* or *"I'm not talking about this,"* you know how silencing that can be. These tactics are designed to keep you second-guessing yourself.

If you are in a relationship – personal or professional – where your emotions are routinely dismissed, know that you are not overreacting. Your feelings matter. Support is available, and I encourage you to explore the resources on my website (www.evestanway.co.uk) for tools, prompts, and guidance to help navigate these challenges.

## Alex's Path to Healing Through Dialogue

Sometimes, a person's inner world tells a very different story from the one they present to others. Alex was one of those people.

Their style was bold – bright colours, bold patterns, statement accessories. Confidence, individuality, presence. Yet when Alex spoke, their voice was quiet, hesitant, as if trying to take up as little space as possible.

This contrast stayed with me. It was clear that Alex's softly spoken nature was not just a personality trait – it was a reflection of something deeper.

Growing up, Alex had been labelled *"the quiet one."* Their family, though loving, had little patience for big emotions. *"Keep it to yourself." "Don't make a fuss."* Alex's understanding of self-expression developed silently, shaped by these phrases.

Despite their vibrant exterior, Alex carried years of self-doubt, unsure if their thoughts and feelings were worth sharing. *"It feels like I am two different people,"* they admitted. *"The person I want to be and the person I think I'm allowed to be."*

### Unpacking the Silence

Through reflection, Alex saw how this disconnect had shaped their relationships and self-image. Silence had once been a shield – protection from rejection or criticism. But over time, it had become a barrier, keeping them disconnected from others – and from themselves.

Their first step was naming what had been buried. Through journalling and guided exercises, they began to untangle years of unspoken emotions: frustration, sadness, fear of being judged. Naming these emotions allowed them to see them not as weaknesses, but as natural, human responses.

Speaking up was harder. In therapy, during emotional but safe conversations, Alex practised sharing their thoughts and feelings, even when it felt uncomfortable. *"I worried people would dismiss me,"* they said. *"But when I started speaking up, I realised they were actually listening."*

Each time they used their voice, confidence grew. They were no longer waiting for permission to exist fully.

### Finding Balance

As they grew more comfortable expressing themselves, Alex also learned that being heard was not about oversharing or seeking approval. It was about speaking from a place of self-respect.

Over time, their bold clothing was no longer just an external statement – it reflected an internal shift. They no longer felt like they were hiding. *"I finally feel like me,"* Alex said.

### The Takeaway

The labels we are given as children – *quiet one, troublemaker, too sensitive, too much* – can shape us in ways we do not always realise. The masks we wear to protect ourselves can become the very things that hold us back.

But with time, patience, and courage, we can take those masks off.

Alex's story reminds us that reclaiming our voice is not about becoming someone new – it is about rediscovering who we have always been.

Because understanding someone's outer world only tells part of the story. It is in the layers beneath – the long-held beliefs and unspoken fears – where real transformation begins.

# The Magic Three Framework for Breaking Silence

## The Magic Three Framework in Action

We have all been in situations where someone's indecision affects us. Perhaps you have a friend who keeps changing their mind – about making plans, about important decisions, about what they want.

You understand they are struggling, and you do not want to be unkind. But their constant shifts leave you feeling frustrated, uncertain, and drained.

How do you address this without creating conflict?

This is where the **Magic Three Framework** helps.

**Step 1: Clarify – Get clear on your own feelings and needs.**

Before speaking, take a moment to understand what is really bothering you. Is it the last-minute cancellations? The uncertainty? The emotional energy it takes to keep adjusting?

*"I feel stressed because I never know if our plans will happen. This uncertainty makes it hard to plan my time."*

Having clarity keeps the conversation focused on your experience, rather than making it about what the other person is doing wrong.

**Step 2: Communicate – Express your feelings in a way that invites understanding.**

Instead of saying:

*"You are so indecisive – it is exhausting."*

Try:

*"I understand that making decisions can be tough, and I want to be supportive. But when plans keep changing, I feel unsettled. Could we find a way to make things more predictable?"*

This approach acknowledges their struggle while also asserting your need for stability. It avoids blame and shifts the conversation toward problem-solving.

**Step 3: Correct – Reinforce your boundary calmly if the pattern continues.**

If they change plans again at the last minute, you might say:

*"I noticed we had to change plans again today. I completely understand if things come up, but I need clearer expectations moving forward."*

This keeps your boundary firm without resentment or accusations. If they continue to struggle with decisiveness, you may need to adjust how much energy you invest in making plans with them, but you will have made your position clear.

### *Why This Works*

People do not always change overnight. Some feel uncomfortable being told their behaviour is frustrating. Others resist making adjustments, even when they know they should.

Repeating your boundary in a calm, non-confrontational way helps them process your request without feeling attacked. Over time, this approach reduces tension, regulates emotions, and encourages more balanced conversations.

## The Magic Three in Practice

The goal of this framework is not to control others – it is to help you express your needs with clarity and confidence.

- ✓ Clarify what is truly bothering you.
- ✓ Communicate your feelings in a way that builds understanding.
- ✓ Correct by reinforcing your boundary calmly and consistently.

Using these steps will transform frustrating situations into productive conversations – helping you be heard while maintaining your relationships.

# The Benefits of Breaking Silence

## Emotional and Psychological Relief

Keeping emotions bottled up creates an invisible weight – one that builds slowly until it becomes unbearable. When you finally speak, it is not just about *getting something off your chest*. It is about freeing yourself from the tension of holding it all in.

Sharing your feelings does not mean they disappear overnight. But it does mean you are no longer carrying them alone. The act of expression – whether through conversation, writing, or even self-reflection – allows emotions to move, rather than remain trapped.

Daring to speak is more than release; it is a way to reclaim yourself. When you voice what matters, you reinforce your own worth. Each time you put words to your experience, you strengthen your sense of self.

## Building Self-Worth Through Expression

Silence can make you feel invisible. Over time, it sends a message – not just to others, but to yourself – that your emotions do not matter.

Each time you advocate for your needs, you send yourself the opposite message:

- ✓ *"I am allowed to take up space."*
- ✓ *"My feelings are worth expressing."*
- ✓ *"I matter."*

This is the foundation of self-worth – the quiet but unshakable belief that you are valuable, no matter what.

Unlike self-esteem, which is shaped by external validation, self-worth is an internal anchor. The more you express your truth, the stronger that anchor becomes.

## Stronger Relationships Through Honest Conversations

Breaking silence does not just benefit you – it transforms the way you connect with others.

When you share openly, you invite people to see the real you. This kind of honesty signals trust, making relationships feel safer and more genuine.

Silence, on the other hand, creates distance. When you hold back emotions – whether out of fear, politeness, or habit – you leave a gap between what you feel and what you show. Over time, this unspoken tension can lead to misunderstandings, resentment, or emotional disconnection.

Being heard is a fundamental part of belonging. Expressing your emotions not only strengthens your own voice but encourages the people around you to do the same. This builds a cycle of openness, where conversations become a source of connection rather than conflict.

Healthy relationships are not about avoiding discomfort. They are about making space for honesty.

## The Courage to Speak

Breaking silence is a choice – one that requires both courage and self-compassion.

Each time you speak up, you affirm your right to be heard. You make space for honesty, connection, and self-respect.

This journey is not about saying everything all at once. It is about learning that your words have value, your feelings are real, and your voice deserves to be part of the conversation.

The more you step into that space, the more natural it becomes.

Because the moment you allow yourself to be seen for who you truly are – you also allow yourself to be free.

# The Role of Grounding for Managing Overwhelming Emotions

Daring to speak can feel intense. The emotions that surface – relief, anxiety, vulnerability – may arrive in waves, sometimes stronger than expected. In these moments, grounding techniques offer a way to stay steady, present, and in control.

Grounding is about reconnecting with the here and now. When emotions run high, your mind may race, and your body may react – your heart pounding, your breath quickening. Grounding helps you shift focus away from this internal storm and back to something tangible:

- ✓ The steady rhythm of your breath.
- ✓ The weight of your body in a chair.
- ✓ The cool air on your skin.
- ✓ The sounds around you.

By anchoring yourself in these small, physical sensations, you interrupt the cycle of stress before it takes hold.

## Why Grounding Works

When faced with emotional intensity, your nervous system automatically activates the fight-or-flight response. This can leave you feeling trapped between two extremes:

- Wanting to run from the conversation.
- Wanting to push through with force.

Neither response leads to meaningful dialogue. Grounding techniques help break this pattern, shifting your body into a calmer, more intentional state. When you feel steady, your thoughts become clearer, and you can act with purpose instead of reacting out of fear or stress.

> *"When you react, someone else is in charge.*
> *When you act, you reclaim control."*
>
> Stoic Philosophy

With regular practice, grounding becomes a powerful tool for emotional resilience. Over time, you will find it easier to stay composed, even in tough situations.

## Grounding for Difficult Conversations

Grounding does not just help you feel calm – it creates the space for honest, meaningful conversations.

When you feel centred, you:

- ✓ speak with clarity instead of from panic
- ✓ listen without feeling defensive
- ✓ approach challenges with focus and presence

Difficult conversations are not just about the words you say – they are about how you show up. Grounding gives you the stability to express emotions honestly, without being consumed by them.

If grounding feels difficult – especially if you have experienced trauma – you are not alone. Additional prompts, tools, and support are available in the resources section of my website: www.evestanway.co.uk/shoreline. These techniques can be explored at your own pace, with guidance for seeking further assistance if needed.

> ### Holding the Storm Within: Key Takeaways
>
> **Roots of Silence:** Silence often originates from childhood experiences where emotional expression was dismissed or discouraged, leaving lasting impacts.
>
> **The Physical Toll of Suppression:** Suppressed emotions manifest in the body as tension, fatigue, and other stress-related symptoms.
>
> **Breaking the Silence:** Voicing emotions and needs, even gradually, can lead to profound healing and greater self-awareness.
>
> **Emotional Reconnection:** Recognising and validating suppressed emotions helps individuals reclaim authenticity and emotional resilience.

## Eve's Safe Harbour:
## The Moment That Changed Everything

When Diana's reply finally arrived, I held my breath as I unfolded the letter. Her words were gentle, full of kindness. She told me she did not think any less of me for what had happened and that she was proud of me for being honest.

Something inside me shifted.

Silence had felt like protection, but all it really did was keep me alone. Finding courage to speak, no matter how difficult, created space – for understanding, for connection, for relief.

Diana's response taught me something profound: mistakes do not define us. It is what we do next that matters. When we allow ourselves to be seen – our vulnerabilities, our fears, our flaws – we give others the chance to meet us with the same kindness we long for.

Looking back, I can see now that silence did not keep me safe; it kept me stuck. I had been hiding behind a wall I thought would protect me, but all it did was shut me off from comfort, understanding, and trust. The moment I spoke up, something changed. The fear was still there, but so was something else – freedom.

## Returning to the Moment of Release

So, what happened after I spoke my truth?

Writing that letter lifted a weight, but the relief was not instant. It took years to understand that speaking up is not a one-time act – it is a practice. It was not just about that moment with Diana. It was about every time I chose to face my fears, be honest with myself and others, and stop hiding.

The courage I found in speaking up did not just change my relationship with Diana – it changed how I saw myself. It was many years, before I fully understood this lesson, that true connection and understanding only happen when we allow ourselves to be known.

Daring to speak was not a quick fix. It was the start of something deeper – a new way of being, a new way of showing up in my life and in my relationships.

## Poetic Reflection on Emotional Repression

## Rainbow in My Brain

*When despair rains down on hope,*
*A prism of shadows in my mind begins to glow.*
*Refracted colours of my feelings blur,*
*Murk into brown, as tears distort my sight.*

*I reach for the light, and*
*With each step, it slips away.*
*I am unloved – can you feel that truth?*
*Please hear me, believe me, see me,*
*To release red-golden warmth,*
*Split of light, that embraces the dark.*

*My despair hangs heavy and low,*
*Then hope showers down, and colours emerge.*
*To paint the horizon of my life, my soul,*
*Living creative force, essence of me.*

*I was taught to feel despair,*
*So, I would never see my light.*
*Now, as hope rains down,*
*I see my emotions clearly.*

*The brown and the dark, my friends also,*
*For all colours reflect the truth.*
*Can you see the rainbow?*
*It is glorious!*

# Part 3

# MAPPING THE CURRENTS: UNDERSTANDING WHAT LIES BENEATH

*"A difficult conversation is a journey through discomfort, one where we must face our fears of rejection, disappointment, and even of being truly seen."*

Eve Stanway

## Facing the Challenge of Difficult Conversations

By now, you have seen how silence shapes our lives – how it influences our relationships, our self-worth, and even our sense of identity. Now, we take the next step: moving from understanding the cost of silence to learning how to face the conversations we once avoided.

Psychologist Susan David, a leading expert in emotional resilience and the author of *Emotional Agility*, reminds us: *"Courage is not the absence of fear, but fear walking."*

Difficult conversations test this courage – not because they are easy, but because they require us to sit with discomfort rather than turn away from it. Whether it is an unspoken tension, a long-overdue boundary, or an emotional wound that needs addressing, these moments challenge us to stay present, communicate clearly, and handle discomfort without shutting down or lashing out.

It is instinctive to avoid conflict, yet Marshall Rosenberg, the psychologist and mediator behind *Nonviolent Communication*, explains that difficult conversations are not about winning or losing – they are about understanding what truly matters to each person. Many of us have been conditioned to either suppress emotions to keep the peace or express them reactively, leading to defensiveness and further disconnection. This chapter offers tools to help you break that cycle – moving away from avoidance or confrontation and toward clarity, empathy, and resolution.

## Why This Chapter Matters

This is the final chapter of Section One, bringing together everything we have explored so far about why difficult conversations matter and why they can feel so overwhelming.

- ✓ In Part 1, we examined the roots of silence – how we learn to hold back our emotions and avoid saying what we really mean.

- ✓ In Part 2, we uncovered the impact of silence – on our mental health, our relationships, and our self-worth.

- ✓ Now, in Part 3, we turn toward action. How do we face difficult conversations with confidence? How do we navigate discomfort instead of avoiding it?

This chapter will help you:

- ✓ **Understand why certain conversations feel so difficult** and what is really happening in your brain and body.

- ✓ **Recognise your own triggers and reactions** so you can manage them more effectively.

✓ **Learn practical tools** to stay steady and engaged, including "Quick Calm" techniques you can use in the moment.

## From Awareness to Action

When you understand why difficult conversations feel challenging – and how to navigate them – you can start seeing them not as something to dread, but as a path to greater clarity, connection, and self-respect.

This is where we begin the shift – from understanding the problem to preparing for change.

# The Benefits of Undertaking Difficult Conversations

## Why We Avoid Difficult Conversations: James' Story

Have you ever avoided a conversation, hoping the issue would simply fade away – only to find it growing heavier, lurking at the edges of your mind?

At first, ignoring it felt like relief. A weight lifted. A breath released. *Not today*, James told himself. *I will deal with it later.* But later stretched into days, then weeks, and the silence that once seemed like protection became the very thing trapping him.

It started with money. The figures in his accounts did not add up, and the more he looked at them, the tighter the knot in his stomach became. Instead of addressing it, he started avoiding calls and emails from clients and business partners. His phone would ring, and he would glance at the screen, pulse quickening, breath shallow. He would let it go to voicemail. When an email popped up with the subject line 'Urgent', he would skim it and think, *I will sort it tomorrow.*

But tomorrow never came. And with every unanswered message, the problem grew.

His clients, once patient, started chasing him more aggressively. At first, the messages were polite – "Just checking in…" – but soon they became sharper, frustration seeping into their words. Even so, James could not bring himself to reply. Each unread email felt like a weight pressing down on him, each ignored call a fresh pang of guilt.

The longer he stayed silent, the worse it got. His confidence eroded, his anxiety deepened, and soon, he found himself avoiding more than just work. Social events, casual conversations – anything that might bring up the reality he was running from. He convinced himself that facing it would be unbearable. That once he opened the floodgates, the backlash would drown him.

What finally changed was a conversation with a close friend. Someone who noticed the way he had been withdrawing, the exhaustion behind his forced smiles. *"You do not have to have all the answers right now,"* they said. *"You just have to stop running."*

Something in James shifted. For the first time, he saw that his silence was not just affecting him – it was affecting others. His clients were not just frustrated; they were confused, uncertain, and left in limbo. His avoidance was making everything harder, not just for himself but for the people relying on him.

That evening, he sat down at his desk, heart pounding, and began replying to emails. He did not have a perfect plan, but he could at least acknowledge the situation. His fingers hovered over the keyboard before he finally typed, *"I am working on a solution and will update you soon."*

To his surprise, the responses were not filled with anger, as he had feared. Some people were relieved to hear from him. Others even offered support. He realised that facing the conversation – even without all the answers – felt far better than carrying the weight of avoidance.

James' story is not unique. We all know the pull of avoidance, the momentary relief that turns into long-term anxiety. But conversations do not disappear just because we ignore them. They wait in the shadows, growing heavier. And the truth is, the hardest part is often not the conversation itself, but the decision to stop running from it.

The first step may feel uncomfortable, but the relief that follows – the clarity, the confidence, the freedom – is always worth it.

## The Two Conversations in Every Difficult Conversation

Difficult conversations rarely begin with words. They start in the quiet of your own mind, in the racing thoughts, and the uneasy feeling in your stomach long before you ever speak. By the time you open your mouth, you have already had the conversation a hundred times in your head – anticipating reactions, imagining worst-case scenarios, questioning whether it is worth saying anything at all.

And then, there is the second conversation – the one that actually takes place. The words exchanged in real time. The way emotions ripple through the room, shaping the tone and direction of what is said. These two conversations – the internal and the external – are always happening side by side. And if the first conversation is filled with doubt, fear, or frustration, it can make the second feel impossible.

Think about the last time you needed to say something important. Maybe you had been putting it off, telling yourself, *It is not the right time*, or *It will only make things worse*. The more you delayed, the heavier it felt. By the time you finally spoke, the weight of all those unspoken thoughts made it harder to find the right words. Maybe the other person reacted defensively, and suddenly, the conversation was not about the issue at hand, but about managing their emotions – or worse, retreating altogether.

## The Internal Conversation: What You Tell Yourself

Before we ever speak, we shape the conversation in our minds. This internal dialogue is often where the biggest battle takes place. Maybe you recognise some of these thoughts:

- *I should be able to handle this alone.*
- *If I bring this up, they will think I am difficult.*
- *There is no point – they will not listen anyway.*

These beliefs do not come from nowhere. They are often echoes of past experiences – times when speaking up led to conflict, rejection, or being dismissed. They keep us silent, convincing us that avoidance is safer. But the more we avoid, the harder it becomes to speak when it truly matters.

Now, imagine shifting the way you think about the conversation before it happens. Instead of bracing for the worst, what if you asked yourself:

- *What do I actually need from this conversation?*
- *How can I express that in a way that feels honest and true to me?*
- *Is my fear based on fact, or is it based on past experiences that no longer define me?*

When you approach a conversation with clarity – when you step in knowing what you want to say and why – it changes everything. You are no longer at the mercy of your fears. You are anchored in your own truth.

## The External Conversation: What You Say and How You Say It

Imagine standing at the edge of a conversation you know you need to have. Your pulse quickens, your hands tighten, and the words feel tangled in your throat. You already anticipate how the other person might react. Maybe you have been here before – tried to explain, only to be dismissed or met with defensiveness. The weight of those past experiences makes it feel as though history is doomed to repeat itself.

But what if, before speaking, you took a moment to reset?

Instead of rushing into the conversation with tension, you pause. You remind yourself: *I am here to be honest, not to win. I am here to create understanding, not to prove a point.*

The way we begin a conversation shapes where it will go. If you have ever watched someone's expression harden the moment you started speaking, you know how quickly walls can go up. A simple shift in how you frame your words can keep the conversation open instead of shutting it down.

Instead of saying, *"You never listen to me,"* try, *"I want to talk about this because I value our relationship."*

Instead of, *"You are always dismissing my feelings,"* try, *"I need to feel heard, and I want to understand your perspective too."*

Words carry weight. The way we deliver them determines whether they land softly or hit like a blow. When we speak with intention – when we express ourselves with both honesty and care – the conversation has a far greater chance of moving toward connection instead of conflict.

## Closing the Gap Between Thought and Expression

Difficult conversations are not just about finding the courage to speak. They are about learning to listen – to yourself first, so you can approach the conversation from a place of clarity, and then to the other person, so you can create space for genuine understanding.

Before you step into your next conversation, take a moment to reflect:

- *What assumptions am I bringing into this?*
- *What do I truly want to express?*
- *How can I make sure my words reflect my intention?*

The first conversation happens in your mind. The second happens in the world. The more clarity you bring to the first, the stronger and more confident you will feel stepping into the second.

If you want to go deeper, the workbook includes a guided reflection to help you explore your beliefs, clarify your needs, and practice shifting from self-doubt to self-assurance. You can find the full exercise at www.evestanway.co.uk/shoreline.

## The Brain's Role in High-Stakes Conversations

### Understanding the Amygdala Response

Difficult conversations are not just about words. They trigger deep, instinctive reactions in the body – waves of tension that rise before you even realise what is happening. That sudden tightness in your chest, the heat creeping up your neck, the way your mind suddenly goes blank.

These are not signs of failure. They are your brain's way of trying to keep you safe.

Just as silence takes a toll on the body, so does the stress of difficult conversations. The more you understand why your body reacts this way, the more you can work with it, rather than against it. Recognising what is happening inside you makes it possible to stay steady, engaged, and in control – even when emotions run high.

### The Brain's Alarm System

Deep inside your brain, the amygdala stands guard, always watching, always ready to sound the alarm. This small, almond-shaped structure is responsible for processing emotions, especially fear and perceived threats. It moves fast – faster than conscious thought – deciding in an instant whether a situation is safe or dangerous.

In a real emergency, this response is life-saving. Step into a busy road and see a car speeding toward you, and your amygdala will flood your body with adrenaline before you even process what is happening. Your heart will pound, your muscles will tense, and without thinking, you will leap back to safety.

During a difficult conversation, the same system can misfire. A tense exchange with a colleague, a disagreement with a loved one, even the act of setting a boundary, can feel, on some level, like a threat. The amygdala does not know the difference between physical danger and emotional discomfort – it just registers stress and throws your body into high alert.

The heart races. Breathing becomes shallow. Blood drains from the rational part of the brain, the prefrontal cortex, making it harder to think clearly. Words that had been carefully prepared suddenly vanish. The impulse to defend, to fight back, to shut down, or to walk away entirely can feel overwhelming. This is the amygdala hijack – your brain choosing survival over conversation.

## When Your Body Takes Over

The moment the nervous system senses danger, it shifts into survival mode, activating the sympathetic nervous system – the system that governs fight, flight, or freeze. If you have ever felt your mind race uncontrollably, your hands clench, or a wave of frustration rise before you could stop it, you have experienced this first-hand.

Emotional hijacks like this are why arguments spiral out of control, why voices shake when trying to express something important, and why some conversations leave a lingering exhaustion, as though the body itself has carried a heavy weight.

These reactions are deeply ingrained, but they do not have to take over. The nervous system has another mode – the parasympathetic nervous system, which is responsible for calming the body, slowing the heart, and restoring balance. The key to switching from one to the other is simpler than it may seem.

## Finding Your Way Back to Calm

Imagine standing in the middle of a storm, wind howling around you, debris flying past. That is what an amygdala hijack feels like – a force bigger than you, pulling you into its chaos. Even in the fiercest storm, there is always a way to anchor yourself.

Pausing is the first step. Not shutting down or walking away, but taking a moment to regain control. A slow, deep breath is enough to interrupt the spiral. Inhaling through the nose for four counts, and exhaling for six, signals to the nervous system that the danger has passed.

Grounding techniques bring the body back to the present. Pressing both feet firmly against the floor, noticing the texture of an object in the hands, or listening for a steady sound in the environment can help to break the loop of emotional overwhelm.

Slowing the conversation down creates space to think clearly. If emotions begin to escalate, it is entirely reasonable to pause. Saying, *"I need a moment to gather my thoughts"* or *"Let me think about that for a second"* provides the brain with time to process, reducing the risk of reacting impulsively. A simple phrase like *"I can handle this"* helps reinforce a sense of control, counteracting the brain's automatic stress response.

## Rewiring Your Response

Think back to a time when a conversation left you flustered or overwhelmed. Perhaps tension gripped your chest, words tangled, and you walked away wishing for a do-over. Now imagine if, in that moment, you had paused. A deep breath, a moment to ground yourself, a conscious effort to slow down.

The more these small resets are practised, the more natural they become. Before stepping into your next difficult conversation, take a moment to prepare. Breathe in, breathe out, letting the tension ease. Difficult conversations are not a fight to be won. They are an opportunity to engage with clarity and confidence, even when emotions rise.

> *"It is not the words alone that define a difficult conversation, but the courage it takes to speak them, and the strength it requires to listen."*
>
> Eve Stanway

## Quick Calm Strategies for Difficult Conversations

Difficult conversations have a way of stirring something deep inside. A tightness in the chest, a racing mind, a sudden struggle to find the right words. Even before you speak, tension can take hold, making it harder to stay present, to listen, to respond the way you truly want.

Calm is not something you summon on command. It is something you return to – like stepping onto solid ground after feeling unsteady. Small, simple techniques can help you find that steadiness again, guiding your body and mind back to centre when emotions start to pull you away.

### The Rhythm of the Breath

Breathing is the body's built-in reset button, the quickest way to interrupt tension and remind your nervous system that you are safe. A simple technique to regulate your breath is the 4-7-8 method: inhale through the nose for four counts, hold for seven, and exhale slowly through the mouth for eight. The long, controlled exhalation signals to the brain that the urgency has passed.

Imagine filling your lungs as if you were sipping warm tea, holding onto that warmth, then releasing it in a slow, measured breath. With each cycle, the heart slows, the muscles loosen, and the mind clears just enough to find your way forward again. Practising this before you need it makes it second nature in the moments when calm feels furthest away.

## The Weight of Something Real

When thoughts spiral and anxiety grips, grounding yourself in the present moment can bring a sense of control. A physical touchstone – something small, familiar, and solid – can act as an anchor. A smooth stone in your pocket, the cool metal of a ring, the gentle press of your fingertips against your palm. Noticing texture, weight, and temperature pulls your awareness out of racing thoughts and back into the here and now.

If tension rises mid-conversation, you might trace the ridges of a coin between your fingers, press your heels firmly against the floor, or wrap your hands around a warm mug of tea. Even the steady sensation of your own breath moving in and out can be enough to keep you connected. The body understands safety long before the mind does, and small physical cues can help bridge the gap between reaction and response.

## The Mind's Quiet Shoreline

The mind does not always know the difference between what is imagined and what is real. This is why visualisation – when used with intention – can help prepare you for difficult conversations, shaping a steady path before you even step into the moment.

Picture yourself sitting across from the other person, speaking clearly, listening fully, staying present. Imagine your words landing with ease, your body relaxed, your mind open. If resistance arises, see yourself meeting it with quiet confidence rather than tension. This is not about expecting perfection, but about helping your brain rehearse steadiness instead of panic.

For an even deeper reset, visualise a place that brings you peace. A quiet shoreline, where the waves move in their own slow rhythm. A forest path, where the air is cool and filled with the scent of pine. The more vividly you engage your senses – imagining the warmth of the sun, the texture of the sand, the hush of the breeze – the more powerful the effect. Even in the middle of a difficult conversation, a single deep breath paired with this image can restore a sense of calm.

## A Moment of Gratitude

Gratitude can feel out of place in high-stress moments, yet it is one of the simplest ways to shift your emotional state. Fear and gratitude cannot exist in the same breath. Turning your attention – even briefly – to something you appreciate interrupts the cycle of stress, helping your body and mind reset.

Before stepping into a difficult conversation, take a moment to acknowledge something that brings a sense of warmth. The comfort of a favourite song. The feeling of sunlight on your skin. The steady presence of someone who has supported you. Even in the midst of conflict, there is often something to hold onto – an intention for honesty, a hope for understanding, a shared history that still matters.

Gratitude does not erase discomfort, but it shifts the lens through which you see the moment. Instead of focusing only on what is difficult, it reminds you of what is steady, what is good, what is still within your control.

## Returning to Centre

Think back to a time when emotions took over in a conversation. What might have changed if you had placed your feet firmly on the ground, slowed your breath, or reminded yourself of something steady?

These techniques are not about avoiding emotion, but about creating enough space to move through it with clarity. With practice, they become less of a tool and more of a habit – something you return to instinctively when you need it most. A deep breath, a steady hand, a quiet thought of gratitude. Small things, but enough to change the course of a conversation.

For more guided exercises and additional support, visit www.evestanway.co.uk/shoreline.

# Preparing for a Positive Conversation

## Preparing for Difficult Conversations: Finding Clarity Before You Speak

Difficult conversations carry weight. They press against the edges of the mind long before they happen, lingering in half-formed thoughts and quiet worries. The anticipation alone can make the moment feel heavier than it needs to be. Yet, preparation can bring a sense of steadiness – a way to step forward without feeling lost in the tangle of emotions.

Imagine holding a lantern in a dimly lit room. The more you clarify what you need to say, the brighter the light becomes, illuminating the path ahead. Rushing in without that clarity is like stepping into the dark, hoping to find your way as you go. Taking a moment to pause, to think, to gather your thoughts is not just preparation – it is an act of self-respect.

### Finding the Heart of What Matters

Before speaking, let the mind settle. Close your eyes, if it helps, and ask yourself, *What is it that truly needs to be said?* Not everything at once, not the entire history of the issue, but the essence of it. Imagine explaining it in a single breath. If you had just one sentence to express the core of what you feel, what would it be?

There is power in simplicity. A conversation burdened with too many points can lose its shape, drifting away from what truly matters. Distilling your thoughts down to their clearest form – *I need more support with...* or *It is important to me that...* – creates a steady foundation. A clear message is easier to express and harder to dismiss.

### Understanding the Destination

Every conversation has a direction, even if it is uncertain. Taking a moment to visualise where you hope to land can prevent the discussion from spiralling into frustration. What would resolution look like? What needs to shift for the conversation to feel worthwhile? Perhaps it is about being heard, setting a boundary, or finding a way forward together. Even if the outcome remains unknown, knowing *why* the conversation matters keeps the focus steady.

## Anticipating the Emotional Currents

Words do not exist in isolation. They carry emotion, history, and hidden triggers – both for you and for the other person. Some topics feel like stepping onto uneven ground, stirring memories of past conversations that did not go well. A single phrase can reopen old wounds, making it easy to react rather than respond.

Before the conversation begins, take a moment to reflect. Where do you feel tension in your body? What phrases or reactions might make you defensive? If frustration rises, what will help you steady yourself? A deep breath, the feeling of your feet pressing into the floor, a quiet reminder – *I am here to express, not to fight*. Preparing for emotions does not mean suppressing them. It means knowing they may appear and choosing how to meet them when they do.

## Writing for Clarity, Speaking with Confidence

Some thoughts feel clear until spoken aloud, where they tangle and twist, losing their shape. Writing them down first can bring unexpected relief. Try summarising the main message in a short sentence, then ask yourself, *Is this honest? Is this clear? Is this what I truly mean?* Adjust as needed until it feels true.

If the words feel too sharp, soften them. If they feel vague, sharpen them. The goal is not to craft the perfect script but to give yourself a sense of direction. When your thoughts are clear to you, they are easier to express with confidence.

## A Moment of Stillness Before You Begin

Before stepping into the conversation, take a breath. Feel the air fill your lungs, then release it slowly. Let the tension in your shoulders ease, the tightness in your jaw soften. If nerves creep in, place a hand over your chest and remind yourself, *I am prepared. I know what I need to say.*

No amount of preparation guarantees ease. Conversations unfold in real time, shaped by emotions, words, and the unpredictable nature of human response. Yet, having clarity before you begin creates something solid beneath your feet. It allows you to step forward with purpose, knowing that no matter how the conversation unfolds, you have already done the most important work – understanding yourself.

Need more support? Visit www.evestanway.co.uk/shoreline for additional tools and exercises to help you prepare and practice.

*"We have two ears and one mouth
so that we can listen twice as much as we speak."*

Epictetus
1st-century Greek Stoic philosopher

## Eve's Epiphany:
## Embracing the Power of Honest Conversations

By the time I was five, I had already sailed around the world twice – but in two very different ways. The first time was aboard *Anneliese*, a thirty-foot boat, where life was unpredictable, often harsh, and required constant adjustment. The second time, I found myself on the *QE2* – the *Queen Elizabeth 2*, one of the world's most famous luxury ocean liners.

One moment, I was navigating ocean storms aboard a cramped, thirty-foot boat, adjusting to the unpredictability of wind and waves. The next, I was gliding through the polished corridors of the *QE2*, where everything was stable, controlled, and perfectly planned. It was a stark contrast – one I did not fully understand at the time.

It was only years later that I realised how deeply those two journeys had shaped me. One taught me survival; the other showed me what it meant to be a child held safe.

I still remember discovering the children's nursery on board. It was the first time I had ever seen a space designed just for children – where they were not expected to simply fit in around adults, but where they actually mattered. It left an impression on me that took years to understand as my life returned to the unpredictable after this dream voyage.

Those early experiences shaped how I interacted with the world. I learned to focus on pleasing others instead of myself, adapting to whatever was expected of me. Conversations always felt like something children had to manage while adults stayed in control.

As I got older, I found grounding myself incredibly hard. My mind was always on the next thing – solving problems, staying busy, and making sure everyone else was okay. Slowing down felt unnatural. When I first tried grounding exercises, I hated it. My mind raced with to-do lists, my body ached, and I felt restless, like my whole system was rebelling. For a long time, I thought I was failing.

But the truth was, I was not failing – I was finally noticing the stress and tension I had been carrying for years. The things I had avoided – both physically and emotionally – were surfacing.

The change came when I stopped fighting myself. Instead of getting frustrated with my racing mind and restless body, I began to see them as part of the process. I let go of the idea that grounding had to look a certain way and allowed myself to take it at my own pace. That shift – from being critical to being kind – made all the difference. Grounding went from something I dreaded to something I relied on.

At the same time, I started to notice something else: I avoided difficult conversations just as much as I had avoided stillness. I held back from saying what I really felt, from setting boundaries, from expressing my needs. And every time I avoided those conversations, I felt smaller – less confident, less in control, less like myself.

I had spent years believing the lie that avoidance protected me. In truth, it held me back.

The moment I realised that, everything shifted.

I started small – one conversation at a time. None of them were easy, but each one gave me back a little more self-respect. Difficult conversations were not just about resolving problems – they were about building the life I wanted.

Now, I see difficult conversations as opportunities – to connect, to grow, to live more authentically. Grounding is a big part of that. It gives me the steadiness I need to stay present, to speak honestly, and to navigate those tough moments without shutting down or lashing out. It is a process I am still working on – but one I am grateful for every day.

> **Mapping the Currents: Key Takeaways**
>
> **Difficult conversations happen on two levels:** The conversations we have with ourselves (intrapersonal) shape how we communicate with others (interpersonal). Understanding both helps us navigate emotional challenges with more confidence.
>
> **Your brain reacts before you do:** The amygdala's fight-or-flight response can make high-stakes conversations feel overwhelming. Learning to recognise and regulate these reactions can help you stay present and in control.
>
> **Preparation changes everything:** Taking time to reflect, journal, and clarify your thoughts reduces anxiety and improves communication, setting the stage for a more constructive dialogue.
>
> **Honest conversations build stronger relationships:** When we express ourselves with clarity and empathy, we deepen trust, resolve misunderstandings, and create more meaningful connections.

*"The oak fought the wind and was broken,
the willow bent when it must and survived."*

Robert Jordan
*The Fires of Heaven*, 1993

## Poem: Silent Drift

*Mellow morning mist, surprising and obscure,
Hiding shadows of perception, twisting what I know.
Light struggles to break through as my view fails,
Am I flying or falling, like a peregrine, wings tight as it dives?*

*Clearing softly, should I bang a drum,
To warn others of my coming, or drift quiet, unseen?
Fog at sea is not like fog on land.*

*Do those on shore know how weather shapes lives?*

*Out here, we notice it all –
The squall's dark edge.
The danger in the still,
A clear blue sky with no clouds in sight,
It gives no wind to fill your sails, no direction but drift.*

*Listen to the whisper over the water.
Not every journey needs a current to carry you forward.*

# CHARTING THE COURSE: PREPARING FOR THE JOURNEY

Understanding why you hold back is a powerful first step. From here, we can start to explore what makes some conversations feel so hard. Together, we will look at the fears, habits, and "masks" that often shape how we navigate difficult moments. These patterns might feel familiar, even protective, but they can also make it harder to communicate what really matters.

In *The 7 Habits of Highly Effective People*, Stephen Covey wrote, *"Most people do not listen with the intent to understand; they listen with the intent to reply."* It is such a human response – to defend ourselves or try to fix things instead of pausing to fully listen. This instinct can make conversations feel heavier than they need to be.

As we go on, we will look at the emotions that come up during these moments – such as defensiveness or withdrawal – and how they influence what we say and hear. We will also explore the idea of "masking" – those little behaviours or personas we lean on to feel safe. While these habits can offer comfort, they might also get in the way of expressing what truly matters. By reflecting on these patterns and experimenting with small changes, you can decide what feels most right for you.

This is not about doing everything perfectly or fixing things overnight. It is about noticing the small shifts that help you feel clearer and more at ease. With time, conversations that once felt overwhelming might begin to feel more possible and even freeing.

### Poem: The Masks We Wear

*Beneath each layer lies a quiet truth,*
*held back by the need to feel safe.*
*In stillness, a light finds its way through,*
*revealing what was waiting to be known.*

This part of the journey is about noticing what lies beneath the surface and letting yourself move at a pace that feels comfortable. Each small step opens new doors, helping you feel steadier and prepared to navigate what comes next.

# Part 4

# CAMOUFLAGED SAILORS: DISGUISES WE USE TO NAVIGATE EMOTIONAL SEAS

*"We are so accustomed to disguise ourselves to others that in the end, we become disguised to ourselves."*

François de La Rochefoucauld (1613–1680)
French author

### Eve's Reflections by the Shoreline

There was a time when my mask felt like armour – solid, impenetrable, necessary. It kept me upright when the ground beneath me threatened to give way, shielding wounds I could not afford to feel. Strength and silence became my currency for survival, the only way to stay safe in a world that never felt like home. I wore that mask so well, even I believed it.

Then, in my fifties, something shifted. I picked up *Lowborn* by Kerry Hudson, expecting to read someone else's story. Instead, I found my own. The pages felt like a mirror, each word reflecting memories

I had long buried. A truth I had resisted for decades came rushing forward – I had lived through nine out of ten Adverse Childhood Experiences (ACEs).

ACEs shape a life before a child even knows how to name them. Abuse, neglect, chaos – the undercurrent of unpredictability rewires the brain, training it to exist in a state of high alert. *The world is not safe*, it whispers. *Stay small. Stay silent. Adapt, or be discarded.* The ACE Study (Felitti et al., 1998) revealed what I already knew deep in my bones: early trauma does not simply fade. It carves itself into the nervous system, deep as tide-worn grooves in rocks, increasing the risk of lifelong struggles with health, relationships, and self-worth.

As I read, I felt that child again – the one always on the move, stepping into yet another temporary home, inhaling the stale unfamiliarity of borrowed spaces. The quiet one. The helper. The fixer of adult problems. If I was useful, I was tolerated. If I was invisible, I was safe. There was no room for fear, sadness, or longing. Vulnerability was a liability. So, I packed it away, sealed it behind a smile, and built a mask that could weather any storm.

To the outside world, I was thriving. Resilient. Capable. But beneath that carefully constructed exterior was a child who had never stopped running, never stopped scanning the room for danger, never truly believed stability was hers to keep. The mask that had once protected me had become a prison, locking me inside a version of myself that could not afford to be real.

## A New Tide

Years later, I watched my own children grow up in a world so different from the one I had known that it felt almost foreign. Their childhood was filled with warmth and laughter, the soft landing of love catching them each time they fell. They cried when they were hurt, knowing comfort would follow. They expressed anger without fear of rejection. They moved through life with the unshaken certainty that they were safe, seen, cherished.

Their freedom was beautiful. It was also a quiet kind of agony. With every moment of their ease, my own childhood became sharper in contrast. The things I had normalised – fear, instability, the need to earn my place – were not normal at all. Their innocence illuminated the depth of what I had lost.

For years, I told myself the past was done, that it could not touch me now. But the body remembers. The mask that had once been my salvation had fused so tightly to my skin that I no longer knew how to take it off. I had learned how to survive. I had never learned how to simply be.

That realisation was a reckoning. To live fully, I had to face the silence I had carried for so long. I had to grieve the child who had been denied comfort, stability, and love. I had to unlearn the belief that my worth depended on what I could do for others – that my presence was conditional, that needing was dangerous.

## Unmasking

The journey back to myself was not easy. The mask, once so essential, resisted removal. It whispered its warnings: *If you let them see you, they will turn away.*

But I had already spent a lifetime in hiding, and I no longer wanted to live behind barriers of my own making.

The truth about masks is that they serve a purpose. As children, they keep us safe. As adults, they help us navigate difficult relationships, manage expectations, move through spaces where we feel out of place. But over time, they begin to suffocate. They press so closely that we forget where they end and we begin.

Letting go is not an act of weakness. It is an act of reclaiming.

To step into the light, I had to lay down the weight of silence and shame. I had to allow myself to be seen – not for what I could endure, not for what I could provide, but simply for who I was.

And in that moment, I began to breathe again.

This chapter is about recognising those masks – how they shield us, how they shape our relationships, and ultimately, how they hold us back. Peeling them away is not easy; it requires courage, patience, and compassion. Yet, the freedom that lies beneath – to be seen, to be heard, to be whole – is worth every step.

> *"I was chasing my past, trying to piece things together but perhaps the real courage was in simply accepting the things that happen and learning to live with them."*
>
> Kerry Hudson<br>*Lowborn*, 2019

## The Masks We Wear: A Journey Back to Ourselves

Every day, we move through life wrapped in invisible layers – masks we have worn for so long that they feel like second skin. They help us shift between roles, smooth over tension, and navigate the expectations of the world around us. At work, we wear the mask of competence, keeping our worries tucked beneath a polished surface. At home, we may soften into the role of caregiver, protector, or provider, even when exhaustion lingers at the edges of our smiles. Among friends, we adjust again – sometimes light-hearted, sometimes guarded, depending on what the moment calls for.

These masks are not falsehoods; they are adaptations, ways of moving through the world without exposing too much at once. Yet, the weight of them becomes heavy when we no longer remember where the mask ends and we begin. When the need to be accepted overshadows the need to be *known*.

Carl Jung spoke of the "persona" – the face we show to the world. It allows us to function in society, to meet expectations, to belong. But when the persona becomes our only reflection, something inside us begins to dim. The deeper self – the one that laughs too loudly, that aches to express, that carries quiet fears and fierce dreams – gets buried beneath what feels acceptable. Over time, this distance from who we truly are can create a hollow space within us, a quiet ache that whispers, *Is this all I am allowed to be?*

## The Origins of Our Masks

These layers did not appear overnight. They were shaped by early experiences, by moments when vulnerability was met with disapproval or silence. They were reinforced by unspoken rules: *Be agreeable. Do not ask for too much. Do not let them see you struggle.* Society, too, has its demands. It rewards composure, confidence, and fitting in.

Brené Brown describes this in *The Gifts of Imperfection*:

> *"Fitting in is about assessing a situation and becoming who you need to be to be accepted. Belonging, on the other hand, doesn't require us to change who we are; it requires us to be who we are."*

The masks we wear may have once served us – helping us find safety, acceptance, or approval. But they can also become barriers, keeping us at a distance from the very connection we long for. Instead of offering peace, they trap us in patterns of hiding, where we are seen but not fully known.

## Unmasking Ourselves, Gently

The journey back to ourselves is not about tearing the masks away. It is about loosening them, feeling where they have been held too tightly, and allowing moments of softness to emerge. It begins with noticing – when do you shift yourself to fit the room? When do you swallow words instead of speaking them? When do you feel the ache of holding back?

Carl Rogers believed that authenticity is the foundation of true connection. The more we align with who we truly are, the more we invite real belonging. Not the fragile kind built on performance, but the kind that allows us to breathe fully, to be met as we are, to exist without the constant effort of shaping ourselves into what we think we should be.

This is an invitation. To let yourself be seen, in small moments at first. To share the thoughts you once kept hidden. To step, even slightly, into the freedom of living as yourself. The world does not need another perfectly masked version of you. It needs **you**. Fully. Honestly. Courageously.

This is not just an act of self-discovery. It is a quiet revolution.

## The Origins of Our Masks

### How Childhood Shapes Coping Mechanisms

### *The Roles We Play: A Childhood of Shoulders Too Small for the Weight They Carried*

Childhood is meant to be a time of wonder – of scraped knees and wild laughter, of learning by falling and knowing there will be a safe place to land. It is a time when needs should be met freely, without question or hesitation, by those who hold the responsibility of care. A child does not come into the world ready to carry burdens. They arrive open, trusting, reaching out with small hands, expecting to be met with kindness.

Yet, not all childhoods unfold this way. When stress overshadows a home – whether through loss, addiction, illness, or the quiet erosion of love – some children learn that their needs must shrink to make space for the needs of others. They grow up too quickly, taking on responsibilities meant for adults. The child who soothes the angry father, the one who comforts the anxious mother, the sibling who becomes a second parent in a home frayed at the edges. These children learn to be hypervigilant, to scan a room for danger before it arrives, to anticipate moods before words are spoken.

They learn that their safety depends on being competent, capable, and convenient.

This is called *parentification* – when a child steps into the role of caretaker, mediator, or emotional anchor far before they should. The cost of this adaptation is high. A child who becomes a protector often struggles to recognise their own need for protection. A child who learns to comfort others often grows up without knowing how to ask for comfort themselves.

## The Echoes of Childhood in the Adult Self

Perhaps even now, those patterns linger. Do you find it hard to ask for help? Do you carry the silent weight of other people's emotions, feeling responsible for keeping the peace? Do you pride yourself on being *strong*, but secretly long for someone to carry you for a while? These are not flaws. These are survival strategies – ones that were once necessary but may no longer serve you.

So many of us were shaped in childhood by what was demanded of us. Some became the *fixer*, believing that love must be earned through usefulness. Others became the *high achiever*, proving their worth through relentless perfection. Some played the *quiet one*, careful never to take up too much space, while others became the *peacemaker*, smoothing over conflicts at the cost of their own truth. These roles brought stability in the past, but now, they may feel like a cage.

In *On Becoming a Person*, Carl Rogers spoke of the quiet burden of meeting external expectations: *"The curious paradox is that when I accept myself just as I am, then I can change."* Yet for many, self-acceptance feels elusive – buried beneath years of striving, pleasing, and adapting.

## A Childhood That Does Not Belong to You

As I raised my own children, the contrast between their world and mine was stark. Their childhoods were filled with sunlight and certainty. They cried freely, knowing their pain would be met with comfort. They expressed anger without fear of rejection. They were allowed to stumble, to make mistakes, to exist as themselves without needing to prove their worth.

Watching them, I realised something painful: I had never been given that freedom. The world had asked me to be *useful*, not *childlike*. There had never been room for my fragility, only for my resilience. The mask I had built – one of competence, control, and quiet endurance – had served me well. But it had also cost me something precious.

I wonder if this resonates with you. Perhaps you, too, have carried this unspoken rule: *Do not be a burden. Do not need too much. Do not ask for more than the world is willing to give.* Maybe you learned that vulnerability was dangerous, that showing weakness meant opening yourself up to criticism or disappointment.

In *The Gifts of Imperfection*, Brené Brown writes:

> *"When we spend a lifetime trying to distance ourselves from the parts of our lives that don't fit with who we think we're supposed to be, we stand outside of our story and hustle for our worthiness."*

It is exhausting to live this way – to mould yourself into something acceptable rather than allowing yourself to be seen.

## Who Are You Without the Roles?

These identities we wear – caretaker, perfectionist, peacekeeper, achiever – were once necessary. But do they still serve you? Do they bring you closer to the life you want, or do they keep you locked in patterns that no longer fit?

This is not about discarding the strengths you have built. You are strong, resilient, deeply capable. But strength should not come at the expense of softness. You deserve more than survival. You deserve space to breathe, to ask, to rest.

Letting go of old roles does not mean losing yourself. It means expanding. It means making space for the parts of you that were left behind – the parts that long for connection, for honesty, for a life that is not dictated by past survival strategies.

It may feel uncomfortable at first, stepping out from behind the mask. But freedom lives there. Connection lives there. The people who truly love you do not need you to be perfect. They need you to be *real*.

The journey back to yourself begins with a question: *Who am I, beneath everything I was told to be?*

## Reflection Prompt

Think back to a role you adopted as a child. How did it help you navigate your environment? Are there ways it might be holding you back now?

## The Power of Perfectionism and People-Pleasing

The need to be perfect and to please others are masks many of us know well. Often rooted in a deep desire to be accepted, these behaviours may feel like shields that protect us from criticism, rejection, or disappointment. Perfectionism, for example, can push us to hide any perceived flaw, to maintain a polished exterior that we believe others will find more acceptable. People-pleasing, on the other hand, encourages us to put others' needs above our own, hoping that by making others happy, we will secure our place in their lives.

While these masks may seem to offer security, they come at a cost. Constantly striving for perfection, or prioritising everyone else's needs, often leads to burnout, anxiety, and a quiet resentment that creeps in over time. These masks create a barrier between who we truly are and the version of ourselves that we present to the world. We become disconnected from our own needs, desires, and even our sense of self.

Recognising these patterns is a courageous first step toward change. When you allow yourself to lower these masks, even in small ways, you create space to show up as you are. You begin to reclaim your right to express your true thoughts, your honest emotions, and your unique imperfections. By doing so, you invite a different kind of connection – one that does not depend on meeting an impossible standard or constantly seeking approval. You might find that this approach brings a sense of relief and freedom, allowing you to live more fully, grounded in self-respect and genuine connection.

> *"The masks we wear serve us, protecting us from hurt, but they also separate us from the true connections we crave."*
>
> Eve Stanway

## Emily's Story: The Weight of Perfection

From the outside, Emily had it all together. She was the straight-A student, the organised one, the person everyone relied on. Growing up in a home where only the highest achievements were acknowledged, she quickly learned that love and approval were conditional – earned through excellence, never freely given. Mistakes were not lessons; they were failures. Emotions were not expressions; they were weaknesses. So, she became *the perfect daughter*, the one who never stumbled, never wavered, never asked for too much.

At first, it worked. Praise followed her wherever she went. Teachers held her up as an example. Family members boasted about her discipline. Friends admired her dependability. Perfection became her currency, and she spent it well. But beneath the surface, the pressure built. Each success raised the bar higher. Each compliment became an expectation. The mask of perfection, once so reassuring, grew heavier with every passing year.

### *The Fear of Being Seen*

By the time Emily entered adulthood, perfectionism had woven itself into every part of her life. At work, she checked every email three times before sending it. At home, she carried the weight of every unspoken expectation, managing the household, keeping everyone happy, making sure nothing slipped through the cracks. Even in friendships, she played the role of the reliable one, the listener, the fixer – never the one who needed anything in return.

It was exhausting. Yet, the thought of letting go felt even more terrifying. What if she disappointed someone? What if they saw the real her and decided it was not enough? The perfection that once protected her was now a wall – keeping others out, keeping her trapped inside.

If you have ever silenced your struggles, afraid they might make you seem weak or unworthy, then you know the ache of hiding in plain sight. You know the loneliness of being surrounded by people who admire you, but never truly **see** you.

### The Moment of Change

It was a quiet evening when everything shifted. Emily was sitting at the kitchen table, staring at a to-do list that never seemed to end, when her husband placed a hand on hers. *"You look so tired,"* he said gently. *"You don't have to do everything alone."*

The words caught her off guard. She had spent years convincing herself that asking for help meant failing. But in that moment, she realised something painful – she had been carrying a weight that no one had asked her to hold.

That night, she took a deep breath and did something she had never done before. She spoke her truth. *"I feel like I have to be perfect all the time, and I'm so tired."*

To her surprise, her husband did not judge her. He did not look at her any differently. He simply listened. And for the first time in a long time, Emily felt something lift.

### Unlearning Perfection, One Step at a Time

Letting go of perfectionism did not happen overnight. Emily had spent a lifetime believing that her worth was tied to what she **did** rather than who she was. But through reflection and practice, she began to challenge those beliefs.

She started with small shifts – pausing to name her emotions instead of dismissing them. When anxiety crept in over a minor mistake, she would remind herself, *This does not define me*. She began setting boundaries, allowing herself to say no without guilt. She stopped apologising for things that did not require an apology.

The more she softened into herself, the more she noticed something unexpected. Her relationships grew stronger, not weaker. Her friends leaned in closer, relieved to see her as human rather than untouchable. At work, colleagues respected her just as much when she set limits as when she over-delivered. Even her children noticed the change. *"You seem happier, Mum,"* her daughter said one day. And for the first time, Emily realised that by embracing imperfection, she was giving her children permission to do the same.

### What Emily's Story Teaches Us

Perfectionism does not protect us – it isolates us. It convinces us that love must be earned, that vulnerability is dangerous, that mistakes are proof of failure. But true connection does not come from *appearing* flawless. It comes from being real. If you have spent years chasing perfection, ask yourself, *What would happen if I put the mask down, even just for a moment?*

Would the people who love you turn away, or would they come closer? Would you lose respect, or would you gain relief? Would you finally feel what Emily felt in that kitchen, when she let herself be seen and found acceptance waiting for her?

This journey is not about giving up on excellence. It is about expanding beyond it. It is about recognising that you are worthy, not because of what you achieve, but because of who you **already** are.

## The Costs of Covering Up

Hiding who we are can feel like protection, like stepping into armour before walking into battle. Over time, though, that armour becomes heavy. What once kept us safe starts keeping us separate – cutting us off from our true selves, from others, from the very connection we long for.

This disconnection seeps into our lives in ways we do not always notice at first:

- **Emotional Isolation:** You sit among friends, nodding, laughing in the right places, yet feeling apart. The loneliness is not from being alone, but from being unseen.

- **Self-Criticism:** The quiet voice inside whispers, *You should not have said that. You should not feel this way.* Every time we mask our emotions, we confirm the fear that who we are is somehow unacceptable.

- **Stunted Growth:** Growth demands that we face what is difficult. Avoiding our emotions may feel like control, but it is only postponement. The feelings do not disappear – they wait, pressing against the surface, unresolved.

Developmental psychologist Dr Ed Tronick (2007) described how *"mis-attunements are inevitable, but repair is what builds security."* When a caregiver misreads a child's emotions, the distress is not in the mistake but in whether it is recognised and repaired. The same is true in adulthood. Avoiding discomfort does not protect us – it erodes trust, both in ourselves and in our relationships.

## Reflection Prompt

Think of a time when you held back your true feelings. What did it cost you? Did it create distance between you and someone you care about? What might have happened if you had spoken your truth?

## Rupture and Repair: When the Mask Slips

No matter how tightly we hold it, the mask will slip. Sometimes it happens in exhaustion, when patience runs out. Sometimes in anger, when years of swallowed words push past our lips. Sometimes in quiet sadness, when a simple, *I am fine* no longer holds up.

Psychiatrist Dr Daniel Siegel (Siegel & Bryson, 2020) reminds us, *"Relationships are not about avoiding disconnection; they are about how we reconnect."* It is not the rupture that defines a relationship – it is the repair.

### Example: The Mask Slips with Sarah

Sarah had spent years being the *"easy-going"* friend – the one who never made a fuss, who laughed things off, who adjusted so others did not have to. It felt like a superpower, this ability to smooth things over.

Then came the moment when she could not.

A close friend, one she loved dearly, had once again disregarded a boundary. The usual response sat on Sarah's tongue – the automatic *It's fine, don't worry.* But this time, her exhaustion spoke first.

*"Actually, I do mind,"* she said, her voice quieter than she expected. *"It hurts when my boundaries aren't respected."*

Silence stretched between them. Sarah braced herself for awkwardness, for defensiveness, for that familiar flash of regret – the feeling that she had said too much.

Instead, her friend frowned slightly, thinking. Then, after a pause, *"I had no idea you felt that way. I'll be more mindful."*

That moment reshaped their friendship.

Dr Siegel describes these moments as essential: *"Rupture and repair provide the foundation for resilience"* (Siegel & Bryson, 2020). Avoiding these conversations may feel like keeping the peace, but it builds quiet resentment. Repairing them – acknowledging the discomfort, addressing the disconnection – creates real trust.

**Reflection Prompt**

Think of a time when your mask slipped. Did you step into the discomfort and create space for repair? Or did you retreat? If you could go back, what would you say differently?

## Creating Safe Spaces for Vulnerability

Authenticity is a powerful force, but it needs the right conditions to flourish. Not every space, not every person, is safe for vulnerability. The art is not just in *what* we share, but *where* and *with whom* we share it.

1. **Identify Safe Relationships**. Who in your life listens without judgement? Who makes space for you without rushing to fix or dismiss? These are the people with whom your authenticity can take root.

2. **Start with Small Disclosures**. Vulnerability does not require a grand confession. Begin with a small truth – an honest *"That hurt my feelings"* or *"I could use some support right now."* See how it is received. Trust deepens in steps.

3. **Seek Mutual Vulnerability**. Authenticity is an invitation. When you open up, you give others permission to do the same. Real connection is built not on perfection, but on shared honesty.

Dr Tronick (2007) explains, *"We are not meant to be perfectly in sync all the time. It is in repairing mis-attunements that real connection is forged."* True authenticity is not about sharing everything with everyone; it is about discerning who has earned the right to hear your story.

## David's Story:
## The Moment He Chose Honesty Over Defensiveness

A few months after our last session, David called unexpectedly. His voice carried something new – excitement, perhaps even relief.

*"I have to tell you about something that happened at work,"* he said.

David had built his career on control. He was the person who always had the answers, always fixed the problems. Authority, he believed, came from never slipping.

Then came the moment he did.

During a team meeting, a colleague pointed out an error in his work. The air shifted. A moment thick with tension.

*"At first, I froze,"* he admitted. *"I could feel it happening – that instinct to explain, to defend, to push back before anyone could question me."*

The old script played in his mind: *Deny. Justify. Prove yourself.*

Instead, he did something different.

*"You're right,"* he said, steady but certain. *"I missed that. Here's what I'll do to fix it."*

Bracing for judgement, he waited. The response surprised him.

*"I could not believe it,"* he said. *"It was like they trusted me more because I admitted it. I think they respected me more for owning up than they ever would have if I had covered it up."*

For years, David had equated leadership with invulnerability. That day, he saw it differently.

*"Being honest didn't make me weak – it made me real. That's what they respected."*

Hearing the certainty in his voice, I smiled.

*"That's leadership, David,"* I told him. *"Not the kind that commands, but the kind that earns trust."*

Dr Siegel describes confidence as the ability to hold imperfections without fear, stating, *"True strength comes not from never making mistakes, but from knowing you can recover from them"* (Siegel & Bryson, 2020).

Every moment presents a choice – to cover up or to step forward. Neither option defines us, but the ability to discern when to do each shapes the way we move through the world.

Real confidence does not come from appearing flawless. It comes from navigating imperfection with integrity.

> *"To live is the rarest thing in the world. Most people exist, that is all."*
>
> Oscar Wilde (1854–1900)<br>Irish playwright and author

## Practical Strategies for Reclaiming Authenticity

Reclaiming authenticity begins with clarity. It is about recognising where you have been shrinking, where you have been making yourself small to keep the peace, where your voice has been drowned out – even by your own silence.

Setting boundaries is not about building walls. It is about drawing the lines that honour your needs, that define the space where respect can thrive. Strong relationships are not made fragile by boundaries – they are strengthened by them.

The **Magic Three: Clarify, Communicate, and Correct** offers a simple yet powerful way to reclaim your voice. It is the difference between reacting in frustration and responding with intention. It allows you to speak in a way that invites understanding rather than resistance.

## The Magic Three in Action

### 1. Clarify: Understanding What You Truly Need

A vague frustration – *I wish they would respect my time* – becomes a clear, actionable request:

*"I need an hour of uninterrupted time in the mornings to focus on work."*

When you define your needs with precision, you give others something concrete to understand and respect.

### 2. Communicate: Expressing Yourself Without Defensiveness

How you say something shapes how it is received.

Instead of:

*"You never listen to me!"*

Try:

*"I feel most heard when we can talk without distractions. Can we set aside some time to have this conversation?"*

A boundary framed with clarity and respect opens doors. Accusation slams them shut.

### 3. Correct: Reinforcing Boundaries with Confidence

Boundaries will be tested – whether by habit, forgetfulness, or resistance. The key is in how you respond.

Instead of suppressing frustration until it explodes, a steady, calm reminder keeps the boundary in place:

*"I appreciate that you need my input, but I'm in the middle of something right now. Let's talk when I'm done."*

The **Magic Three** is not about rigid rules. It is about creating a rhythm of clarity and consistency, so that expectations are understood, and relationships grow from a foundation of mutual respect rather than assumption.

## Case Study: Amy's Journey to Rebuilding Trust

For years, Amy sat at family gatherings feeling exposed, waiting for the moment her sister would turn her private thoughts into public conversation.

It happened every time. A small detail Amy had shared in confidence, now tossed casually into dinner table conversation. Laughter. Nods. A quick, passing moment for everyone else.

For Amy, a slow, familiar pang.

*Why would she say that? Doesn't she know how much it bothers me?*

She had tried before – had pulled her sister aside, had said *please don't* – but the response was always the same.

*"You're overreacting."* A dismissive shrug. A wave of the hand.

Every attempt to express herself felt like walking into a locked door. The frustration built, but the exhaustion of another circular argument kept her silent.

Maybe it was easier to stay quiet. Maybe she would never change.

But silence did not make the problem go away. It only deepened the distance.

Family gatherings, once something to look forward to, became something Amy dreaded. The lack of trust turned every conversation into a minefield – an unspoken fear that anything she said might be used against her later.

Something had to change.

### Preparing with the Magic Three

Amy knew that emotion had derailed past conversations – her frustration, her sister's defensiveness. This time, she would approach it differently.

She rehearsed her words, prepared for resistance.

*"If I lose my temper, she'll shut down. If I stay steady, maybe she'll actually hear me."*

At the next family gathering, Amy pulled her sister aside.

*"Can I talk to you about something that's been on my mind?"*

Her heart pounded. The urge to back out pressed hard against her ribs.

As soon as Amy brought up the issue, her sister's expression shifted.

*"You're being overly sensitive,"* she said, crossing her arms.

Amy felt the familiar rise of frustration. *Here we go again.* The same script, playing out once more.

But this time, she was ready.

She took a breath.

This was not about winning an argument. This was about setting a boundary that mattered.

### Clarify

*"This isn't about being sensitive,"* Amy said evenly. *"This is about my need for privacy. I need to feel safe sharing things with you, without worrying they'll become conversation topics."*

Her sister sighed, rolling her eyes, but Amy stayed steady.

### Communicate

*"When you share things I've told you in confidence, I feel hurt and exposed,"* she continued. *"I want to trust you with personal things, but I need to know that they won't be repeated."*

A flicker of something – Understanding? Guilt? – crossed her sister's face. The defensiveness wavered, if only slightly.

### Correct

*"I know this might be hard to hear,"* Amy said, *"but I need you to respect this boundary. Moving forward, I need my personal stories to stay private. If that doesn't happen, I'll have to think carefully about what I share with you."*

Saying it out loud felt uncomfortable.

It also felt like freedom.

### A Shift Toward Trust

At first, nothing seemed different.

Her sister shrugged. Changed the subject. The conversation ended without resolution.

But something had shifted.

At the next family gathering, Amy noticed the change. No comments. No offhand remarks about her personal life. No stories casually tossed into the conversation.

Her sister had listened – not because she had agreed in the moment, but because Amy had been clear.

Over time, the tension softened. Trust, once eroded, slowly began to rebuild.

Most importantly, something shifted within Amy herself.

*"I don't feel powerless anymore,"* she thought. *"I can express my needs without everything falling apart."*

Avoiding difficult conversations does not make problems disappear. It only makes them harder to live with.

Setting boundaries is not about controlling others – it is about respecting yourself.

Amy's story is a reminder that change is possible. A single conversation may not rewrite history, but it can begin a new chapter. One where you no longer shrink. One where your voice is no longer swallowed by fear of how it might be received.

With preparation, patience, and a clear focus, you can communicate in ways that strengthen relationships rather than weaken them.

The **Magic Three** is more than a framework. It is an act of self-respect.

A single conversation may not change everything overnight, but each step builds a foundation of trust – one honest moment at a time.

> *"When we allow ourselves to shed our masks, even for a moment, we make room for vulnerability – a quiet but powerful truth that invites others to join us in authenticity."*
>
> Eve Stanway

## Embracing Authenticity in Different Relationships

Authenticity does not mean revealing everything at once or speaking without a filter. It is about knowing when to open up, how much to share, and how to express yourself in a way that strengthens rather than strains relationships.

In some moments, honesty means full transparency. In others, it requires careful pacing, choosing the right words so that both you and the person listening feel safe and understood. The key is finding that balance – between sharing and holding space, between openness and discretion – so that your relationships deepen rather than buckle under the weight of too much, too fast.

### Navigating Personal Relationships: Lesley's Story

Lesley sank into the couch, rubbing her hands together as if trying to shake off the weight of the day.

*"I don't know,"* she said, exhaling hard. *"I feel like I'm dumping everything on my partner lately. I want to talk to her about how I'm feeling, but I don't want to overwhelm her."*

Her voice wavered between frustration and hesitation. She needed to be heard but feared that saying too much would push her partner away.

*"It sounds like you've been carrying a lot,"* I said gently. *"And you want to let her in, but you're also trying to protect her from the weight of it."*

Lesley nodded. *"Exactly. I don't want to just bottle everything up, but I also don't want her to feel like she has to fix it all."*

We explored a way for her to share honestly without overwhelming the conversation, using the **Magic Three: Clarify, Communicate, and Correct**.

- **Clarify:** Before diving into everything, she could start with the core of what she needed. Instead of spilling every detail at once, she could say: *"I've been feeling really drained lately, and I need some support."*

- **Communicate:** Framing the conversation this way would help her partner understand how to respond. *"I don't need solutions right now, just someone to listen."*

- **Correct:** Setting a gentle boundary would give them both space to process. *"I want to talk about this, but I also want to make sure I check in with you too."*

Lesley exhaled, some of the tension lifting from her shoulders.

*"So, I can let her know I'm struggling without overwhelming her?"*

*"Exactly. It's about pacing yourself. That way, the conversation stays open instead of feeling too heavy all at once."*

Later that week, she tried it. To her surprise, her partner's response was one of relief.

*"I've wanted to help,"* she said, *"but I wasn't sure how. This makes it easier to be there for you."*

The conversation did not just help Lesley feel heard – it deepened their connection.

## Maria's Story:
## Strategic Honesty in Professional Environments

Maria had always been the one people relied on. The one who took on extra projects and stayed late to ensure everything got done. At first, it felt like a strength – proof of her dedication. Over time, it became exhausting. The long nights stretched on, and the stress began to show.

One afternoon, her manager, Oliver, stopped by her desk.

*"Maria, you're doing great, but I've noticed you've been staying late more often. Is there anything I can do to help?"*

Her first instinct was to brush it off. *I'm fine*, she almost said. But the fatigue in her bones told a different story.

She took a breath and used the **Magic Three** to guide her response.

- **Clarify:** *"I really appreciate the support, Oliver, and I want to keep delivering quality work. But I've realised I'm stretching myself too thin."*

- **Communicate:** *"To stay on track, I need to adjust my workload. I'd love to talk about prioritising tasks and possibly delegating a few."*

- **Correct:** *"I want to make sure I'm working at my best, without risking burnout. If we could discuss how to balance things, I'd feel more in control."*

She braced herself for resistance, but Oliver simply nodded.

*"That makes sense. Let's figure out how to balance things."*

Maria left the conversation feeling lighter, knowing she had protected her well-being and professional reputation. She had not just set a boundary – she had reinforced her value by ensuring she could do her job well without burning out.

## Honesty Without Overload

Lesley and Maria's stories reveal two important truths:

- **Personal relationships thrive on honesty, but honesty does not have to mean emotional overwhelm.** Thoughtful communication helps others listen with care, rather than shutting down under the weight of too much information at once.

- **Professional boundaries do not make you unreliable.** Asking for help, setting limits, and communicating clearly allows you to work at your best while maintaining credibility and respect.

Authenticity is not about spilling everything at once – it is about choosing when and how to be open in a way that serves both you and the relationship. With intention, balance, and self-awareness, difficult conversations can become opportunities for deeper trust and stronger connections.

## Curiosity and Play in Rediscovering Authenticity

### Peeling Back the Mask: A Journey to Authenticity

Masks are woven into the fabric of daily life. Some are deliberate – a polished version of ourselves presented in professional settings. Others form unconsciously, shaped by years of adapting to expectations. These masks are not inherently wrong. They help us navigate difficult conversations, protect our emotions, and function in a world that does not always make space for vulnerability.

Yet, a mask can become so well-worn over time that we forget what exists beneath it. Peeling back these layers is not about stripping away every defence but about allowing your true self to breathe again. Authenticity is not an all-or-nothing act; it reveals itself in small moments – when you speak honestly when you engage in something that lights you up, when you choose to express rather than suppress.

Shedding these protective layers allows your nervous system to settle, reconnecting you with long-silenced emotions. This is a process of rediscovery, not reinvention. There is no rush. With each interaction, you illuminate different facets of yourself, permitting growth rather than forcing change.

## Reconnecting with Your True Self

Authenticity begins with curiosity and play. Engaging in activities that interest you can uncover hidden aspects of your identity. Playfulness provides a space free from judgement, where you can explore parts of yourself that may have been neglected or forgotten.

- **Exploring Interests:** When was the last time you did something simply for the joy of it? Whether painting, dancing, hiking, or learning a new skill, pursuing interests without pressure can help you reconnect with the parts of yourself that feel most alive.

- **Redefining Success:** For many, success has been measured by external approval – pleasing family, meeting professional expectations, or fitting into societal moulds. Authenticity means shifting this perspective, defining success based on what truly matters to you. When you align with your own values rather than those imposed by others, you strengthen your connection to your core self.

## Reflection Prompt

Think of three activities or interests you have always wanted to try but hesitated to pursue. What held you back? How might engaging in these pursuits help you feel closer to your authentic self?

This journey is not about discarding the past but embracing all the parts of yourself – both the ones you have shared with the world and those you have kept hidden. Each conversation, each choice, each moment of honesty brings you closer to the person beneath the mask.

## Eve's Breakthrough: The Masks I Wore

I once heard an actor say that his work's joy came from being anyone, slipping into different roles and becoming something new. The thought lingered with me, but for a different reason. We all wear masks – not for entertainment, but for survival.

I did not realise how many masks I had collected for much of my life. Through journalling – especially using Julia Cameron's *The Artist's Way* – I began uncovering the identities I had worn since childhood.

I had been *"the helpful girl"*, always eager to please. *"The cheerful traveller"*, adapting to my parents' unpredictable lifestyle. *"The capable one"*, who did not need guidance or comfort. Beneath these masks, I was scared, lonely, uneducated, and often hungry. But I learned quickly: showing fear was dangerous, asking for help led to rejection, and my value lay in how well I could meet the needs of others.

For years, I believed something was wrong with me. The truth was, my masks had protected me. They allowed me to navigate a world that did not always feel safe. But they also distanced me from myself. The more I played these roles, the harder it became to know where they ended and where I began.

Journalling became a way of peeling back these layers, slowly, gently, without shame. Some days, it was painful – realising how much I had hidden, how much of my life had been shaped by survival rather than self-expression. Other days, it felt like opening a window after years of stale air, letting in something fresh, something real.

## Wearing Masks with Intention

I no longer see masks as something to discard completely. They are tools. They allow us to step into different roles – parent, partner, friend, professional. They help us navigate spaces that may not be safe for full vulnerability. The problem is not the mask itself; it is when we forget that we are more than the persona we present.

Now, I use my masks consciously. I allow myself that protective layer when I need to be composed in a difficult conversation. When I step into my role as a coach, I bring confidence and clarity. But I also know when to take the mask off – to let my guard down with close friends, to allow myself to be held, to be seen.

Authenticity is not about being unfiltered all the time. It is about knowing that beneath any mask, my true self remains intact and understood. The goal is not to erase the masks completely, but to create spaces where we do not need them.

With the right balance, masks do not separate us from others; they enhance our ability to connect, giving us the confidence to engage while preserving the space to be real.

*"As we open our minds to the creative process,*
*we see that the purpose of art is not to impress but to express.*
*It is not to present a version of ourselves that is acceptable*
*but to allow the true self to emerge."*

Julia Cameron (1948– )
Author, Artist and Director

### Camouflaged Sailors: Key Takeaways

**Recognising the Masks:** Childhood roles often create protective layers that shield us but limit genuine connection. Awareness is the first step to letting go of masks that no longer serve us.

**The Cost of Hiding:** Suppressing your true self leads to self-criticism and emotional isolation. Small steps toward vulnerability build healthier self-worth and deeper connections.

**The Magic Three for Boundaries:** Clarify your needs, communicate with "I" statements, and calmly reinforce boundaries to reduce conflict and build trust in relationships.

**Rediscovering Authenticity:** Exploring genuine interests and redefining success based on your values reconnects you with your true self, promoting growth and meaningful relationships.

## Poem: Girl of Light and Glass

*Girl of light and glass,*
*golden glow, you move,*
*soft as warmth in morning's breath,*
*but then —*
*In a moment fixed, still shut down,*
*all passes through.*
*Nothing touches*
*your empty vessel.*

*What happened then?*
*Transparent vacancy,*
*hair, looks, clothes,*
*caught in awkward quicksand,*
*flow gone.*
*Behind the mask, a reset needed,*
*but the lock is hidden, lost.*

*I spent a lifetime*
*knowing myself enough*
*to find my own key.*
*I hope my love can reach you.*
*As my love has found me. At last,*
*To live a full life, not a half-life.*

# Part 5

# FINDING A SAFE HARBOUR: TOOLS TO ANCHOR EMOTIONAL SECURITY

> *"A thoughtful conversation is built in the quiet moments before it begins; clarity, intention, and a plan form the bridge from thought to words."*
>
> Eve Stanway

## Introduction: Preparing for Meaningful Communication

You are on the brink of a conversation that feels impossible, held back by fear, doubt, or the echoes of past attempts that did not go as planned. It is tempting to retreat into silence, but deep down, you know the cost of avoiding what needs to be said. This chapter will give you the tools to step forward purposefully and confidently.

Tools such as anchoring yourself in curiosity, building strength through a willingness to work out what you want to say and finding the right words. Using intentional boundaries – like "healthy masks" – to create a safe space for honesty. You will learn how to say "no" as an act of self-respect and use practical exercises to speak up when the stakes feel high.

This is not about getting it perfect; it is about having a plan and following it. Preparation, not perfection. With the right tools, you can turn discomfort into progress, silence into understanding, and fear into action.

## Understanding the Emotional Landscape of Difficult Conversations

Have you ever felt like you are hitting a wall in a conversation, where no matter what you say, it feels like the other person has shut down or stopped listening? Or perhaps you have found yourself retreating into silence, unsure of how to continue or too overwhelmed to speak. This is stonewalling, and it is one of the biggest barriers to meaningful communication.

Stonewalling happens when defensiveness, fear, or frustration takes over, leaving one or both people unable to engage. It can feel like the conversation is at a dead end, but it does not have to stay that way. The key is to recognise when it is happening and understand what lies beneath it.

When emotions run high, conversations often trigger deeper fears – about being misunderstood, judged, or even losing a sense of control. These moments are rarely about the surface disagreement. They are shaped by the values and insecurities we carry: the need to feel competent, respected, or safe. When these vulnerabilities are challenged, shutting down can feel like the only option.

So how do you move forward when you feel like you are talking to a wall, or when you feel the urge to stonewall yourself? The answer lies in slowing down, grounding yourself, and creating space for both sides to feel heard. It is not about forcing a resolution but about staying present, asking the right questions, and showing patience even when tensions run high.

Melanie and Kristy were in the middle of a tense discussion about a disagreement at work. As the conversation escalated, Melanie noticed Kristy's arms folding tightly across her chest and her responses becoming clipped and defensive. The energy in the room felt heavy, and Melanie realised they were heading into a stalemate.

Instead of pushing forward, Melanie paused.

**Clarify:** *"Kristy, I can see this is getting really tense, and I don't want us to walk away from this feeling worse. How about we take a break, get some fresh air, and come back to it when we've had a moment to process?"*

Kristy hesitated, visibly torn, before nodding. *"Yeah, I think that would help. I'm feeling pretty overwhelmed right now."*

After stepping away for a short break, they sat down again, both more composed. Melanie began by softening her tone and speaking calmly.

**Communicate:** *"I've had some time to think, and I really want to make sure I'm hearing you clearly. Could you tell me more about your perspective? I want to understand where you are coming from."*

Kristy's body language shifted slightly, and she met Melanie's gaze. *"Thanks. I was just feeling like my concerns weren't being taken seriously."*

Melanie nodded, staying open.

**Correct:** *"I can see now that I wasn't fully acknowledging what you were saying earlier, and I am sorry if that made you feel dismissed. Let's figure out how we can move forward in a way that works for both of us."*

This simple reset – acknowledging the tension, taking a break, and returning with fresh focus – allowed both women to approach the conversation with clearer minds. Melanie's willingness to clarify her intention, truly listen, and repair any misunderstandings created a safer, more respectful dynamic. The shift from defensiveness to mutual understanding was a result of slowing down, checking assumptions, and prioritising care over conflict.

When we are challenged by difficult conversations, they push us to examine how we view ourselves and others. These moments can feel uncomfortable but also create space for change. Laura's story shows how deeply rooted patterns can begin to shift.

## Laura's Journey to Connection Through Curiosity

Laura came to me feeling overwhelmed and stuck. She had always prided herself on being strong, shaped by her mother's often-repeated phrase, *"There is no time to wallow."* Laura repeated it to herself whenever life felt hard, a mantra she relied on to push through. Over time, she even found herself saying it to others, though it never felt right. *"I would never want to say it to someone who was struggling,"* she admitted. *"It feels so unkind, but I can't stop saying it to myself."*

This belief – that resilience meant holding everything in – helped her manage work, family, and responsibilities for years. However, the cracks began to show. Laura described constant headaches, exhaustion, and feeling emotionally disconnected from her husband and children. *"It's like I'm here, but not really here,"* she said. *"I don't know if this is just how life is supposed to feel or if something is wrong with me."*

One evening, she shared a moment that marked a turning point. Watching her children play, she was struck by how free and open they were with their emotions. *"I can't remember the last time I cried or even let myself really laugh,"* she said. *"I've just been holding everything in."*

In therapy, letting her guard down was a struggle. *"I've spent so long pretending I'm fine,"* she admitted, *"I don't know how to start without falling apart."* I encouraged her to start small – to notice and name her feelings as they arose, without judging herself. At first, it felt strange and uncomfortable. As she began identifying emotions like frustration, sadness, and exhaustion, she realised they were not signs of weakness. They were signals pointing to what she truly needed.

This growing awareness gave Laura the courage to open up to her husband. One evening, she said, *"I feel so overwhelmed."* She braced herself for his reaction and was met with kindness.

*"I've seen that you're struggling,"* he said, *"but you didn't seem to want to talk about it. Tell me what you need."* For Laura, it was a moment of clarity: her silence had not protected her family; it had created distance.

Setting boundaries was another step forward. The first time she told her children, *"I need some quiet time,"* she felt a pang of guilt. Afterward, she noticed how much calmer and more present she felt. Over time, these small acts of self-care became acts of self-respect. They also taught her children that taking care of yourself is not selfish – it is necessary.

Reflecting on her journey, Laura began to see her mother's advice differently. *"It got me through a lot, but it's not how I want to live now,"* she said. *"I want my children to know it's okay to feel. Strength isn't about hiding your emotions – it's about showing up, even when it's hard."*

The beliefs we learn in childhood can help us survive but may stop serving us as we grow. Laura's story shows how these patterns shape our lives and how questioning them can lead to change. By letting go of the ideas that no longer fit, she found the courage to share her feelings with the people who cared most.

## Cultivating Curiosity as a Foundation for Difficult Conversations Is Essential

Curiosity creates an open mental space that helps reduce defensiveness. When you approach a conversation with curiosity – toward yourself, the other person, and the situation at hand – you are more likely to keep a receptive and flexible mindset. Curiosity allows you to explore why you feel the way you do, what you genuinely hope to achieve, and how the other person might be experiencing the situation. Rather than viewing the conversation as a battle to be won, curiosity transforms it into a collaborative exploration.

Curiosity also encourages you to look beyond your immediate reactions. For example, if a friend frequently cancels plans, instead of assuming they do not care, you might ask yourself, *"What else could be happening for them?"* This shift in perspective makes room for empathy and compassion, helping you see the situation from a broader angle. Curiosity invites you to question assumptions and make space for understanding, which often leads to a more constructive and meaningful exchange.

Through curiosity, you build a bridge that allows for deeper connections and reduces the tension that can arise from misinterpretation. It turns even challenging conversations into opportunities for growth, discovery, and strengthened relationships.

### Practical Exercises for Cultivating Curiosity

1. **Self-Reflection Before the Conversation:** Write down three questions you are genuinely curious about regarding the other person's perspective. Examples might include, *"What might be preventing them from meeting my expectations?"* or *"How might they be perceiving my actions?"*

2. **Curiosity Practice Prompt:** Think of a recent disagreement. Reframe your initial reactions with questions such as, *"What might I not be seeing?"* or *"How could I approach this conversation from a place of curiosity rather than criticism?"*

*"Planning is bringing the future into the present so that you can do something about it now."*

Alan Lakein (1932–2024)
American author and time management professional

# Embracing Self-Affirmation as a Tool for Confidence

## The Power of Self-Affirmation in Difficult Conversations

Self-affirmations, much like goal setting, serve as a guiding compass, focusing our thoughts on where we aim to go. Just as goals give us a target, affirmations help us anchor our beliefs, reinforcing that our journey is meaningful and that our efforts will lead somewhere worthwhile. When we nurture this belief, we create a foundation where tackling challenges feels not only possible but valuable – each step affirming that we can and should meet our aspirations with courage.

This is where "fake it until you make it" comes into play. Although it might feel shaky at first, this practice can help convince your mind and body that you are capable, even if you are not quite there yet. Our nervous system is tuned to protect us from both real and imagined threats, so having a positive focus is crucial. Combined with tools like the **Magic Three: Clarify, Communicate, and Correct**, self-affirmations help us prepare to face any issues that arise. In doing so, we are not merely addressing immediate challenges; we are shaping a path toward resilience and stronger connections.

Affirmations do not need to feel "true" initially. Think of them instead as a blueprint for how you wish to see yourself. Over time, as you repeat these affirmations, they start to shape your mindset, subtly shifting your experiences toward smoother, more authentic conversations. Self-affirmations ground us in our core values and sense of self-worth, providing a buffer against rejection or misunderstanding. Before stepping into a challenging conversation, affirming both your right to be heard and your own value will lower your anxiety, helping you to approach the situation with calm and respect.

When you affirm that your feelings and perspectives are valid, you bring a layer of self-respect that directly impacts how you communicate. It is the difference between speaking from a place of insecurity and speaking from a place of strength. With self-affirmation as part of your toolkit, you are no longer merely surviving difficult conversations but engaging in genuine connection, confidence, and clarity. Affirmations remind you that your voice matters and that your efforts to build understanding and connection are worthy, grounded in your sense of purpose and inner truth.

## Practical Affirmations for Conversation Preparation

Self-affirmations serve as gentle yet powerful reminders of your worth, your right to be heard, and your intentions in approaching difficult conversations. These can be simple phrases that anchor you in self-respect and purpose. Here are a few examples:

- **Affirming Self-Worth:** *"My feelings are valid, and I have the right to express them."*

- **Grounding in Intention:** *"I am here to both understand and be understood. I am open to finding clarity together."*

- **Creating Safety for Vulnerability:** *"It is safe for me to share my needs. I trust myself to handle the outcome."*

## Exercise: Self-Affirmation Journalling

1. **Define Your Intentions:** Before entering the conversation, take a moment to journal about what you truly hope to accomplish. Be specific – whether your goal is to assert a boundary, share your emotions, or reach a mutual understanding, define this intention clearly to create a personal roadmap for the conversation.

2. **Affirmation Practice:** Choose an affirmation that resonates and repeat it aloud or write it down several times. This repetition helps embed it in your mind, allowing the words to ground you in your own worth. Remind yourself that your value remains intact, regardless of how the conversation unfolds.

felt and consider how setting a boundary might have changed the experience. This exercise helps clarify why and when "no" serves you best.

## Reflection Prompt

Think of a recent situation when saying "no" would have supported your self-care. How might you approach a similar scenario next time?

Reframing "no" as an act of self-respect allows us to express it gently and with compassion. Rather than seeing "no" as a rejection, we can begin to view it as a loving boundary – one that nurtures healthier, more balanced relationships with ourselves and others. Saying "no" then becomes a choice that honours our well-being, making room for what truly matters and creating space for deeper, more genuine connections.

> *"By failing to prepare, you are preparing to fail."*
>
> Benjamin Franklin (1706–1790)
> American writer, inventor and statesman

## Practising Authenticity Through Role-Play and Exercises

### Role-Play as Preparation for Real Conversations

Preparation is a gift you can give yourself. When preparing for a challenging conversation, feeling a blend of hope and unease is natural. We often step into these moments carrying the quiet wish to be truly heard, alongside a worry about how our words may land. Practising beforehand, especially with a supportive framework like the **Magic Three: Clarify, Communicate, and Correct**, can ground you in your intentions and offer a steadying influence, allowing you to speak kindly and calmly.

# Reframing "No" as Self-Care

## Understanding "No" as a Boundary, Not a Rejection

Saying "no" often feels uncomfortable. Many of us are conditioned to fear disappointing others, worrying that "no" will come across as selfish or unkind. Yet, saying "no" is frequently an essential act of self-care – a way to protect our energy, time, and mental well-being. When we reframe "no" as a boundary instead of a rejection, we begin to recognise it as a way of honouring our own needs rather than letting others down.

Reframing "no" requires a shift in perspective: instead of seeing it as depriving others, we can start to view it as giving something valuable back to ourselves. This becomes especially crucial in situations where saying "yes" would undermine our own well-being, values, or priorities.

## Example: Using "No" to Honour Self-Care

Take Emma, who often found herself saying "yes" to extra tasks at work, even when her plate was already overflowing. She felt reluctant to say "no" because she worried it would make her appear unhelpful. But as she started to view "no" as a boundary that protected her mental health, she felt empowered to decline additional tasks. By saying "no," Emma could focus fully on her existing responsibilities, reducing her stress and improving the quality of her work. In saying "no," she was, in fact, saying "yes" to her own well-being.

## Exercises for Practising "No" as Self-Care

1. **Role-Play Saying "No":** Practise saying "no" in a calm, confident manner, either with a trusted friend or in front of a mirror. Reinforce this boundary by using an affirmation such as, *"Saying no is a way of honouring my needs."*

2. **The "No" Journal:** Reflect on moments when you said "yes" but wished you had said "no." Write down how each situation

authentically while keeping certain layers protected. This might mean staying composed during a difficult conversation with a colleague or keeping some emotional distance when sharing with a friend who may not respond empathetically.

## Balancing Openness and Protection

Imagine discussing a sensitive topic with a family member who tends to respond critically. Rather than diving into vulnerable details, using a healthy mask means presenting your perspective calmly and without excessive emotion. It lets you share what feels safe while setting a clear boundary that keeps your inner self protected. This approach can help you express your needs without opening yourself up to judgement or feeling vulnerable.

## Reflection Prompt

Consider a recent conversation where you felt overly exposed or misunderstood. If you had approached it with a healthy mask, how might it have felt different?

Remember, your ability to set boundaries and protect your emotional space is not a limitation. It is a tool for resilience and self-respect. Healthy masks give you the strength to engage, connect, and stay true to yourself without compromising your emotional safety.

*"Preparation gives us the gift of pause, grounding our thoughts so that when we speak, we are not just reacting but expressing our true intentions."*

Eve Stanway

## Reflection Prompt

Reflect on a recent challenging conversation. How might self-affirmation have shifted your approach? Write down an affirmation you could use in a similar situation next time. This will help build confidence and reinforce your commitment to approaching future conversations with self-assurance.

Affirmations help you enter conversations with an open heart and a steady foundation, reminding you that, whatever the outcome, your voice and perspective hold genuine worth. This practice is not about forcing an outcome but about cultivating a mindset of self-respect, clarity, and resilience, creating room for more authentic and fulfilling dialogue.

## The Concept of Healthy Masks as Boundaries

### Navigating Healthy Emotional Boundaries

There is power in choosing what to share and what to hold back, a strength that comes not from hiding who you are but from honouring your emotional well-being. When you engage in challenging conversations, you do not need to lay everything bare; authenticity does not require overexposure. This is where establishing healthy boundaries – and sometimes using what we call "healthy masks" – comes in.

A healthy mask is not about being inauthentic. It is about protecting parts of yourself that might feel too vulnerable in the moment or too precious to risk in potentially unsupportive spaces. Think of it as an emotional buffer, one that lets you connect without feeling overexposed.

### Knowing When to Use a Healthy Mask

In certain relationships or environments, you might sense that showing everything could lead to misunderstanding or judgement. In these situations, a healthy mask can allow you to engage

## Why Practise Difficult Conversations?

In times of tension, we can lose track of the message we wish to convey as emotions take over. When words become tangled, our intentions may be obscured, and moments of connection may slip by. Practising these conversations beforehand gives you a compassionate space to find your voice, refine your language, and adjust your tone. This practice is a way of caring for yourself, ensuring that when you finally step into the conversation, you are better able to stay composed, respond rather than react, and hold space for both yourself and the other person.

Each step of preparation is not about perfection but about honouring your feelings and needs. This gentle approach also nurtures authenticity, helping you enter the conversation more present, anchored, and willing to truly listen. In practising, you allow room for the heart as much as the mind – making space to be both clear and compassionate, toward yourself and toward the person you are speaking with.

## Using the Magic Three in Practice

1. **Clarify:** Start by identifying your core message. Take a moment to define what you want to convey clearly. For instance, if you need more respect for your time, be specific: *"I need time in the mornings to focus without interruptions."*

2. **Communicate:** Practice expressing your needs using "I" statements, focusing on how certain behaviours make you feel rather than assigning blame. If interruptions frustrate you, instead of saying, *"You're always interrupting me,"* try, *"I feel more productive when I have uninterrupted time."*

3. **Correct:** If boundaries are crossed again, practise reinforcing them with kindness and clarity. Say, *"I would really appreciate if we could save non-urgent questions for after my morning work hours."* This approach maintains your boundaries without creating defensiveness.

How might this work in action?

## Samantha, the Overwhelmed Parent

Samantha sat at the kitchen table, staring at the pile of dishes in the sink. It was nearly 10 pm and she still had emails to respond to and laundry to fold. Her son, Ethan, was upstairs, headphones on, completely oblivious to the chaos around him. She felt a familiar wave of frustration rising, but beneath it was something deeper – loneliness and sadness. When had it started feeling like she was on her own in this house?

She thought back to their latest argument, just a few hours earlier. *"Ethan, can you please unload the dishwasher before I get home?"* she had asked as she left for work that morning. When she returned, the dishwasher was untouched.

*"I forgot, okay?"* he had snapped when she brought it up, his tone dripping with irritation. *"Why do you always make such a big deal out of everything?"*

His words stung more than she wanted to admit. Samantha found herself retreating, muttering something about doing it herself, while Ethan shrugged and disappeared into his room.

### Recognising the Pattern

That night, unable to sleep, Samantha replayed the scene in her mind. She felt stuck – she wanted to connect with Ethan, but every time she tried, it seemed to spiral into conflict or dismissal. It hit her that she had been focusing so much on the small tasks Ethan was ignoring that she had lost sight of what she truly needed: to feel respected and supported.

*"I cannot keep doing this,"* she whispered to herself. *"But how do I change it without pushing him away?"*

### A Moment of Courage

The next morning, Samantha decided to approach Ethan differently. She waited until they were both in a good mood – Saturday morning, over pancakes. *"Ethan,"* she began hesitantly, *"can I talk to you about something?"*

He raised an eyebrow but nodded, his mouth full of syrupy pancake. *"Sure."*

Samantha took a deep breath. *"I have been feeling pretty overwhelmed lately. Between work and keeping the house running, I feel like I'm carrying a lot on my own. I know I have been nagging, and I hate it. I just… I need us to work together more. Not because I want to boss you around, but because it feels really lonely doing it all by myself."*

Ethan looked up from his plate, his expression softer than she expected. *"I didn't realise you felt that way,"* he admitted quietly. *"I just thought you were mad at me all the time."*

Samantha blinked back tears. *"I am not mad at you, Ethan. I just miss feeling like we are a team."*

### Building Something New

The conversation was not perfect. Ethan rolled his eyes when she suggested setting up a weekly chore schedule, but he agreed to give it a try. They brainstormed together – what tasks he could manage, what times worked best, and how to remind each other without arguing.

Over the next few weeks, there were slip-ups. Ethan forgot to take the bins out twice, and Samantha found herself biting her tongue to avoid slipping back into nagging. Instead, she would say, *"Ethan, I know we agreed on this, and I need you to follow through. It makes a big difference to me."* Slowly, he started responding – sometimes with a bit of grumbling, but often with action.

One evening, as they cleaned up dinner together, Ethan surprised her. *"I know I forgot the bins last week,"* he said, avoiding her gaze. *"I'll get them out tomorrow morning."*

Samantha smiled, feeling a warmth she had not felt in a long time. *"Thank you, Ethan. It really means a lot."*

Samantha's story is not about instant transformation or a perfect resolution. It is about finding courage in moments of vulnerability and recognising that change takes time and consistency. By stepping back from the conflict and sharing her feelings openly, Samantha and Ethan began to rebuild a connection rooted in mutual understanding and respect.

## Reflection Prompt

Think of a recent situation where you held back in expressing a need. How might practising the **Magic Three** have helped you feel more prepared and assertive?

## Reinforcing Self-Respect

Role-playing is not only a form of preparation; it is an act of kindness toward yourself, a way to affirm that your voice and boundaries matter. Each time you practise, you are gently reinforcing your own worth and your right to be heard. By the time you enter the conversation, you bring with you a foundation of confidence and calm, ready to express yourself with clarity and self-respect.

Approaching conversations in this way – grounded in authenticity and preparation – transforms them into spaces where growth and connection can flourish. Each conversation becomes an opportunity to honour your values, strengthening the foundation for relationships that truly resonate with who you are.

# Self-Care After the Conversation

## Reflecting on the Outcome and Learning From Experience

Difficult conversations can leave us feeling drained, so self-care is key to finding balance again. Taking a moment to reflect helps you process the experience and recognise what went well, as well as areas to improve. This reflection keeps you grounded, reminding you of your worth regardless of how the conversation went.

1. **Reflect on the Conversation**

   After the conversation, take a few minutes to jot down your thoughts. What felt genuine? Were there moments where you wish you had said something differently? Reflecting helps you understand what worked and what to adjust for next time.

   Example: After a tense conversation with her colleague, Tamara wrote, *"I felt calm when I set boundaries, but I could have listened more in the middle of the conversation. Next time, I'll pause more before responding."*

2. **Practise Self-Compassion**

   Remember, no conversation is perfect, and that is okay. Recognise the courage it took to engage and be kind to yourself as you process. Showing yourself compassion is a powerful way to honour your effort, no matter the outcome.

   Example: Tamara reminded herself, *"It's okay that I didn't get everything right. I showed up and stayed respectful, and that's what matters most."*

## Reflection Prompt

After a challenging conversation, ask yourself, *"What did I learn from this experience? How can I carry this insight into future interactions?"*

## Celebrating Small Wins

Each difficult conversation, no matter how it ends, presents an opportunity for growth. Recognising small wins – such as staying calm, expressing your feelings, or simply showing up – builds confidence and resilience. Celebrating these small victories reminds you of your progress, encouraging you to continue building genuine and assertive communication.

## Example: Celebrating Progress

After an open and honest conversation with her partner about a recurring issue, Sarah took a moment to acknowledge her progress. She realised that her ability to articulate her feelings without self-censoring was a step forward, independent of her partner's response. By celebrating this small victory, she reinforced her self-worth and felt encouraged to keep pursuing authentic conversations.

## Reflection Prompt

Reflect on a recent difficult conversation. Identify one small victory or moment of progress. Write down how this accomplishment can support you in future interactions.

Taking time to reflect and celebrate after challenging conversations is more than a practice; it is an affirmation of your growth and resilience. These moments of self-care help you recognise that, step by step, you are strengthening your ability to communicate with courage and clarity.

---

### Finding a Safe Harbour: Key Takeaways

**Curiosity as a Compass:** Embracing curiosity helps unravel misunderstandings and creates space for authentic dialogue during difficult conversations.

**Healthy Masks as Boundaries:** Understanding that some "masks" protect rather than suppress allows individuals to establish boundaries without losing authenticity.

**The Power of "No":** Reframing "no" as an act of self-care instead of rejection empowers individuals to prioritise their needs without guilt.

**Aftercare for Conversations:** Engaging in self-reflection and nurturing rituals after challenging conversations strengthens emotional resilience and promotes healing.

## Eve's Shift of Mind

A crossroads in my life came when I was struck by a serious case of bacterial pneumonia while my daughter was still a toddler. I was forty years old, healthy, active, and seemingly doing everything "right," yet I became as unwell as I had ever been. There was no clear reason for it. Looking back, I can see how illness became my body's way of forcing me to confront a lifetime of putting others first at the expense of myself.

As a child, I took on the role of caregiver for my father and younger brother after my mother left. I became the *"helpful older sibling,"* believing my worth was tied to how much I could do for others. This pattern followed me into adulthood. My health, dreams, and personal time were all sacrificed in the belief that saying "No" was selfish or shameful.

It took pneumonia – and years later, a skin cancer diagnosis – for me to understand how dangerous this belief was. Neglecting myself was not just unhealthy; it was life-threatening. Constantly sacrificing my needs not only hurt me but also let others down. By refusing to prioritise my well-being, I was depleting the energy and care I could offer to those who truly mattered.

I began to rewrite the script. Through affirmations and reflection, I saw that setting boundaries was not about rejecting others but about affirming my right to thrive. Have you ever heard the following? *"The graveyard is full of people who thought they were indispensable."* My experience taught me the truth of this. Anyone who cannot respect your "No" or your need to care for yourself is not supporting your well-being. They are not safe for you, and their presence should be limited.

Today, putting my needs first shows self-respect. It has allowed me to show up as my best self for the people and dreams that truly matter. If there is one lesson I would share, it is this: saying "No" is not selfish; it is the ultimate expression of self-love, a boundary that protects your health, your spirit, and your life.

> *"Every difficult conversation holds a choice: to face the moment with authenticity and respect or to avoid the truth that could lead to growth."*
>
> Eve Stanway

## Poem: Hope Reclaimed

*Child with gold curl and peachy skin,*
*Sweet breath defined you. Glowing with life,*
*Ready to be warmed by love,*
*You turn, you seek.*

*Yet silence greets you.*
*Unheard words slip into the void,*
*Vanishing before they find a home.*

*Slowly, your petals curl inward,*
*A shield against the empty space.*
*Body and brain reshape to fit a world*
*Where quiet feels safer than speaking,*
*And hope is wrapped in layers,*
*Tucked so far from reach,*
*You forget it was ever yours.*

*Sharp words that slap,*
*Unanswered questions dust upon on your tongue.*
*You shrink away from that swaddled bundle,*
*Until hope becomes a lesson in foolishness.*

*Yet something lingers –*
*A whisper inside, too soft to ignore.*
*A lifetime of moving forward,*
*And still, the absence pulls.*
*Bag searched, pockets felt,*
*Something too crucial to leave behind.*

*So you turn back, each step cracking open silence,*
*Edging past pain and fear,*
*Letting your voice rise – hesitant, then stronger.*
*You kneel before that dusty box,*
*Lifting hope with steady hands,*
*Holding it close,*
*For always.*

# Part 6

# PLOTTING YOUR COURSE: HOW TO NAVIGATE STORMY SEAS

*"Seek first to understand, then to be understood."*

Stephen R. Covey (1932–2012)
American author, educator and
the 'father' of personal development

## Introduction: The Power of Preparation

### Eve's Voice in the Maze

When I began working as a typist in London in my twenties, I felt like an imposter lost in an endless maze. Each morning brought a new desk in an unfamiliar office, new faces I could barely remember, and systems that seemed alien. My pulse quickened as I settled into each new seat, the hum of office chatter around me a constant reminder that I was out of my depth. Yet, I played my part, projecting an air of competence I barely believed in. Each keystroke felt like a performance, and every glance at my screen reminded me that I was making it up as I went along.

It never crossed my mind that I could ask for help or training. My childhood had taught me that admitting ignorance was shameful, a weakness that others might use against me. The thought of exposing my inadequacies sent a cold flush to my cheeks. *What if they saw me for what I was – a fraud who did not belong?* Instead of risking vulnerability, I turned to instinct and sheer grit, solving problems as they arose and praying my guesses were correct.

## The Mask of Competence

Despite the internal storm, I succeeded – or at least, I appeared to. Years of moving from place to place with my parents had sharpened my observational skills. I could pick up on patterns quickly, adjust to new processes, and once I learned something, I never forgot it. I became a master of projecting calm confidence. People trusted me, drawn to the steadiness I displayed. What they could not see was the turmoil underneath, the exhausting act of holding everything together.

For all my ability to adapt and appear composed, there was one area where I could not pretend. When it came to expressing my needs or asking for support, it felt like standing at the edge of a cliff. The ground beneath me felt unstable, my heart raced as though it might burst, and my breath caught in my chest. Words tumbled out of my mouth in a chaotic rush, leaving me flustered and exposed.

## The Roots of Silence

This hesitation was not new. Its roots stretched back to childhood, to moments when my cheeks burned with humiliation as I froze under the weight of being wrong. In a world where no one felt safe enough to ask for guidance, not knowing was terrifying. Judgement loomed like a shadow, and silence became my shield. It protected me from the sting of criticism but trapped me in a loneliness I could not escape.

I learned to rely on myself, building walls of self-reliance that kept others out. Admitting I did not know something, or that I needed help, felt like opening the gates to a flood of shame. Instead, I pushed through in silence, hiding my fears behind a mask of capability.

## Ending the Silence

Eventually, the silence became unbearable. I realised that if I wanted to grow, I would need to face my fear. It was not a dramatic moment, no sudden epiphany. It began with small steps – writing down what I wanted to say, untangling the knot of thoughts that made my words stumble. I would rehearse, sometimes in my head, sometimes out loud, and with each small act of preparation, the fear began to loosen its grip.

Clarity became my anchor. By focusing on what mattered most, I found I could steady myself, even when anxiety crept in. My heart still raced, my breath still caught, but I learned to ground myself in those moments. A deep breath, a reminder of the purpose behind my words, and a deliberate pause before speaking allowed me to find my voice. Though the fear never entirely left, it no longer controlled me.

## The Cliff Became a Bridge

What once felt like standing at the edge of a cliff now became something else entirely – a bridge. Speaking up no longer felt like a terrifying plunge but a connection to something bigger. Each time I shared my thoughts with intention, I opened the door to new opportunities, new understanding, and even a new-found freedom within myself.

The girl who once stayed silent out of fear had found her voice. It was not perfect, and it was not always easy, but it was mine. And with each conversation, I proved to myself that vulnerability could be a strength, not a weakness. The maze I had once wandered aimlessly now felt navigable, with every step forward bringing me closer to the person I wanted to be.

*"Healing does not mean the damage never existed. It means the damage no longer controls our lives."*

Tara Brach
*Radical Acceptance,* 2003

## Understanding Perceptions and Motivations

Imagine standing on opposite sides of a window. You each see the same world beyond, but the view is framed differently depending on where you stand. This is the essence of a difficult conversation – two people with unique perspectives shaped by their individual experiences. One person might feel an urgent need to address an issue, while the other hesitates, unsure why the discussion is necessary or even uncomfortable about what it might reveal.

These differences can feel like an invisible wall, creating tension before the first word is spoken. But what if you approached the conversation with curiosity? Instead of focusing on your own view, you step to their side of the window. You ask, *"What do you see from here?"* In that moment, the wall starts to dissolve, replaced by a shared understanding. Listening with the intention to understand, not to respond, can transform a conversation from a standoff into a bridge.

## The Invisible Weight of Shame

Shame is a silent force that can sneak into a conversation without warning. It whispers that we are not good enough, not smart enough, not worthy enough. It tightens our chest, quickens our breath, and makes our skin flush with heat. In those moments, the conversation becomes less about the words being spoken and more about the fear of being exposed – of having our vulnerabilities laid bare.

For the person feeling shame, it can feel like standing under a spotlight, every flaw magnified. This often triggers a fight-or-flight response: we lash out defensively or retreat into silence, hoping to protect ourselves from further discomfort. But this self-protection comes at a cost. Shame, left unspoken, lingers in the shadows, eroding confidence and creating distance in relationships.

On the other side of the conversation, if the person you are speaking to feels shame, they may misinterpret your words as judgement or criticism, even if that was never your intention. Their body language might shift – averted eyes, crossed arms, a defensive tone. These are signs that shame has entered the room, and if unacknowledged, it can derail even the most carefully planned dialogue.

## Creating a Safe Space for Dialogue

Now, imagine instead that the conversation begins in a space of safety. The tone is calm, the body language open, and the intention clear: this is not a battle but a shared exploration. When people feel safe, they lower their defences. They lean in rather than pull away, opening themselves to understanding and connection.

Creating this sense of safety starts with your presence. Your body language – relaxed shoulders, an uncrossed posture – signals that you are approachable. Your tone – steady, warm, and unhurried – invites trust.

Even the way you breathe can influence the atmosphere; slow, even breaths help to keep your own nervous system calm, which in turn helps the other person feel grounded.

For those who have experienced criticism or rejection in past conversations, this reassurance is vital. If they sense that judgement is absent, they are more likely to engage honestly. Instead of bracing for impact, they begin to share. They see that the goal is not to point fingers but to understand one another.

## The Courage to Face Shame with Sensitivity

Recognising shame – whether in yourself or the person you are speaking with – is a pivotal step. In yourself, it requires self-compassion, a gentle reminder that vulnerability is not weakness but strength. When you feel the heat of shame rising, pause. Place a hand on your chest, breathe deeply, and ground yourself in the knowledge that it is okay to feel exposed. You are human, and this moment does not define your worth.

For the other person, sensitivity is key. Words carry weight, and even well-meaning ones can unintentionally deepen their discomfort. Phrases like, *"I understand this is hard,"* or, *"It is okay to feel this way,"* can create an opening for them to step out of the shadows of shame and into the light of the conversation. Avoid blaming language or harsh tones that might push them further into retreat.

## The Power of Safety in Conversations

When safety is present, conversations become transformative. Think of safety as the soft ground where trust can take root. It allows both people to share their truths without fear of rejection. In this space, the focus shifts from winning or losing to understanding and connection.

The success of a conversation lies not just in the words exchanged but in the feelings it leaves behind. Did the other person leave feeling seen? Did you feel heard? These are the marks of a meaningful dialogue, one that creates a foundation for deeper relationships and lasting growth.

## Overcoming Resistance: The Quiet Battle We Face

Resistance is like a shadow that lingers at the edge of every difficult conversation. Sometimes, it rises from within – a voice whispering doubts, fears, and reasons to hold back. At other times, it comes from the person sitting across from us – a wall of defensiveness, avoidance, or even emotional overload. Whether internal or external, resistance is not something to conquer but something to understand. It is a guide, pointing to the places where vulnerability, fear, or unspoken truths reside.

As Professor Steve Peters writes in *The Chimp Paradox*, *"Emotions are not the enemy; they are messengers. Listen to them, understand them, and then decide how to respond."* This captures the essence of resistance.

The emotions we feel when we face it – fear, frustration, doubt – are not obstacles to be overcome but signals inviting us to pause and reflect. They call us to understand the unspoken truths that lie beneath the surface of our interactions, offering us the opportunity to engage with greater clarity and care.

## The Shape of Internal Resistance

Picture this: you are preparing to have a conversation you have avoided for weeks, perhaps months. As the moment approaches, a voice begins to stir inside you. *Am I ready? Will they listen? What if I say the wrong thing?* The closer you get, the louder the questions grow, until they feel like a thick fog, clouding your thoughts and freezing your resolve.

This is internal resistance – the quiet battle within. It shows up in many forms. Sometimes it is self-doubt, whispering that your voice does not matter or that the risk of speaking up outweighs the potential for change. Other times, it is the fear of conflict, a deep discomfort with the idea of upsetting the balance, even if that balance is already fraying. And then there is the relentless hum of imposter syndrome, feeding the belief that your perspective is less valid, less important, or less worthy than others.

Resistance within feels heavy, like a weight pressing down on your chest. It tightens your throat, quickens your breath, and tempts you to stay silent. Yet, beneath this resistance is often something vital – a truth you are afraid to share, a need you fear will be dismissed, or a hope you dare not admit aloud.

## Moving Through the Resistance

The first step in facing internal resistance is to name it. Imagine shining a light into a dark room. Fear, doubt, and anxiety lose some of their grip when you acknowledge them: *I am scared of being misunderstood. I am afraid of making things worse. I am worried they will not care.* By naming these feelings, you begin to take back control.

Next, ask yourself a simple but powerful question: *What might happen if this conversation goes well?* Instead of fixating on the risks, imagine the relief, understanding, or growth that might emerge. Shifting your focus from fear to possibility creates space for hope, making the act of stepping forward feel less daunting.

Preparation also helps. Think of preparation as laying a steady foundation beneath your feet. Grounding techniques, quiet moments of reflection, or even rehearsing aloud can calm your mind and anchor you. Resistance may not vanish entirely, but it becomes more manageable, like a current you can wade through rather than a wave that pulls you under.

## The Pushback of Others

Resistance is not only an internal experience; it often lives in the reactions of others. Perhaps you have seen it in a sudden wall of defensiveness, where their posture stiffens and their words become sharp. Or in avoidance – a quick change of subject or a dismissive shrug, as though the topic is too hot to touch. Sometimes it shows up as emotional overload, an outpouring of anger or tears that derails the conversation before it can begin.

These reactions are not about you. They are the other person's response to their own discomfort, fear, or vulnerability. Understanding this can help you stay steady. Their resistance is not a rejection of you but a reflection of their internal struggle.

## Navigating External Resistance

When faced with resistance from others, staying grounded is key. Begin with empathy. Acknowledge the difficulty of the conversation and express why it matters to you. A simple statement like, *"I know this is not easy, but it is important to me that we talk about it,"* can soften their defensiveness and create an opening for dialogue.

Listening is your superpower here. Even when their words sting or their tone feels dismissive, listening actively shows that you value their perspective. It is not about agreeing but about understanding.

Responses like, *"I can see this is hard for you,"* or, *"I understand this feels overwhelming,"* can create a sense of safety without diminishing your own voice.

If emotions run too high, it is okay to pause. Saying, *"Let's take a moment and revisit this when we are both ready,"* shows care without compromising your boundaries. It allows space for both of you to regroup and return with a clearer mind.

## The Courage to Face Resistance

Resistance, whether it comes from within or around us, is a natural part of any meaningful conversation. It signals that something significant is at stake – something worth navigating, no matter how uncomfortable it may feel. Facing it requires courage, yes, but also compassion – for yourself and for the person sitting across from you.

As Viktor Frankl writes in *Man's Search for Meaning* (2004):

> *"Between stimulus and response there is a space. In that space is our power to choose our response. In our response lies our growth and our freedom"*

This space is where resistance and courage meet. By pausing to reflect, by choosing to move through the discomfort, you transform resistance from a barrier into an opportunity. It becomes a bridge to deeper understanding, connection, and growth.

The resistance may not disappear, but as you move through it, you will find that it no longer controls you. Instead, it becomes part of the journey – a reminder of the strength it takes to face what is difficult and the growth that awaits on the other side.

# Self-Reflection:
# Preparing for Difficult Conversations

## The Quiet Strength of Reflection

Before stepping into a challenging conversation, imagine pausing for a moment of stillness. Picture yourself setting aside the noise – the rising emotions, the fears of what might go wrong, the urge to rush in and say your piece. In this moment of pause, you create space to ask yourself the questions that truly matter: *What am I feeling? What am I hoping to achieve? Am I ready to listen as much as I want to be heard?*

Self-reflection is not about perfecting a plan or rehearsing every word. It is about creating a quiet buffer between your initial impulses and the message you genuinely want to convey. Think of it as stepping back to view the full canvas rather than fixating on a single brush stroke. In this space, you gain clarity – not just about your feelings and needs, but about your willingness to engage with the other person as an equal participant in the conversation.

## Listening with Intention

Listening is not merely waiting for your turn to speak. It is stepping into the other person's world, even if only for a moment, to see things as they see them. Imagine sitting across from someone whose perspective challenges your own. You feel the tightness in your chest, the urge to jump in with your counterpoint. But instead, you breathe. You ask yourself, *What might I learn if I truly listen?*

Listening with intention means more than hearing the words they say. It means recognising the emotions beneath their words, the unspoken truths they might be afraid to reveal. It is the choice to value their voice as much as your own. When you listen this way, you send a powerful message: *I see you. I respect you. I am here to understand, not just to be understood.*

## Moving from Reflection to Action

Reflection prepares you for the conversation, but it is action that bridges the gap between clarity and connection. Imagine stepping into the moment with a clear mind and a steady heart. You are not striving for perfection. Instead, you are grounded in your intentions, ready to express yourself with honesty and calm.

Start with the simplest of truths: *What do I need to say, and why does it matter?* Perhaps you feel hurt, frustrated, or misunderstood. Maybe you want to rebuild trust or find a way forward together. Whatever it is, clarity helps you hold onto that purpose, even when the conversation takes unexpected turns.

## Techniques for Grounded Conversations

1. **Name the Heart of the Matter.** Begin by focusing on what matters most. Think of your emotions as clues, pointing toward what lies beneath. If anger flares, could it be masking hurt or disappointment? If frustration rises, might it reveal a longing for connection? Naming the heart of the matter – whether aloud or in your mind – helps you stay rooted in the truth of what you need to express.

2. **Focus on Your Intentions.** Approach the conversation with a clear purpose. Maybe your intention is to rebuild trust, understand their perspective, or simply share how you feel. Hold this purpose gently, like a lantern lighting the way forward. It will guide you, even if the path becomes unclear.

3. **Stay Open to Their Perspective.** Imagine the other person speaking. Can you hear their words without rushing to respond? Can you sit with their emotions, even if they challenge your own? Staying open does not mean you abandon your needs. It means you make space for both voices, creating room for mutual understanding.

4. **Speak with Calm and Care.** When it is your turn to speak, let your words reflect the clarity and compassion you have cultivated. Instead of saying, *"You never listen,"* try, *"I feel*

*unheard, and I would like us to talk about this."* This approach shifts the conversation from blame to connection, inviting the other person to meet you in a shared space of honesty.

## The Ripple Effect of Reflection

When you take the time to reflect before a conversation, something remarkable happens. The edges of tension soften. The urgency to defend yourself fades. You begin to see the other person not as an obstacle, but as a partner in navigating the complexity of human connection.

Imagine this: a difficult conversation begins, and instead of spiralling into frustration, it unfolds like the opening of a book. Each word, each pause, each moment of listening, reveals a new page. You may not agree on everything. You may not find a perfect resolution. But you will have shared something real, something honest, and that is where growth begins.

By grounding yourself in self-reflection and approaching with openness, you create the conditions for a conversation that transcends conflict. It becomes an exchange of understanding, a chance to honour both voices, and an opportunity to build something stronger than before.

# Staying Open: A Path to Connection

You are walking into a conversation you have been dreading. The weight of all the possible outcomes sits heavily on your chest. What if they do not listen? What if they misunderstand? What if they walk away? Your mind begins to spiral, narrowing your focus until all you can see is a single, rigid outcome – the one you fear the most.

Now, pause. Take a moment. Imagine instead that you approach this conversation with curiosity. What if you let go of the need to control every twist and turn? What if you step into it not as a battle to be won, but as a shared journey to be explored? When you stay open, when you allow space for the unexpected, the conversation shifts. Tension softens. Defences lower. Connection begins to form.

## The Strength in Openness

Openness is not about giving in or losing your voice. It is about making room for both your perspective and theirs to coexist. Think of it as holding a lantern in the dark – lighting the way for both of you to see more clearly. When you let go of the need to force a single outcome, you create space for understanding, even when the subject feels uncomfortable or uncertain.

Openness means trusting the process. It means saying, *"I do not have all the answers, but I am willing to listen."* It is an act of courage, not weakness, to step into a conversation with curiosity rather than certainty.

## Clarity: Your Anchor in the Storm

In a conversation where emotions are running high, without clarity, it is easy to get swept away – words spill out too fast, or you freeze, unsure of what to say. However, when you know what matters to you, when you are clear on what you want to express, it feels like you are standing on solid ground.

Clarity is not about having a script or memorising perfect phrases. It is about understanding your thoughts, feelings, and intentions. It is about knowing why the conversation matters to you. Maybe you want to say, *"I need you to understand how this is affecting me,"* or, *"I would like to hear your side of things so we can find a way forward."* Simple, clear, honest words can steady the storm and guide the conversation back to purpose.

## Some Techniques for Staying Open

### 1. Clarify What Matters Most

Before the conversation, take a quiet moment to reflect. Ask yourself, *"What is my goal here? What do I truly want to say?"* Let the answers rise gently, like air bubbles drifting to the surface, while the heavier thoughts sink and settle, like pebbles resting on the riverbed.

When you are clear on what matters most, you can stay focused even when the conversation feels chaotic.

### 2. Communicate with Calm and Curiosity

Imagine your voice as a thread, weaving connection between you and the other person. Keep it steady, even if emotions rise. Instead of saying, *"You never listen to me,"* try, *"I feel unheard, and I would like to talk about that."* This shifts the tone from accusation to invitation, encouraging the other person to step into the conversation rather than retreat from it.

### 3. Course-Correct with Kindness

Conversations rarely go exactly as planned. There will be moments when misunderstandings arise, or emotions flare. When this happens, pause. Take a breath. Then gently guide the conversation back on track. You might say, *"I think we might be talking past each other. Let me try to explain what I mean."* These small acts of kindness – to yourself and to them – keep the dialogue constructive and grounded.

## The Beauty of Intention

Clear intentions help you create a space where both voices can be heard. It is not about convincing or changing the other person; it is about understanding. *"I want to share how I feel, and I want to hear your thoughts,"* you might say. This kind of openness allows trust to grow, even when the conversation feels difficult.

Staying open does not mean you abandon your boundaries or needs. It means you hold them firmly while still inviting the other person to share theirs. This is where real connection happens – when both people feel valued, respected, and understood.

## A Shared Journey

Conversations are not just exchanges of words; they are bridges between people. They can be messy, awkward, even uncomfortable. Yet, within that messiness lies the potential for something extraordinary. When you stay open, when you bring clarity and curiosity to the table, you turn a moment of conflict into a chance for connection.

So, the next time you feel your chest tighten and your mind cling to a single outcome, pause. Take a breath. Ask yourself, *"What could I discover if I let go of control?"* The answer might surprise you. It might even change everything.

> *"Difficult conversations are the crucibles where relationships either fracture or fortify – what survives is forged in honesty, tempered by empathy."*
>
> Eve Stanway

# Emotional Data:
# Recognising Feelings as Essential Information

## Understanding Emotions as Data, Not Burdens

Your emotions are a compass, each feeling pointing you toward something significant. Resentment, sharp and heavy, might be drawing your attention to a boundary that has been crossed. Anxiety, like a fluttering in your chest, could be urging you to seek greater security or clarity. These emotions are not random intrusions or inconveniences; they are messengers, quietly illuminating your needs, values, and boundaries. When you begin to see emotions as "data" rather than burdens, you unlock their potential to guide you with self-awareness and empathy.

Think of a moment when anger flared up inside you, hot and unrelenting. Instead of dismissing it as "bad" or "wrong," what if you paused? What if you let the heat settle and asked, *What are you trying to tell me?* Perhaps it is pointing to a sense of injustice, or a need that has gone unmet for too long. The same applies to sadness, often seen as a weight to carry or something to suppress. What if, instead, you leaned into it? Perhaps it is highlighting something you have lost, asking you to honour what once mattered deeply.

## Listening to the Signals Within

Like the colours on a canvas, each emotion adds depth and dimension to your inner world. When you view them with curiosity instead of judgement, they reveal truths that might otherwise remain hidden. Anger, sadness, fear – they are not flaws but signals. Anger might pulse in your temples, sadness might sit heavy in your chest, and fear might tingle in your fingertips. These physical sensations are clues, inviting you to explore what lies beneath the surface.

When stepping back from your emotions, like a scientist observing a fascinating phenomenon, you can approach them with curiosity, instead of labelling your feelings as "bad" or "weak". You can ask *What is this trying to tell me?* This shift in perspective transforms emotions from obstacles to allies, each one helping you better understand your inner landscape.

## The Power of Observing Without Judgement

Observing your emotions without judgement is like stepping into a quiet room after a storm. The noise of self-criticism fades, and in its place, you find clarity. When you stop seeing anger as an explosion to avoid or sadness as a pit to escape, you make space to listen. These feelings are not here to disrupt you; they are here to guide you.

Let's say you feel a wave of frustration rise, tight and restless in your chest. Instead of pushing it down or letting it erupt, you pause. You breathe. You ask, *Why are you here? What do you need me to see?* Maybe it is telling you that your time is being disrespected or that your efforts are not being acknowledged. This moment of reflection shifts the dynamic. You are no longer at the mercy of your emotions; you are working with them, learning from them.

## Emotions as a Mirror to Your Values

Embracing emotions as data, you begin to see them as mirrors reflecting your deepest values. Resentment might highlight your need for fairness, while fear might point to a value you hold dear, like safety or stability. Every feeling, even the uncomfortable ones, is an invitation to understand yourself better. It is like tuning into an inner frequency you might have ignored before, one that speaks in quiet but profound truths.

By listening to these signals, you enter conversations with greater clarity and empathy. You understand not only what you feel but also why you feel it. This self-awareness becomes a tool, allowing you to communicate with intention and engage with others from a place of understanding rather than reactivity.

## The Gift of Emotional Data

Your emotions are not here to burden you; they are here to inform you. They are like a map, guiding you toward your needs, boundaries, and values. When you learn to listen – really listen – you discover a deeper connection to yourself and a clearer way to engage with the world. Emotions are not obstacles to overcome; they are a gift, offering insights into what truly matters to you.

The next time a feeling rises, whether it is anger, sadness, or fear, pause. Notice how it feels in your body. Breathe. Ask yourself, *What are you trying to show me?* In that moment, you may find not just a path forward but a way to connect more deeply – with yourself and with others.

> *"Healthy emotional expression is vital to recovery.*
> *It releases stored pain, reconnects us to our true feelings,*
> *and strengthens our ability to feel safe in relationships."*
>
> Peter Walker
> *Complex PTSD: From Surviving to Thriving*, 2013

## Dealing with Emotional Overwhelm in Real-Time

### When Emotions Take Over: Staying Grounded in the Storm

Even when you prepare for a conversation with the utmost care, there will be moments when emotions swell unexpectedly. A sudden flush of frustration, a pang of anxiety, or the tightening grip of anger can feel like an unstoppable wave. Your heart might race, your breath may quicken, and your thoughts might spiral. It is in these moments, when emotions rise like a storm, that finding a way to stay grounded becomes crucial.

Imagine you are in the middle of a conversation, and the tension begins to rise. Words are exchanged, but suddenly you feel overwhelmed. It is as if the room shrinks, the sound of your own heartbeat drowns everything out, and clarity slips through your fingers. The urge to lash out, shut down, or simply flee can feel overpowering. Yet, there is a way to steady yourself and regain control – tools that can help you calm the storm within and continue the conversation with intention and clarity.

## Emotions as Signals, Not Barriers

Remember, your emotions are not the enemy. They are signals, pointing you toward something deeper. Anxiety might be telling you that this conversation matters. Frustration could signal that a boundary feels crossed. Even anger, intense and fiery are often a call to protect something you value. Recognising these emotions as guides rather than obstacles allows you to respond rather than react.

## Simple Ways to Calm the Storm

### *Breathe Slowly and Deeply*

When the world feels like it is spinning too fast, your breath can anchor you. Close your eyes for a moment and inhale deeply through your nose for four counts. Hold it for seven counts. Then exhale slowly, releasing the tension, for eight counts. This simple rhythm – the 4-7-8 method – can bring an immediate sense of calm, slowing your racing heart and quieting your thoughts.

Picture this: you are mid-discussion, and anxiety grips you. As you breathe, you feel the ground beneath you solidify. The moment softens, and when you speak again, your voice carries clarity instead of panic.

### *Stay Present with Grounding Techniques*

When emotions threaten to overwhelm, focus on the physical world around you. Notice the sensation of your feet on the floor, the texture of the chair beneath you, or the coolness of the air on your skin. Let your senses remind you that you are here, in this moment, and safe.

Imagine touching a desk's smooth surface or curling your toes against the floor. These small actions can tether you to the present, allowing the emotional storm to pass without pulling you under.

### Pause to Regroup

Sometimes, the best way to stay in control is to take a step back. If the conversation feels too heated, it is okay to say, *"I need a moment to gather my thoughts."* Step away, breathe, and return when you feel steadier. This is not avoidance – it is self-care, giving both you and the other person a chance to reset.

Envision gently raising a hand to pause the conversation, like calling a time-out in a game. When you return, the air feels clearer, and you can approach the discussion with renewed focus.

### Recognising and Naming Emotions

A crucial step in managing overwhelm is naming what you feel. Saying to yourself, *"I am feeling anxious"* or *"I am noticing frustration rising"* can create just enough distance from the emotion to stop it from taking over. When you name your feelings, you take the reins, choosing how to respond rather than letting the emotion control you.

Picture a moment of rising tension in a conversation with someone close to you. Instead of snapping or withdrawing, you take a deep breath and silently say, *"I feel overwhelmed."* With this small act of recognition, you regain your footing.

### Inviting Calm with Compassion

In emotionally charged moments, it is tempting to judge yourself harshly for struggling. *"Why am I reacting this way?"* you might think. Instead, try offering yourself kindness. Remind yourself that difficult conversations are, well, difficult. It is okay to feel upset. It is okay to stumble. When you treat yourself with compassion, you invite calm into the chaos.

## The Power of Simple Tools

These small, simple actions – breathing, grounding, pausing, naming your emotions, and offering yourself compassion – are like life rafts in a stormy sea. They will not erase the intensity of the moment, but they will steady you enough to navigate through it. Each technique is a reminder that, even when emotions rise, you have the power to guide the conversation back to clarity and connection.

## Preparing for a Collaborative Conversation

### Building Trust and Connection

When conversations matter to you, the stakes feel high, and the words seem to be heavy with importance. Maybe your palms grow clammy as you prepare to speak, or your chest tightens as you search for the right words. Perhaps the other person leans in, their gaze steady, their expression soft? Or do they look away, jaw set, arms crossed, their presence distant?

Trust begins in these small, almost imperceptible moments – the flicker of an eye, the nod of a head, the softening of a tone. It is built not through grand gestures but through the quiet reassurance that someone is listening, truly listening, not just waiting for their turn to talk.

Conversations are not just about words; they are about what lies beneath them. The pauses, the sighs, the way a voice wavers or steadies – it all tells a story. When we approach these moments with curiosity rather than certainty, we open a door. *"I wonder why this feels so hard for them to say?"* or *"What might they be feeling right now?"* These questions invite connection.

Imagine sitting across from someone whose opinion opposes your own. You might feel the tension in your shoulders, the urge to interrupt bubbling in your throat. What happens if, instead, you take a breath? What happens if you let their words hang in the air for a moment, giving them the weight they deserve? In that pause, trust grows. It says, *"I am here. I am listening. Your voice matters."*

## Using Emotional Data for Collaborative Conversations

Emotions often speak before we do. A clench in the stomach, a tightening in the chest, a heat rising to your face – your body knows what it feels long before you find the words. These signals are not distractions; they are guides. They point to what you value, what you fear, what you need.

Picture this: you are in the middle of a conversation that feels tense. The other person's tone sharpens, their hands fidget. You notice your own pulse quicken, a flush of irritation blooming in your chest. In this moment, it is easy to react – to fire back with words that sting or shut down entirely. But what if you paused? What if you took a moment to ask yourself, *What am I really feeling here? And what might they be feeling too?*

Emotions are like the undercurrents of a river. If you ignore them, they will pull you off course. But if you tune in, they can guide you. When someone says, *"I feel like you never listen to me,"* their words might be tinged with frustration, but beneath them is a quieter truth: *"I feel unseen."* If you can respond to the need rather than the complaint, the conversation shifts. *"I want to understand how you feel,"* you might say, meeting their gaze, softening your tone. That small moment of connection can dissolve defensiveness, inviting something deeper into the space between you.

Trust grows when emotions are acknowledged. It grows when you look past the surface of someone's words and listen for the story their heart is trying to tell. You might not always agree, but understanding is not about agreement – it is about recognition. *"I see you. I hear you. You matter."* These unspoken truths transform the most challenging conversations into opportunities to build something stronger than resolution: connection.

> *"When we honestly ask ourselves which person in our lives means the most to us, we often find that it is those who, instead of giving advice, solutions, or cures, have chosen rather to share our pain and touch our wounds with a warm and tender hand."*
>
> Henri Nouwen (1932–1996)
> Dutch professor, writer and theologian

## Setting the Stage:
## Timing and Setting for the Conversation

### Choosing the Right Time and Place for a Difficult Conversation

The timing and setting of a conversation can make all the difference. While it might be tempting to dive in and address an issue immediately, especially when emotions are high, waiting for the right moment is often the better choice. A calm, focused environment – free from distractions – gives both people the best chance to engage meaningfully and feel heard. It is not just about convenience; it is about creating space for a thoughtful and respectful exchange.

At times, you may feel pressure to talk right away, especially if the other person is anxious or eager to resolve things. They might push for answers or demand to know what is going on, leaving you feeling unprepared or second-guessing yourself. This can lead to guilt about delaying or worry that waiting will make things worse. However, taking a step back is not avoidance – it is about ensuring the conversation happens when both of you are ready.

If you find yourself cornered into an untimely discussion, it is important to stay calm and set a clear boundary. Often, the other person's urgency comes from their own stress or anxiety about the situation. A firm but compassionate response, such as, *"I know this is important to you, and I want to talk about it too, but I think we will have a better discussion when we are both calm and ready,"* can create understanding without escalating tensions.

Choosing the right moment honours both the value of the conversation and your mutual need to feel heard. Waiting is not about avoiding the issue – it is about giving it the care and attention it deserves.

## Tips for Creating a Supportive Environment

1. **Choose a Quiet, Private Space**

   Select a setting that feels neutral and secure, where both of you can speak freely. Privacy is essential for creating a safe environment where you both feel comfortable opening up without interruption. Avoid busy or public places where distractions might hinder the flow of conversation.

2. **Schedule at a Time with Few Distractions**

   Resist the urge to discuss sensitive matters during stressful or busy moments, such as right after work or during a hectic day. Instead, find a time when both parties can be fully present. This means having the mental and emotional bandwidth to engage in a way that honours each other's perspectives.

3. **Prepare Resources if Needed**

   If the conversation involves specific topics, concerns, or solutions, consider gathering any relevant information in advance. Having materials or notes on hand can help guide the conversation, keep it focused, and allow you to refer to facts rather than relying solely on memory or emotions.

## Managing Your Own Anxiety and Self-Doubt

When planning a difficult conversation, it is normal to feel anxious or to second-guess your timing and approach. You might worry about making the other person wait, fearing that they could misinterpret your delay or grow impatient. These feelings are natural, but remember that delaying until you feel prepared is often beneficial. By taking the time to self-reflect and calm your nerves, you are more likely to enter the conversation with clarity and confidence.

Second-guessing is common, especially if the other person pressures you to reveal details prematurely. However, allowing yourself to process your emotions and intentions can ultimately lead to a more constructive conversation. If you feel guilty or anxious, remind yourself that setting the right time and place is an act of care. Giving both of you the chance to approach the conversation thoughtfully is far more valuable than rushing into it unprepared.

## Reflection Prompt

Think of a past conversation where timing played a role in how things unfolded. How might a different time or setting have influenced the outcome? Reflect on how planning and patience could have created a more supportive environment for both of you.

In choosing the right time and place, you create a foundation for genuine connection, where both parties feel respected and heard. By managing your own anxiety and setting boundaries around timing, you honour the conversation's importance and prepare for a dialogue that encourages understanding and mutual respect. This thoughtful approach lays the groundwork for growth and empathy, turning a potentially difficult exchange into an opportunity for positive change.

---

### Plotting the Course: Key Takeaways

**Preparation as a Lifeline:** Engaging in self-reflection and journalling ensures emotional readiness and clarity before initiating high-stakes conversations.

**Emotions as Data:** Viewing emotions as informative rather than overwhelming equips individuals with insight to navigate the conversation thoughtfully.

**Real-Time Strategies:** Techniques like box breathing and mindfulness offer stability in the heat of emotionally charged moments.

**Setting the Stage:** Timing, location, and purpose are key to creating safe and collaborative conversations.

## Eve's Childhood Thoughts

Reflecting on my childhood, I see now how much unfiltered adult emotion surrounded me. At the time, it felt normal – just the rhythm of life – but I was exposed to things no child should witness. Whether it was my parents, the boating environment, or simple chance, I saw deregulated emotions, arguments that spiralled into fights, and conflicts left unresolved. As a parent, I would never have let my own children see, hear, or feel those moments of chaos.

Growing up in that environment, it became second nature to adapt, to appease, to hold tension in silence, or to try and fix what was broken. Preparation, calmness, and managing emotions in the heat of conflict did not come naturally; they felt foreign. For those of us who grew up in a storm of unresolved emotions, stepping into difficult conversations as adults can awaken the inner child still shaking with fear.

There is a better way to face conflict. It is possible to hold your ground without losing your calm, to resolve misunderstandings without the weight of blame, and to approach tense moments with clarity and confidence.

The next chapters will guide you on this journey, helping you chart a new course – one that leads to peace, connection, and understanding.

> *"The task of a companion in distress is not to make it better but to make it less lonely to bear."*
>
> Dr Kathryn Mannix
> author and palliative care specialist

## Poem: Hope Danced

*Hope danced with a tip-tap smile*
*On the tongue of a girl who said to her friend,*
*Shall we play? Shall we dance?*
*Shall we listen to music?*
*Shall we remember the fun we had?*

*They sank their toes into the sand*
*Listening to the ripple of the sea on the shore.*
*The words danced, they tripped to the sea*
*And splashed in the surf,*
*Running forwards as the waves drew back.*

*And laughing, thrilled as the splash caught their heels,*
*Hope danced in the sunlight,*
*Ripple of the wave in her hair*
*As the light glanced off.*

*Hope danced in the heart*
*As it beat like a drum,*
*Sounding the rhythm of her life.*

*Hope sang as the gulls dipped*
*And soared over the tide.*
*Hope spoke as she lifted the shell to her ear*
*And listened.*

# NAVIGATING THE WAVES: FACING THE CONVERSATION

## Preparing for the Voyage

Now we get to the heart of it. Where preparation turns into action – where understanding and planning meet the reality of speaking up. Here we move into the practicalities of having difficult conversations, equipping you with tools to stay receptive, calm, and steady even when emotions flash and flare.

You will explore how to set clear boundaries, navigate resistance, and remain open to reciprocity while expressing your truth. Examples offer step-by-step guidance tailored to different relationship dynamics – partners, family, friends, and colleagues – helping you adapt your approach to fit the moment and the person you are speaking with.

When conversations feel stuck or overwhelming, this section will help you keep going. You will find strategies to handle defensiveness, adjust your tone, and rebuild trust, even when progress seems slow. These tools are designed to support you in staying present and resilient, knowing that clarity and understanding often emerge gradually through repetition and persistence.

To support you, explore the glossary for key terms and concepts, and take a look at the extra exercises and templates available on the website: www.evestanway.co.uk. You will find insights and practical strategies.

This is where your voice becomes the wind in your sails, steady and purposeful, guiding you through the waves and past the hidden shoals. Each step forward brings clarity and courage, showing that even the hardest conversations can chart a course to understanding and growth.

### Poem: A Voice Prepared

*In the stillness, the sea gathers its breath.*
*The sails rise, steady and deliberate,*
*Carried not by haste, but by intention.*
*Calm replaces the storm within.*

*This is no battle, but a journey*
*To reclaim understanding and clarity.*
*The waves speak, and we listen,*
*Finding truth in their quiet echo.*

# Part 7

# RAISING THE FLAGS: SETTING SIGNALS FOR CLEAR COMMUNICATION

*"Do unto others as you would have them do unto you."*

Matthew 7:12 (KJV)

### Eve's Cold Tea: Why Boundaries Matter

I stood in my kitchen, fingers wrapped around a mug of tea that had long since gone cold. The steam had vanished, the warmth drained away. The thousandth cup I had let sit untouched.

I detested cold tea.

Yet here I was again – standing, listening, nodding – absorbing someone else's frustration, their needs, their expectations. My own needs? Left on the back burner, just like my tea.

I remembered something Libby Purves once wrote in *How Not to Be a Perfect Mother* (1986):

*"There are two kinds of mothers – the ones who drink their tea hot, and the ones who always let it go cold. Taking care of yourself is not selfish; it is how you stay strong enough to care for others."*

Where were my boundaries?

You might think boundaries are about big moments – refusing an unfair demand, walking away from toxicity, drawing a line in the sand. But boundaries lived in the small moments too. In the cold cups of tea. In the time we gave away without hesitation. In the silent contracts we never meant to sign.

I had spent years teaching people that my time was available, my energy unlimited, my needs secondary. Without realising it, I had sent the message: *I will always listen, I will always help, I will always say yes.*

Something had to change.

## Why Boundaries Matter

Boundaries are not barriers. They are the lines that protect what matters most. They define where we end and another person begins, offering both clarity and protection.

Yet, setting them can feel like walking a tightrope – especially with those we love.

With strangers, boundaries feel simple. There is no emotional history, no deep connection to protect. It is easy to say *"No, thank you,"* or *"That doesn't work for me."* The stakes are low.

With loved ones, boundaries feel more like a storm-tossed sea. The weight of shared history, love, and loyalty tugs at our balance. We tell ourselves that discomfort is the price of love, that saying no is selfish, that keeping the peace matters more than protecting our energy.

But what is the real cost of always saying yes?

## The Silent Cost of Ignoring Boundaries

When boundaries are weak, resentment grows.

John Gottman, a leading researcher in relationships, found that small, unspoken frustrations often build into the very patterns that destroy connection – criticism, defensiveness, contempt, and stonewalling (Gottman and Silver, 1999). When we do not express our limits clearly, emotions do not disappear. They fester.

- The yes you gave when you meant no becomes silent frustration.
- The obligation you accepted with reluctance becomes exhaustion.
- The unspoken resentment seeps into the way you interact, pulling distance between you and the very people you wanted to stay close to.

Ignoring your own needs does not make relationships stronger. It makes them fragile, imbalanced, and unsustainable.

## The Myth of the 'Good' Person

Many of us grew up believing that being good means being agreeable.

- *Don't make a fuss.*
- *Be nice.*
- *Keep the peace.*

These messages seep into adulthood, shaping how we navigate relationships. Saying yes becomes a reflex, even when we are exhausted. Saying no feels loaded with guilt.

Brené Brown's research (2012) on vulnerability reminds us that true connection is built on authenticity, not compliance. She writes, *"Daring to set boundaries is about having the courage to love ourselves, even when we risk disappointing others."*

Boundaries are not rejection. They are self-respect.

## Boundaries Are Bridges, Not Walls

When expressed with clarity and respect, boundaries do not create distance. They create healthier, more secure relationships.

Imagine standing at the shore of a vast ocean. Boundaries are the shoreline – defining where the water meets the land. Without them, the waves would swallow everything, pulling the landscape into chaos.

- Boundaries do not push people away. They invite them to meet you in a place of mutual respect.

- Boundaries do not make you unkind. They allow you to show up fully, without resentment or depletion.

- Boundaries do not mean losing relationships. They mean redefining them in a way that serves both people.

The words you use matter. A simple *"please"* or *"thank you"* when setting a limit signals that you value both your needs and the other person's feelings. Small acts of care – like a steady tone, a moment of acknowledgment – can transform a difficult conversation into one of understanding.

## The First Step in Holding Your Ground

Boundaries are not always easy to set, and they are not always received well. People who benefited from your lack of boundaries may resist when you start to put them in place.

That does not mean you are wrong.

You have every right to protect your time, your energy, your well-being.

This chapter will show you how to:

- ✓ Identify the boundaries that matter most to you.
- ✓ Express them clearly and calmly, without guilt.

- ✓ Handle resistance with confidence and grace.
- ✓ Recognise when a relationship cannot meet your needs.

Your voice matters. Your limits matter. You deserve to take up space in your own life.

Are you ready to hold your ground?

For those looking to explore these concepts further, additional resources, examples, case studies, and journal reflection prompts are available in the accompanying workbook. Visit www.evestanway.co.uk/shoreline to deepen your understanding and begin building your own boundary-setting toolkit.

## Clarify:
## The First Step in Defining Boundaries

Clarity is the foundation upon which all boundaries stand. It is the compass that keeps you steady, the map that marks where you feel safe, and the anchor that holds you firm when the tides of expectation pull at your resolve. Without it, boundaries feel uncertain – like drawing lines in shifting sand, only to watch them disappear beneath the weight of obligation, guilt, or fear.

The process begins with self-reflection – a quiet pause to look inward and untangle your limits, values, and needs. It is the moment you realise that not everything that is asked of you must be given.

Life without defined boundaries can feel like wandering through a dense fog. Conversations grow tangled, weighed down by unspoken tensions. Relationships become draining rather than nourishing. Yet, when you take the time to identify what truly matters – what lights you up and what dims your spark – boundaries become more than lines; they become a framework for freedom, built with intention and aligned with your deepest sense of self.

Defining your boundaries is not about restriction; it is about recognition. It is like stepping from shadow into sunlight – suddenly, you can see with sharpness and certainty what is right for you and what is not. This clarity transforms the way you communicate, making your words stronger, your presence steadier, and your relationships more balanced.

**Key Insight:** Boundaries are not just rules; they are expressions of your inner truth. They guide others toward relationships built on mutual respect, understanding, and emotional integrity.

## The Power of Clarity: Anna and Sasha's Story

Anna arrived, her shoulders hunched with exhaustion, her face tight with frustration. She set down her bag with a sigh, her energy drained in a way that words could not fully explain.

For years, her friendship with Sasha had been a source of joy, but something had shifted. Their conversations had become one-sided – Sasha's worries and struggles filling every silence, leaving no space for Anna's thoughts, her laughter, or her needs.

Anna loved Sasha. She wanted to be there, to support her, to be the friend she had always been. Yet something in her felt depleted, unseen, unheard. Guilt gnawed at her – was she selfish for wanting more balance? Would speaking up make her seem unkind?

Then came the realisation that stopped her mid-thought: *Staying silent was not saving the friendship – it was suffocating it.*

Anna spent time reflecting on what she truly valued in friendships. She realised she needed reciprocity, moments of joy, light-hearted conversations alongside the deeper ones. She wanted a friendship that felt balanced, where both voices were heard.

She took a deep breath and chose clarity over comfort.

One evening, as Sasha launched into another heavy conversation, Anna gently interrupted. She spoke not from frustration, but from care – for Sasha, and for herself.

*"I really value our friendship, and I want to be here for you. But I feel like our conversations have been focused on the heavy things lately. I miss the laughter and the fun we used to share. Can we try to bring some of that back?"*

The words landed softly, like a pebble skipping across the surface of the water. Sasha blinked, absorbing the moment. Then, something shifted.

*"I didn't realise I had been doing that,"* she admitted. *"I guess I've just been so caught up in everything. I miss that too."*

The weight between them lifted. The friendship found new balance – not by ignoring difficulties, but by making space for both joy and vulnerability.

Anna's clarity did more than repair a friendship – it empowered her. She learned that voicing her needs did not push people away – it brought them closer.

## Your Own Map to Clarity

Think about your own relationships. Where are you feeling drained instead of nourished? Where have you been silencing yourself to keep the peace?

Clarifying your boundaries is not about changing others; it is about recognising what you need and having the courage to ask for it.

- What drains you? What situations leave you feeling exhausted or unheard?

- What sustains you? What conversations, actions, and connections feel balanced and fulfilling?

- What do you truly need? What kind of relationships make you feel seen, valued, and respected?

The answers to these questions form the blueprint of your boundaries. They are not walls to keep others out, but doorways to more honest, fulfilling relationships.

For the full story of how Anna transformed her friendship and practical tools to clarify your own boundaries, visit the workbook section on my website at www.evestanway.co.uk/shoreline.

*"Moving forward is a test of patience and acceptance, where clarity unfolds gradually, and the pieces of a changed dynamic settle into a new whole."*

Eve Stanway

## Communicate: Expressing Boundaries Openly and Respectfully

### The Importance of Communication in Boundary Setting

Communicating your boundaries can feel like stepping into unknown waters – daunting at first, yet deeply rewarding when navigated with care. Open and respectful communication is like casting a light into the room, allowing others to see your needs clearly. It highlights understanding and mutual respect, while also affirming your self-worth and showing that your feelings matter.

Using "I" statements is a powerful way to share your boundaries without casting blame or stirring defensiveness. These statements keep the focus on your experience, creating a bridge of connection rather than a wall of conflict. For example, imagine the difference between the sharpness of saying, *"You are always late,"* versus the openness of, *"I feel frustrated when our meetings start late because it makes it hard for me to manage my time."* The first can feel like a push; the second feels like an invitation to collaborate.

Other techniques can help make your message land with greater clarity and impact. When stating a boundary, be as specific as possible – vague words can leave the conversation feeling foggy and unresolved. Instead of saying, *"I wish you would listen more,"* try, *"I need you to give me your full attention when I am speaking."* The clarity cuts through ambiguity like a ray of sunlight through clouds.

Sharing the reason behind your boundary can deepen understanding. For instance, *"I value honesty in our conversations, so I need us to be open about any issues we are facing,"* brings your boundary to life by grounding it in your values. This helps others see the heart behind your words and invites them to engage with empathy.

When you communicate boundaries, it feels like finding your footing after walking on shifting sands – steady, clear, and intentional. These tools not only strengthen your voice, but also create pathways for deeper, more respectful connections.

## Non-Verbal Communication: The Silent Messages We Send

Words may be the framework of a conversation, but non-verbal communication is the heartbeat. Your body language, tone of voice, and facial expressions often speak louder than the words themselves, revealing truths that lie beneath the surface. In setting boundaries, these silent signals either reinforce your message or undermine it, making them essential tools in effective communication.

### *Body Language and Boundaries*

Imagine standing tall with an open posture, your hands relaxed, and your gaze steady. These cues convey confidence and respect, creating an atmosphere where your boundaries feel solid and secure. Now picture the opposite: arms folded, eyes shifting away, or a voice wavering with hesitation. These signals can cloud your message, making it seem uncertain even when your words are clear. Your physical presence is like a canvas; paint it with calmness and openness to match the clarity of your boundaries.

### Reading Non-Verbal Cues From Others

Communication flows both ways, and tuning into the other person's body language can feel like reading an unspoken language. A tense jaw, crossed arms, or a furrowed brow might signal discomfort or resistance. Recognising these signs is like spotting storm clouds on the horizon, giving you a chance to adjust – soften your tone, offer reassurance, or pause to let them process. These small shifts can turn a challenging conversation into a more collaborative exchange.

### Mirroring for Connection

Mirroring subtly connects people by quietly matching their energy and movements, creating a shared rhythm. If their posture is relaxed, mirroring their openness can strengthen the bond. Their stiffness and curtness can be countered by your calm demeanour, creating a reassuring presence. Think of mirroring as a dance, where each movement builds trust and understanding with no need for spoken words.

### Body Language

It is understandable to worry that setting boundaries – especially with loved ones – might create tension or damage the relationship. You may fear being seen as distant, demanding, or even selfish, particularly when discussing deeply personal issues. For many, these fears arise from a genuine desire to preserve harmony and avoid conflict, even at the cost of their own emotional needs. Changes in body language can be a silent way of expressing these fears.

However, it is crucial to challenge this perspective. Boundaries are not about distancing yourself from others; they are about creating a foundation for mutual respect and deeper understanding. Far from damaging relationships, when approached with care and empathy, boundaries strengthen them by building trust and clarity. They provide the space for both individuals to feel seen and valued.

## A Snapshot: Rachel's Story

Rachel often felt like a ghost in her own workplace – present, but somehow invisible. In meetings, her ideas hovered in the air unheard, bypassed as if she had never spoken. Tom, her colleague, made decisions that should have included her, moving projects forward without so much as a nod in her direction. Each overlooked suggestion, each unanswered email, chipped away at her confidence, leaving her frustrated and unseen.

Tom likely thought he was being efficient, but for Rachel, his actions carried the weight of dismissal.

### The Moment of Choice

Confronting him felt impossible. The thought of speaking up sent a sharp pulse of anxiety through her chest. She imagined his defensive glare, the way he might wave off her concerns, the way her own voice might betray her – cracking, uncertain, too easily drowned out.

Yet the alternative – remaining silent – had become unbearable. The tension had settled into her shoulders, a constant, nagging presence, tightening every time she swallowed back unspoken words.

Something had to change.

### Finding Her Voice

When she finally approached Tom, her movements were careful, deliberate. Her feet pressed firmly to the ground, a silent reminder to stay steady. She adjusted her posture, lifting her chin, though her stomach coiled with nerves.

Locking eyes with him, she took a slow breath, keeping her voice calm and measured.

*"Tom, I feel frustrated when decisions about our projects are made without my input. I value our work together, and I believe we can achieve even greater success through more open collaboration."*

She saw it the moment her words landed – the tightening of his jaw, the arms crossing over his chest like a shield. A flicker of resistance, quick and instinctive.

For a moment, doubt crept in. Had she misstepped? Would he shut her down before she even had the chance to explain?

Instead of retreating, she softened.

*"I know this may not have been intentional, and I appreciate how much you take on. I just want us to work in a way that brings out the best in both of us."*

### Shifting the Dynamic

Something shifted. The rigidity in his stance eased, his shoulders lowering by an inch, then another. His fingers uncurled, no longer gripping his arms so tightly. His expression, once guarded, became thoughtful.

*"I didn't realise how that was coming across,"* he admitted, his voice quieter now, carrying a note of genuine regret.

It was enough.

Rachel left the conversation feeling as though a weight had been lifted. The thick fog of silence had cleared, replaced by something lighter – possibility.

In the weeks that followed, she noticed small but meaningful changes. Tom looped her into decisions, checked in more often, acknowledged her contributions in meetings. Their working relationship, once lopsided, began to balance.

She had not demanded, accused, or retreated. She had simply made herself seen.

Body language is as powerful as words when navigating difficult conversations. Rachel's grounded presence – her steady posture, deliberate eye contact, and composed tone – allowed her to turn vulnerability into quiet strength. Her approach did not just demand respect; it invited collaboration.

True confidence is not about volume. It is about knowing you have the right to take up space.

*"We do not learn from experience... we learn from reflecting on experience."*

John Dewey (1859–1952)
American philosopher and educational reformer

## Correct:
## The Role of Correction in Boundary Setting

Boundaries are not static but living frameworks that adapt as relationships grow and evolve. Maintaining boundaries requires gentle reinforcement – like tending a garden, where consistent care keeps the structure intact and the connection thriving. This is where correction plays a vital role. It is the act of reminding others of the limits you have set, not with force but with clarity and calm.

Correction is not about drawing hard lines in the sand but about guiding others toward mutual respect. It is a way of communicating, *"This matters to me, and I hope it can matter to you too."* When approached with empathy, correction becomes a bridge, allowing both people to engage with honesty and care. A steady tone, deliberate pauses, and warm eye contact can turn a moment of potential conflict into an opportunity for deeper connection.

Clearly defined and consistently upheld boundaries demonstrate to others the importance of respecting your emotional space. This process is not about shutting others out but creating a structure that allows relationships to flourish. Correction, when done with care, can turn misunderstandings into moments of growth and trust.

## A Snapshot: Daniel's Story

Daniel felt as though he was being pulled in two directions. His brother Liam's frequent calls during work hours disrupted his focus, leaving him feeling stretched thin and frazzled. Each interruption was like a knock at the door of his concentration, pulling him away from his responsibilities. At first, Daniel tried to set a boundary, explained that he needed uninterrupted work time, but Liam dismissed it with, *"It's just a quick chat."*

Over time, the frustration built like a pressure cooker, leaving Daniel questioning himself. Was he being unreasonable? Was it selfish to ask for space? Yet, after some reflection, he realised that Liam's actions were not defiance but simply a habit. Liam valued their connection and had not understood his calls' impact.

With this perspective, Daniel decided to approach speaking to Liam in person about how he was feeling. He arranged to meet and after chatting for a bit, he said, *"Liam, I love that we're so close and can talk anytime, but my workdays have been feeling overwhelming. I'd like us to set a time to catch up when we can both really focus on the conversation."* His voice was calm, his tone warm, and his posture relaxed, signalling that this conversation was rooted in care, not criticism.

Liam's expression shifted – his shoulders softened, and his tone grew thoughtful. *"I didn't realise it was stressing you out that much,"* he said. Together, they agreed on a weekly evening catch-up in person or phone call, when both could be fully present.

The result was transformative. Daniel felt less overwhelmed during the day, and their conversations became richer and more intentional. What had felt like a source of conflict became a chance to deepen their bond. Correction, Daniel learned, is not about shutting someone out but about creating room for balance and connection.

Correction is like gently adjusting the sails on a ship – it keeps relationships on course without creating turbulence. Responding to boundary violations with calm empathy encourages others to respect both your needs and theirs.

# Overcoming Resistance When Setting Boundaries

Setting boundaries can feel like standing at the edge of a storm, with resistance swirling around you. Whether it comes from within or from others, resistance is a natural part of the process. Learning to navigate this turbulence with calm and clarity helps you remain steady, assertive, and true to your needs.

## Internal Resistance: The Struggle Within

Internal resistance often feels like a knot in your stomach or a whisper of doubt in your mind. It asked, *"Am I being unreasonable?"* or warns, *"What if they get upset?"* This resistance can come from old wounds or the fear of disrupting harmony. It pulls at you, making you second-guess your right to assert your needs.

To move past this resistance, start by recognising it for what it is – a sign that you are stepping outside your comfort zone. Take a deep breath and imagine your boundaries as roots grounding you to the earth. Reframe your thoughts: setting boundaries is not selfish; it is self-care. Each time you express your needs, you strengthen those roots, reminding yourself that your feelings matter.

**Key Idea:** Embrace the discomfort, let it pass like a wave, and focus on the goal – a healthier, more balanced version of yourself and your relationships.

## External Resistance: Pushback from Others

External resistance can feel like facing a gale-force headwind; defensiveness, anger, or guilt-tripping blowing back at you as you set your boundaries. While the unsettling nature of these reactions – a tense silence, perhaps, or a hasty shutdown – can be disconcerting, understand that they usually signal the other person's discomfort, not a problem with your needs.

To weather this resistance, steady yourself with a calm tone, an even gaze, and firm resolve. Picture yourself holding an umbrella in the storm – protecting your emotional space while allowing the winds of discomfort to pass. Restate your boundary clearly, like anchoring a signpost in shifting sands: *"I understand this is hard for you, but I need to stick to this decision for my well-being."*

Repetition is a powerful tool. When someone keeps pushing, calmly repeating your boundary becomes like steady waves reshaping the shoreline – gentle yet firm. By showing empathy without compromising your needs, you model respect for both yourself and the other person.

**Key Idea:** Empathy does not mean bending to the storm. It means holding your ground while recognising the other person's feelings.

## A Snapshot: Max's Story

For Max, setting a boundary with his colleague felt like being pulled into quicksand. Each time he said no to working late, his colleague pushed back with guilt-laden comments: *"You're not being a team player."* Max felt the familiar tug of guilt and hesitation, but he knew he could not continue stretching himself thin.

Instead of sinking into self-doubt, Max steadied himself. He imagined his boundary as a lighthouse guiding him through the haze of resistance. Calmly, he repeated his message: *"I need to prioritise my time outside of work to feel balanced. This isn't about not being a team player – it's about my well-being."*

At first, his colleague bristled, but Max's calm and consistent approach diffused the tension. Over time, his boundary became clear, and his colleague began to respect it. Max's resolve not only protected his emotional energy but also strengthened his confidence.

For Max, meeting resistance with clarity and persistence turned a moment of pushback into an opportunity to reinforce his needs.

Resistance, whether internal or external, is part of the boundary-setting journey. It may stir discomfort, but it is also an opportunity to grow stronger in your convictions. Like a tree bending in the wind, you can remain rooted while adapting to the challenges around you.

## Managing Boundaries in the Heat of the Moment

When emotions rise – yours or the other person's – it can feel like stepping into a storm. The air feels charged, your chest tightens, and your thoughts begin to race. These moments, when boundaries are challenged or emotions run high, are the true test of staying grounded. Recognising and managing emotional overwhelm in real-time is essential to holding onto your boundaries without losing connection.

### Recognising Emotional Overwhelm

Emotional overwhelm speaks through your body before your mind has time to catch up. Perhaps your palms grow clammy, your breath quickens, or a knot tightens in your stomach. These sensations are signals – a flare warning you to pause before the conversation slips into chaos.

In these moments, taking a pause is like pressing a reset button. Box breathing, for example, can help: inhale deeply for four counts, hold the breath for four, exhale slowly for four, and then pause for another four. As you breathe, notice the soothing rhythm like waves ebbing and flowing, gradually calming your nervous system.

If the storm feels too intense, give yourself permission to step back. You might said, *"I need a moment to gather my thoughts,"* or *"Let's take a short pause and come back to this."* This creates a pocket of stillness, allowing you to regain composure and approach the conversation with intention.

## Managing Your Internal Dialogue

When emotions rise, your inner critic often joins the fray, whispering doubts like, *"Am I being too rigid?"* or *"Maybe I should just let this go."* These thoughts can be like static noise, pulling you away from your purpose.

Reframe these doubts into affirmations that anchor you to your right to set boundaries. Remind yourself:

- *"I am allowed to protect my energy and well-being."*
- *"Standing firm may feel uncomfortable, but it is an act of self-respect."*

Imagine these affirmations as a steady hand on your shoulder, guiding you back to clarity amidst the chaos. By focusing on your purpose, you shift your attention away from the discomfort and toward the importance of the boundary.

## Recognising and Responding to the Other Person's Emotional State

When the other person reacts strongly, their emotions can feel like a tidal wave crashing into your resolve. Raised voices, tense expressions, or sharp words may tempt you to meet their intensity. Instead, tune in to their signals and respond with empathy while holding your ground.

If you notice defensiveness or agitation, acknowledge their feelings without abandoning your needs. You could say:

- *"I can see this is upsetting for you, and I want us to work through it together."*
- *"Let's revisit this conversation when we are both feeling calmer."*

This approach is like throwing a lifeline into turbulent waters. It shows care for their emotions while reinforcing the boundary you have set, creating space for understanding rather than conflict.

## Mirroring Calmness and Staying Grounded

In emotional conversations, your presence is like a lighthouse in a storm. If you remain steady, open, and calm, it can influence the tone of the entire interaction.

Keep your posture relaxed, your tone steady, and your gaze soft but direct. Picture your calmness radiating outward, like the stillness of a deep lake even as the surface ripples. By staying grounded, you may notice the other person beginning to mirror your composure, de-escalating the tension and creating room for connection.

**Key Insight:** Your calm presence acts as a stabiliser, keeping the conversation from being swept away by heightened emotions.

## Holding Your Ground: Emma's Story

Emma could feel the tension rising.

Her best friend's voice had sharpened, frustration spilling into every word. The conversation had taken an unexpected turn – what began as a simple boundary had become emotional, charged with defensiveness and hurt.

Emma's heart pounded. A familiar tightness crept into her throat. The instinct to retreat was strong. She had spent years avoiding conflict, choosing silence over discomfort, swallowing her needs to keep the peace.

This time, she made a different choice.

She placed a steady hand on her stomach, grounding herself as she inhaled slowly, feeling the air expand through her ribs. With each breath, she reminded herself:

*"This boundary is important for my well-being."*

Her voice was gentle but firm as she spoke.

*"I know this might be difficult to hear, and I don't want to upset you. But this is something I need for myself. Let's take a pause and come back to this when we are both ready."*

The weight of the moment settled between them. Silence stretched, but Emma did not rush to fill it.

The sharp edge in her friend's expression softened. The resistance in her posture eased. With time and space, the conversation shifted – not into argument, but into understanding.

Emma had not given in. She had not shut down. She had held her ground with grace, clarity, and calm persistence.

## Recognising Emotional Overwhelm in the Moment

Difficult conversations have a way of stirring the body before the mind even catches up.

A racing heart. Clenched fists. A tight chest. These are not just sensations; they are signals – your nervous system preparing for conflict, readying you for fight, flight, or freeze.

The key to maintaining boundaries is not avoiding emotion but learning to manage it. Recognising these physical cues allows you to pause before reacting, to shift from impulse to intention.

- If your breath becomes shallow, **slow it down**. Inhale deeply, feeling your stomach rise and fall.
- If tension builds in your hands or shoulders, **unclench them**. Drop your shoulders, open your palms.
- If your mind spirals into doubt, **anchor yourself in self-affirmation**:
    - *"It is okay to assert my needs."*
    - *"I do not need to over-explain or apologise for my boundaries."*
    - *"Staying calm helps me stay in control."*

Emma's ability to self-regulate in the moment helped her turn a difficult conversation into a constructive one. When emotions are high, calmness is not weakness – it is strength.

## The Power of Calm Repetition

Boundaries are not always respected the first time.

Sometimes, people push back. They test the limits. They ignore the request or pretend they did not hear. This is where many lose confidence, believing they must either escalate or give in.

There is a third way: calm repetition.

Imagine you have asked someone to turn down their music because it is too loud, and they ignore you. Rather than reacting with frustration or resentment, you take a breath and restate your boundary:

*"I really need the volume lowered so I can focus. Please turn it down."*

No over-explaining. No justification. Just a steady, repeated request that reinforces its importance.

Each time you restate your boundary with calm confidence, you strengthen it. Boundaries are like muscles – the more you use them, the stronger they become.

## Why Calmness Is a Superpower in Boundary-Setting

These moments – when you hold firm without anger, without apology, without giving up – are the moments where your boundaries take root.

- When you stay steady, others take your boundaries seriously.
- When you remain calm, you keep control of the conversation.
- When you persist, relationships adapt to the new dynamic of mutual respect.

Every time you choose clarity over conflict, calm over chaos, and persistence over panic, you create space for trust, understanding, and stronger relationships.

Are you ready to hold your ground?

# Practical Applications of The Magic Three in Boundary Setting

## The Magic Three: Clarify, Communicate, and Correct

We have explored how to take a moment to recognise your feelings and needs (*Clarify*), how to express yourself clearly and kindly using "I" statements (*Communicate*), and how to gently reinforce your boundaries while staying calm and giving the other person time to process (*Correct*).

It is not always easy, especially when emotions are involved, but each step is a chance to create better understanding and connection. You are already taking those steps by reflecting and practising these skills.

1. **With Partners**

   Romantic relationships are like tending a garden – boundaries help things grow stronger and healthier. But it is common to feel stuck in patterns that seem impossible to change. When you have tried to address an issue many times, it can feel easier to put up with it than to risk another uncomfortable conversation. If that sounds familiar, you are not alone. These struggles are common, and while change can feel hard, it is possible.

   **Example:** Maybe your partner often asks what needs to be bought from the shops instead of checking for themselves. It can be tempting to keep answering because it feels quicker, even if it builds frustration over time. Instead, you might say, *"I know it is easier to ask, but I need you to take the lead on this. It is okay if it is not perfect – what matters is that you try."*

   If the pattern continues, calmly remind them: *"I really need you to handle this yourself. It helps me feel like we are sharing the load."* You may need to repeat this gently and consistently, but even small efforts can lead to change.

These situations are so common, and it is normal to feel disheartened when things do not change right away. But every time you clarify, communicate, and calmly reinforce your boundary, you are creating room for improvement. Boundaries are not about being perfect; they are about honouring your needs. Change takes time, but your steady efforts can make a real difference. You can do this.

2. **With Family Members**

   Family relationships often carry the weight of history, where patterns run deep like grooves in stone. Setting boundaries here requires patience and a steady hand.

   **Example:** If you are working from home and constantly interrupted, you might say, *"I love how close we are, but I need focused time during the day. Can we set an evening time to connect?"*

   When family members forget, gently reminded them: *"I really look forward to our evening chats – it helps me unwind. Let's save our conversations for then."* This approach keeps the connection alive while protecting your personal space.

3. **With Friends**

   Friendships thrive when there is mutual respect, but they can feel unbalanced if one person leans too heavily for support.

   **Example:** If a friend relies on you daily for emotional support, you could said, *"I care deeply about you, but I've been feeling drained. I need some time to recharge so I can be a better friend. Let's plan to talk every few days instead of every day."*

   If the friend resists, you might correct by saying, *"I value our friendship, and I want to be fully present when we talk. Giving myself time to recharge helps me do that."* This sets a compassionate but firm boundary that honours both your needs.

4. **With Colleagues**

   Boundaries at work help create clarity and reduce frustration or burnout.

   **Example:** If a colleague often delays tasks you need completed, it can disrupt your workflow. You might say, *"This task is important for meeting our deadlines. I need it finished by [specific time or date] to keep things on track."*

   If delays continue, you could calmly follow up with, *"I noticed the task wasn't done on time. Can we agree on a clear timeline to stay on track and avoid last-minute stress?"*

By staying calm and clear, you show the task's importance, set boundaries, and encourage teamwork.

## Rachel's Journey: The Magic Three in Action

Rachel first encountered the power of the **Magic Three** in her professional life. Her colleague, Tom, often made key decisions on joint projects without consulting her, leaving her feeling overlooked and frustrated. Instead of stewing in resentment, she applied the **Magic Three**:

- **Clarify:** She recognised her core need was to feel included in decision-making.

- **Communicate:** She addressed the issue directly, using calm and respectful language.

- **Correct:** When Tom slipped back into old habits, she gently reminded him of their agreement.

The change was not immediate, though over time, their dynamic shifted. Tom began involving her in discussions, acknowledging her input, and treating her as a valued collaborator. Encouraged by this success, Rachel wondered whether the same approach could help her marriage with Lewis.

## Bringing the Magic Three Home

Rachel and Lewis shared a deep love, though certain conversations – about household responsibilities, finances, and long-term plans – often ended in frustration. When Rachel raised concerns, Lewis would brush them aside, offering a half-hearted nod or a distracted *"We'll sort it later."* The lack of engagement left her feeling unheard and disconnected.

At first, Rachel withdrew, convincing herself that pushing the issue would only create tension. Silence did not solve anything. Avoiding the conversation widened the gap between them. If she could use the **Magic Three** to strengthen her professional relationships, she wondered if the same approach could create change in her marriage.

### Step One: Clarify – Understanding What She Needed

Rachel realised her frustration was not just about chores or money – it was about feeling ignored. She needed to know that her thoughts and concerns mattered. Before approaching Lewis, she took time to reflect:

- *What do I really need from this conversation?*

- *What would help me feel valued and understood?*

This reflection led her to a key realisation: conversations with Lewis had to involve active listening and mutual respect. That was the foundation she needed to set.

### Step Two: Communicate – Opening the Dialogue

One evening, when they were both relaxed, Rachel took a deep breath and began. She avoided accusations or ultimatums, focusing instead on her feelings.

*"I love the life we have built together,"* she said, her voice warm but steady. *"When I bring up concerns about the house or our finances, and I feel like I am met with silence or a shrug, I feel alone in this. I need us to work through these things together."*

Lewis stiffened slightly, caught off guard. For a moment, Rachel worried she had said too much. Holding the pause, she allowed him space to absorb her words rather than rushing to fill the silence.

He exhaled and nodded. *"I didn't know you felt like that,"* he admitted, his voice quieter than before.

For the first time, Rachel saw something shift. Lewis was not shutting down – he was listening.

### Step Three: Correct – Reinforcing the Boundary

The conversation had opened a door, though old habits take time to change. Over the next few weeks, Rachel noticed that Lewis still interrupted or brushed past her concerns at times. Instead of letting resentment build, she addressed it in the moment.

One evening, when he cut her off mid-sentence, she placed a hand on the table, grounding herself before speaking.

*"Remember how we talked about taking turns to share our thoughts?"* she said gently. *"I want to make sure that we both feel heard and that our opinions carry equal weight."*

Her tone was calm, not confrontational. Instead of feeling criticised, Lewis nodded in understanding.

At first, these adjustments felt awkward, like learning a new dance with unfamiliar steps. Over time, something remarkable happened. Lewis began pausing before responding, listening with intention rather than waiting for his turn to speak. Rachel, in turn, felt more confident sharing her thoughts, no longer bracing for dismissal.

The invisible wall that had been growing between them softened, replaced by a renewed sense of partnership.

## The Power of Boundaries in Connection

Boundaries, when approached with care and patience, are not walls that separate but bridges that strengthen relationships.

Setting boundaries can feel like walking a tightrope – balancing personal needs with the desire for connection. True connection is not about erasing yourself for the comfort of others. It is about standing firm in what matters to you while inviting them to meet you there.

By using the **Magic Three**, Rachel was able to say, *"This is important to me,"* without pushing Lewis away. Creating space for honest conversations allowed him to step closer.

> *"What we call the beginning is often the end.*
> *And to make an end is to make a beginning.*
> *The end is where we start from."*
>
> T.S. Eliot (1888–1965)
> American-British poet, essayist, critic and publisher

---

### Raising the Flags: Key Takeaways

**Boundaries as Anchors:** Establishing clear boundaries creates mutual respect and ensures emotional safety in relationships.

**The Magic of Clarity:** Articulating boundaries and needs with precision minimises misunderstandings and defensiveness.

**Navigating Resistance:** Learning to remain calm and open in the face of pushback strengthens trust and keeps dialogue constructive.

**Repairing Missteps:** Revisiting and correcting miscommunication reinforces respect and deepens connection.

## Eve's Light Bulb

It was not one dramatic event, but a slow accumulation of moments that brought me to breaking point. My children pushed every limit, their defiance relentless, and each tantrum felt like a small challenge I was losing. The frustration simmered under the surface, growing with every "no" to my "no."

Yet, it was not just their behaviour – it was what it stirred inside me. Old wounds from my childhood reopened, dragging me back to a time when I had no voice, no choice, and no one to help me understand my feelings. In those moments with my children, I was not just parenting – I was battling my past.

Then came the moment of clarity. My tone was too sharp, my words too harsh, and I saw it reflected in their startled eyes. The guilt hit me like a physical blow. I realised I was becoming the very parent I had promised myself I would never be. That gut-wrenching realisation forced me to confront my pain, not just for my children's sake, but for my own.

I knew I had a choice: I could repeat the patterns I had learned, or I could change them. The path forward was hard. I walked for hours, sorting through my emotions, and wrote endlessly to untangle the mess inside me. Slowly, I started to take small steps.

When frustration surged, I paused. I told myself, *"You are the adult now. You can choose differently."* Some days I succeeded; others, I failed. But gradually, I learned that boundaries are not about control – they are about trust. They are not a way to impose power but a way to create safety and connection, something I had never known as a child.

This process has been messy and imperfect, but it has changed everything. I know how overwhelming it feels to stand in conflict, unsure of what to say or do. I know the fear of feeling like you are failing. But every pause, every effort to respond calmly rather than react, is a step toward transformation.

If this story feels familiar, know that you are not alone. You are not failing – you are learning. Forgive yourself for the moments you wish you could undo. Each time you pause and try again, you are rewriting your story. With every small shift, the storm within will begin to calm. You will find your way – not in spite of your past, but because you dared to rise above it.

## Reflection Prompt

Was there a moment when you realised something needed to change? Perhaps it was during a moment of self-awareness, when you recognised the cost of staying silent or accommodating others at your expense. What would it mean to honour that need now with kindness and self-compassion?

## Poem: Lesson at Sea

*In my own sea, I sailed towards dreams,*
*Glimpsing shores just beyond my reach.*
*Hope steadied me as I traced my course,*
*Love lingering in the whispering waves.*

*Yet the sea murmured its quiet warning,*
*Still, I pressed on, bracing for the storm.*
*When it struck, I stood unshaken –*
*For I am strong, and hope is my lighthouse.*

## Part 8

# KEEPING THE HELM STEADY: STRATEGIES FOR EMOTIONAL STABILITY

> *"You do not have to control your thoughts.*
> *You just have to stop letting them control you."*
>
> Dan Millman, (1946– )
> American author and personal development lecturer

### Eve's Aha

Looking back, my childhood wasn't shaped by a desire to get things right – it was driven by a crippling fear of getting things wrong. Perfectionism became my sea wall, built high and unyielding to protect me from the storm of judgement I feared would crash over me if I made a mistake. My imposter syndrome rose to crash against that wall, flooding my mind, whispering that I didn't belong, I wasn't enough, and that it was only a matter of time before I'd be found out.

The problem with a sea wall, however, is that it doesn't stop the tide. It simply forces the water to find another way, wearing away at the foundation. That fear – of being seen, of getting things wrong – eroded my confidence. By the time I faced any difficult conversation, I had already battered myself with waves of self-criticism, chipping away at my sense of self. Harsh self-talk left me anxious, small, and brittle – fragile against the vast, relentless forces of doubt.

The turning point came when I realised that the sea wall wasn't helping me; it was holding me back. It kept me distant from my emotions, from others, and from myself. Then I learned the power of wholeheartedness. Brené Brown describes wholehearted living as engaging with life from a place of worthiness, embracing imperfection, and showing up with courage and vulnerability (Brown, 2010). Wholeheartedness allowed me to lower that sea wall. I began to see failure as feedback – gentle waves lapping at my feet, showing me where to step next.

Every mistake, every stumble, became part of a natural ebb and flow, teaching me how to grow stronger, steadier. Wholeheartedness gave me permission to stop striving for perfection and instead show up as myself – messy, real, and human. It was not about letting the tide overwhelm me but about learning to stand firmly in it, feeling its rhythm and trusting my ability to stay grounded.

For many of us – especially those who grew up self-reliant – this idea feels foreign. When your childhood teaches you that vulnerability is dangerous, the instinct is to build walls, rush to solutions, and avoid sitting with discomfort. Yet, those quick fixes often fail to address the emotions beneath the surface. Psychologist Daniel Goleman (1995) calls this an "emotional hijack," when the brain's fight-or-flight response overrides reflection. That instinct to protect can stop us from processing what truly needs attention, leaving conversations unresolved and connections frayed.

Wholeheartedness offers a different way forward. It asks us to trust that vulnerability. Remaining calm and open creates the space to process emotions rather than suppress them. Imagine the moment before a conversation begins: instead of bracing against the tide, you take a deep breath. You feel the ground beneath you, the cool air brushing your skin, and the steady rhythm of your heartbeat. In that pause, you allow yourself to settle, to let the water touch you without fear.

When I embraced this approach, I entered conversations not as someone trying to shield myself from mistakes but as someone willing to be present, feel the discomfort, and engage fully. My clients often describe a similar transformation. When they stop hiding behind perfectionism and allow themselves to show up with self-compassion, they find that they are stronger than they imagined. They stop fighting the tide and start moving with it.

You don't need to have all the answers to navigate high-stakes conversations. You need to show up – honestly, wholeheartedly, and willing to learn, with the courage to keep moving forward – one breath, one pause, one conversation at a time.

## Building Emotional Resilience

*"Calmness is the compass that guides us through even the stormiest interactions; it allows us to respond with thought rather than react with fear."*

Eve Stanway

### Emotional Resilience: Strengthening Yourself for Difficult Conversations

You feel it before you even speak – your heart pounding, your palms damp, a tightness curling in your stomach. A storm of emotions rises beneath the surface, tempting you to retreat, to put the conversation off for another day. Yet emotional resilience is not about running or suppressing. It is about standing firm, feeling every wave of discomfort without being carried away by it. It is the steady ground beneath your feet when anxiety and uncertainty try to pull you under.

Imagine yourself at the edge of a conversation you know will be challenging. Perhaps with a partner, a friend, or a colleague. Your pulse quickens. A voice in your mind urges, *Forget it, another time.* Emotional resilience is what allows you to take a breath, acknowledge what you feel, and move forward anyway – with composure, insight, and quiet strength. Like any skill, it takes practice. The more you engage with your emotions instead of avoiding them, the steadier you become. Here are some simple but powerful techniques to help you build this strength:

1. **Practice Self-Compassion**

    Difficult conversations stir up anxiety, doubt, even fear – but these emotions only prove that you care. Instead of silencing them, meet them with kindness. If you are nervous about raising a sensitive issue, remind yourself, *This is hard for anyone. It is okay to feel this way.* Let go of the idea that you must be perfect. Self-compassion replaces the harsh inner critic with a steady, reassuring voice, allowing you to approach the conversation without self-judgement.

2. **Label Your Emotions**

    When emotions surge, take a moment to name them. Are you feeling frustration? Sadness? Disappointment? Labelling emotions reduces their intensity, giving you distance from their grip. If anger bubbles up before confronting a loved one, pause and acknowledge it: *This is anger.* It sounds simple, but by naming emotions, you step outside their pull and regain control.

3. **Use Visualisation to Prepare**

    Picture yourself moving through the conversation with calm and clarity. Visualisation is a powerful grounding tool – mentally rehearsing how you want to show up. If you anticipate defensiveness, imagine yourself breathing deeply, staying steady, and listening without reacting impulsively. See yourself responding with grace, even when tension rises. Visualising success reminds you that you are capable, even when the moment feels hard.

4. **Reflect Through Journalling**

    Look back at past conversations where you stayed composed, even when it was difficult. Did you manage to stay calm during a heated family discussion? Did you hold your ground in a stressful work meeting? Write about what helped – was it deep breathing? Staying focused on your intentions? Reflecting on your resilience reminds you that you have navigated challenges before and can do so again.

These techniques are stepping stones – small but powerful. By creating space to feel, understand, and process your emotions, you build the foundation for conversations that are not ruled by fear but guided by clarity and strength.

If you are ready to go deeper, explore the workbook on my website (www.evestanway.co.uk/shoreline) to find guided exercises to help you put these ideas into practice and make them part of your everyday life. Emotional resilience is not something you "get right"; it is something you nurture. Start small, trust yourself, and know that with every step, you are building the strength to face whatever lies ahead.

## Managing Real-Time Anxiety: Finding Calm in the Moment

When conversations turn tense, your body often speaks before you do. Your chest tightens, your stomach churns, heat rises in your face. Maybe your hands grow clammy, or your voice trembles, just slightly. These physical reactions are not mistakes. They are signals – your body sensing discomfort, bracing for what is to come.

Fighting these sensations only feeds the tension. Your body is not betraying you; it is trying to protect you. By working *with* these reactions, rather than against them, you can find steadiness, clarity, and the presence needed to navigate the moment. Simple techniques can help you stay grounded, easing the panic that makes words hard to find.

## Techniques for Easing Anxiety in Real Time

1. **Box Breathing**

   Imagine the steady rhythm of waves washing against the shore. Box breathing follows that same rhythm, slowing your heart rate and calming your thoughts. Breathe in deeply for a count of four, hold for four, exhale slowly for four, and pause for four before starting again. With each cycle, your body registers safety, your mind steadies, and tension softens its grip.

2. **Grounding Yourself in the Present**

   When anxiety rises, your mind often races – flashing between fears of what might happen and echoes of what has already been. Grounding techniques pull you back to *now*. Try the 5-4-3-2-1 method: Name five things you can see, four you can touch, three you can hear, two you can smell, and one you can taste. Engaging your senses in this way interrupts anxious spirals, anchoring you in the present moment.

3. **Progressive Muscle Relaxation**

   Tension lives in the body – locked in your jaw, hunched in your shoulders, curled in your fists. Progressive muscle relaxation helps release it. Start with your toes – tighten them for a few seconds, then let go. Move upward, tensing and releasing your legs, stomach, shoulders, and face. As your muscles soften, so does your mind, making space for ease and clarity.

## Experimenting with Calm

Before your next difficult conversation, try one of these techniques. Does focusing on your breath help you find steadiness? Do grounding exercises keep you present? Practicing these tools ahead of time makes them easier to reach for when you need them most.

Tension is not failure. It is an invitation – to pause, reconnect, and step forward with calm and clarity.

## Setting Realistic Expectations for High-Stakes Conversations

Difficult conversations take real courage. It is not easy to step into the unknown, to risk feeling exposed, or to say something that might be met with silence, resistance, or even anger. The weight of past experiences can make it even harder. If you grew up in a home where important conversations were avoided, shut down, or turned into conflict, it is natural to carry that history with you. The mind races ahead, filling in worst-case scenarios before a single word has been spoken. I used to do the same – playing out every possible disaster in my head, leaving no space for the possibility that things might go well.

The truth is, meaningful conversations take time. Rarely does one moment fix everything – and that is okay. A small step forward, a single point of clarity, or the sense that you have been heard is already a triumph. With practice, patience, and the **Magic Three: Clarify, Communicate, and Correct**, these conversations will start to feel more natural. Not every disagreement needs to be a battle. Sometimes, the air will crackle with challenge, and the other person may see the exchange as a contest to be won. But true dialogue is not about victory – it is about steady, respectful engagement, even when views differ.

Throughout my life, I have found strength in poetry – lines that anchor me when conversations feel too charged or uncertain. One that has stayed with me since childhood is Kipling's *If*. I first read it at ten years old, in *Rewards and Fairies*, and even then, something in it resonated. As I have grown, its words have taken on new meaning, reminding me to stay calm, hold my ground, and trust in myself – especially when stepping into the hardest conversations.

> *"If you can keep your head when all about you*
> *Are losing theirs and blaming it on you..."*

Rudyard Kipling (1865–1936)<br>English journalist, author and poet

## Making Room for Progress

One of the biggest traps in high-stakes conversations is expecting too much too soon. You might step in hoping for a breakthrough – total understanding, a perfect resolution. When that does not happen, the weight of disappointment can feel crushing. Instead, focus on movement, not miracles. Conversations, like relationships, unfold over time. The first exchange might only nudge the door open, just enough for light to seep through. Trust builds in these small moments, in the pauses between words, in the willingness to keep returning.

The person in front of you brings their own history, fears, and limitations. They may not meet you where you want them to – at least not yet. And that is okay. You might feel your heart race, your stomach tighten, your hands clench. This discomfort is not failure; it is proof that you are present, that this matters. Instead of fighting these feelings, let them anchor you. They are signs that you are engaged, that you are choosing courage over retreat.

Showing up with openness and respect is the real success, regardless of the outcome. These conversations are not about quick fixes; they are about something deeper – building trust, strengthening resilience, and shaping relationships that can withstand discomfort and grow stronger because of it.

# Remaining Calm Under Accusations or Misinterpretations

*"Calmness is the cradle of power."*

Josiah Gilbert Holland (1819–1881)
American novelist, biographer and mentor

## Navigating Misunderstandings: Staying Calm Amid Accusations

When someone misinterprets your words or throws an accusation your way, it can feel like the ground beneath you has suddenly shifted. Your chest tightens, your pulse quickens, and a sharp urge to defend yourself rises. These reactions are instinctive – your body sensing a threat and bracing for battle. But accusations, especially false ones, have a way of pulling you into quicksand. The more you struggle to explain, the deeper you may sink, even when you have done nothing wrong.

Accusations are powerful because they destabilise. They make you question yourself, planting seeds of doubt even when you know your truth. Maybe someone denies what you have said, twists your intentions, or challenges your memory. These moments can feel like hitting an invisible wall, leaving you lost in a fog of frustration and disbelief. But steadiness is possible. Imagine planting your feet on solid ground – pausing, breathing, resisting the pull to react on instinct. That pause is where clarity lives.

## Understanding and Responding

Accusations often shift the conversation away from the real issue, trapping you in a defensive spiral. But staying calm does not mean surrendering. It means choosing your response, rather than letting someone else's words dictate your emotions. Instead of pushing back immediately, create space. A simple, steady response like, *"I can see this has upset you,"* acknowledges their feelings without conceding to their viewpoint. If a misunderstanding is at play, try *"I think we may see this differently – can I share how I see it?"* These responses keep the conversation open rather than closing it down in conflict.

When someone flatly denies your experience, it can feel like your reality is being rewritten in front of you. In those moments, return to your truth. Ask yourself, *What do I know for certain? What matters most right now?* Staying anchored in your values helps you hold your ground, even in the face of resistance.

## The Emotional Toll and Finding Clarity

Accusations – whether deliberate or unintentional – can drain you. They strike at your identity, making you second-guess your intentions, your values, even your own memory. These moments test patience and emotional resilience, but they are not about proving your worth. They are about staying true to yourself.

Navigating these conversations is not about perfection; it is about intention. By pausing, breathing, and choosing how you respond, you reclaim your steadiness. You do not need to solve everything in one conversation. Progress happens in small steps. Simply knowing you are showing up with clarity and self-respect is already a victory.

## Taking Breaks During High-Stakes Conversations

### Finding Clarity in the Pause

In the heat of a difficult conversation, emotions rise fast – your pulse quickens, your breath shortens, and your mind races ahead, grasping for the right words. In these moments, taking a pause is not weakness; it is power. A pause is not about shutting down or stepping away. It is a deliberate moment to breathe, to steady yourself, to let the dust settle before you step forward again with purpose.

Imagine pressing pause in the middle of a storm. The winds do not disappear, but for a moment, they stop pulling you under. This small act of stillness stops tension from escalating, giving you the space to re-centre. As you pause, notice what is happening inside you. Is frustration tightening your chest? Is defensiveness curling in your stomach? Instead of pushing these feelings away, acknowledge them. They are not barriers – they are signals, guiding you back to your intention. Ask yourself, *Why did I enter this conversation? What truly matters here?*

## The Power of Returning with Intention

When you step back in, do so with purpose. A pause is only as powerful as what follows. Maybe you choose to listen more closely, speak with greater calm, or gently steer the conversation back to where it belongs. Picture it as resetting the compass, finding true north again after the conversation started drifting off course.

A pause is an act of care – for yourself and for the conversation. It shows that you are committed to responding with thought, not just reacting on impulse. Every time you choose to pause, you strengthen your ability to navigate tension with steadiness, building a foundation for deeper, more meaningful conversations. You do not need to be perfect. You just need to create space – for clarity, for connection, for a way forward.

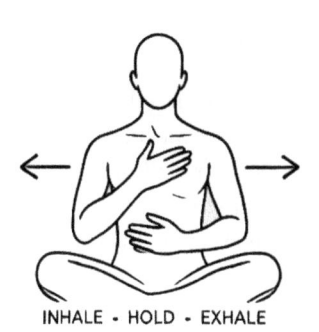

INHALE · HOLD · EXHALE

# Listening Is Your Superpower!

Every conversation holds the potential for connection, but truly engaging requires more than just hearing words – it requires listening with your whole presence. Active listening is not passive; it is a gift. It is stepping into someone else's world and saying, *"I am here with you, and I care."* When we listen deeply, we create something powerful – an act of kindness that can soften tension, shift perspectives, and turn even the hardest conversations into moments of understanding.

Douglas Stone, a leading voice on communication, reminds us, *"You cannot move the conversation in a more positive direction until the other person feels heard and understood"* (*Difficult Conversations*, 1999). His words carry a simple but profound truth: real change begins when people feel seen. Imagine a colleague sharing their frustrations about a project – voice tight, hands fidgeting. Instead of rushing to fix the problem, you pause and reflect, *"It sounds like this is weighing heavily on you, and you are feeling alone in the effort."* In that instant, their shoulders drop, their expression softens, and the energy between you shifts. They feel safe – not because you solved anything, but because they felt heard.

## The Power of Presence

Active listening is not about having the perfect response. It is about small, intentional acts of care: meeting someone's eyes, leaning in slightly, nodding in recognition, allowing space for silence. These subtle gestures say, without words, *"I value what you are sharing."* Yet, in the heat of a tough conversation, the urge to jump in – to correct, to defend, to fix – can be overwhelming. As Daniel Goleman explains, *"The emotional brain responds to an event more quickly than the thinking brain"* (*Emotional Intelligence*, 1995). That split-second pause – a deep breath, a moment of stillness – gives your rational mind the chance to catch up, allowing you to respond with intention rather than to react impulsively.

Open-ended questions can invite even deeper understanding. Asking, *"What has this been like for you?"* or *"How can I better understand what you are feeling?"* signals that you are not here to debate or dismiss – you are here to listen. And when you listen fully, you send an unspoken message: *"I see you. I hear you. What you feel matters."*

## Listening as an Act of Care

Active listening does not ask for perfection – only presence. It takes courage to slow down, to resist the pull of defensiveness, to make space for another person's truth. Yet in doing so, you remind both them and yourself that connection is possible, even in the most difficult conversations.

So next time a conversation feels heavy or fraught, take a breath and remember: listening is your superpower. One pause, one word, one act of care at a time, you have the ability to transform the moment.

*"In staying clear, we protect our boundaries, communicate our needs, and offer our best selves to the conversation."*

Eve Stanway

### Keeping the Helm Steady: Key Takeaways

**Staying Grounded:** Simple practices like box breathing and grounding techniques help manage anxiety during intense discussions.

**Resilience Through Practice:** Building emotional resilience involves learning from each difficult conversation rather than fearing failure.

**Listening Actively:** Developing deep listening skills helps de-escalate tension and nurtures understanding within in contentious moments.

**Realistic Expectations:** Acknowledging that progress takes time prevents frustration and encourages patience with oneself and others.

## Eve's Moment of Grounding

There have been moments in my life when navigating a difficult conversation felt like stepping into Alice's Wonderland. Everything I thought I understood seemed to shift, and the rules I relied on vanished, leaving me confused and unsure of my footing. In those moments, I learned that staying grounded takes more than willpower – it requires focus, faith, and the support of people who truly see you.

Alice's words, *"I can't go back to yesterday because I was a different person then"* (Carroll, 1865) have stayed with me. They remind me that every experience shapes us, especially the hard ones. We are not meant to go back – we are meant to step forward, carrying the clarity and strength we find along the way.

I used to seek validation from the most critical voices in my life, as though winning their approval would prove my worth. Over time, I realised how damaging this was. True allies encourage growth without making you feel small. As Shahida Arabi says, *"When you notice someone does something toxic the first time, don't wait for the second time before you address it or cut them off"* (Arabi, 2020). Learning to trust my instincts and set boundaries has been transformative. It is not easy to walk away from toxic dynamics, but it is far harder to stay in them and lose yourself.

I have found that surrounding myself with those who challenge me constructively and hold space for my growth has made all the difference. True friends will challenge you, yes, but they will also support you, never aiming to diminish you or blame you for how their words land. They encourage you to see the best in yourself while holding you accountable to your values.

These moments of chaos, where nothing seems to make sense, are an invitation to come back to what you know is true: your worth, your integrity, and your resilience. Staying grounded amidst the storm is not easy, but each time you do, you strengthen your ability to navigate the unexpected with clarity and self-respect.

> "Wholehearted living is about engaging in our lives from a place of worthiness. It means cultivating the courage, compassion, and connection to wake up in the morning and think, No matter what gets done and how much is left undone, I am enough."
>
> Brené Brown<br>The Gifts of Imperfection, 2010

## Poem: Mindshift

*I stand now on the solid ground of my own words,*
*held within the rhythm of a beating heart,*
*warmed by the belief that stirs within.*

*Every book written was an act of audacity, a blind leap,*
*a coin tossed into the well of original flow,*
*water shaped and reshaped by time and tide.*

*Thoughts do not rise in a vacuum;*
*No, the DNA of a phrase tumbles through centuries,*
*before landing on my page, carried by the weft and silk of life,*
*pouring through abundant minds.*

*I hold the coat-tails of those who, like me,*
*schemed and scratched,*
*tapped and sighed, gazed anywhere but the task,*
*noticing dust or distraction,*
*stealing another moment to steep the brew of imagination.*

*Am I late to the page, or has my dance been deliberate,*
*a slow waltz of faltering steps, gliding with the music of my soul?*

*It is time to ease off the brakes, to release the strain,*
*to loosen my teeth, swallow, and breathe.*

*Let the words fall gently, resting beneath the glow of the lamp.*
*Trust is not a chore, but a quiet surrender, a softening into the flow.*
*Freedom lies here, in the lineage of all those who have touched the page,*
*scribblers like me, finding their way through every word.*

# Part 9

# STRATEGIES FOR DIFFERENT RELATIONSHIPS: ADJUSTING THE SAILS – NAVIGATING VARYING WINDS OF RELATIONSHIPS

*"We should say that just as fear of conversations can make it hard for us to speak, it can also lead us to consciously or unconsciously shut down other people's attempts to share their feelings."*

Eve Stanway

Navigating relationships can feel like steering a ship through unpredictable seas. Each communication – whether with a partner, parent, friend, or colleague – requires a unique approach. Some relationships demand patience, others assertiveness, and some require us to simply let go. Understanding these dynamics is crucial for building healthier connections. This chapter explores tailored strategies for different types of relationships, offering methods and wisdom to guide you during even the most challenging interactions.

# Introduction:
# Appreciating the Value of Tailored Communication

Not every relationship asks the same of us. The way you talk with a close friend may feel too personal with a colleague, and the gentle words you might share with a child might not suit a partner. Situations such as co-parenting require a still different approach. Each relationship has its own dynamic, its own set of expectations, and sometimes, its own unspoken challenges. Knowing this can be daunting at times; how do we communicate what we need to say while honouring each unique connection in our lives?

Throughout this chapter, we will explore approaches tailored specifically to four core relationships: partners, family members, colleagues, and children. Each of these situations requires its own way of receiving and processing words, and you will be invited to try relationship mapping. This exercise offers a chance to pause, reflect, and see more clearly where different strategies may fit best for the unique people in your life.

As you learn to adjust your approach, remember it is not about masking your true self. Instead, it is about finding a gentle balance – honouring both your authenticity and the needs of each relationship. By embracing this flexibility, you are setting the stage for healthier, more open connections across all areas of life. Together, we will explore how meeting each person where they are can create the space for understanding, respect, and trust, even in the most difficult conversations.

*"To know oneself is, above all, to know what one lacks.*
*It is to measure oneself against truth, not the other way around."*

Flannery O'Connor (1925–1964)
American novelist and essayist

## Relationship Mapping:
## A Framework for Awareness and Connection

Relationship mapping is a practical and reflective tool that helps uncover the deeper emotions, needs, and patterns driving any relationship dynamic. It encourages stepping back from surface-level conflicts to explore the underlying factors shaping interactions. Dr Nicole LePera, in *How to Do the Work*, emphasises, *"Awareness is the foundation of all change. Until we can identify the unconscious patterns driving our relationships, we are destined to repeat them"* (LePera, 2021). Relationship mapping provides the space for this vital awareness, enabling individuals to approach conflicts with empathy and insight.

Begin by asking:

- *What do I feel in this relationship?*

- *What do I need from this relationship?*

- *What might the other person feel and need?*

Consider Erin and Jason, whose frequent arguments about household chores leave both feeling alienated. Erin uses relationship mapping to step beyond the frustration and examines the patterns at play. She discovers her anger stems from feeling unsupported, while Jason's avoidance of chores reflects the emotional exhaustion he feels from work stress. With this new perspective, Erin shares her insights with Jason. Together, they create a compromise – Jason agrees to take on smaller weekly tasks, and Erin acknowledges his need for downtime on weekends.

In a professional scenario, Maria feels overwhelmed by her manager's habit of assigning last-minute tasks, which often leaves her scrambling to meet deadlines. By reflecting on their dynamic, Maria identifies a clash between her need for structure and her manager's reactive decision-making style. Armed with this understanding, Maria approaches her manager with a solution-focused mindset, suggesting ways to balance urgent tasks with her preference for planning and stability.

LePera highlights that such self-reflective practices can dismantle unhealthy cycles and create space for deeper understanding. Relationship mapping transforms conflicts into opportunities for connection, enabling collaborative solutions that honour the needs of all parties involved.

> *"Marriage is not simply a romantic union between two people; it's also a political and economic contract of the highest order."*
>
> Elizabeth Gilbert (1969– )
> American journalist and author

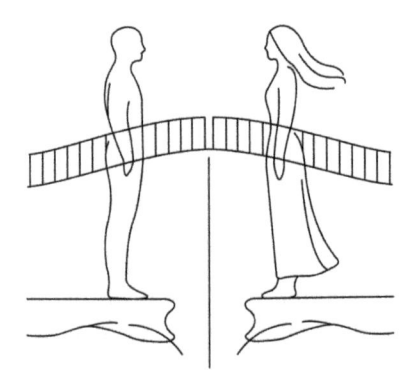

## Communicating with Partners

> *"A great relationship is about two things: First, appreciating the similarities, and second, respecting the differences."*
>
> Anon

### A Forgetful Partner

The MOT deadline is looming. Each passing day tightens the knot in your stomach. You have asked your partner to book it, but nothing has been done. Frustration rises – sharp, insistent, demanding an outlet. You want to snap, *Why do you always forget?* Yet, deep down, you know this approach will only spark defensiveness and distance. So, instead of reacting, you pause, take a breath, and begin to map out the situation.

Relationship mapping allows you to reflect on the dynamics at play. You ask yourself, *What am I really feeling?* It becomes clear – it is not just about the MOT; it is about feeling unsupported, as though the weight is entirely on your shoulders. Then, *What do I need?* You realise you need shared responsibility, a sense that you are in this together. Finally, you consider your partner: *What might they be feeling?* Perhaps they are distracted or overwhelmed, avoiding the task not from laziness, but because they are juggling their own pressures.

Armed with this awareness, you turn to the **Magic Three: Clarify, Communicate, and Correct**.

**Clarify.** Start by naming the issue without assigning blame. *"The MOT date is coming up, and I'm starting to feel stressed because it hasn't been booked yet."* This opens the conversation calmly, inviting collaboration.

**Communicate.** Share how this makes you feel, focusing on your emotions rather than pointing fingers. *"When it is left undone, I feel like I am carrying the responsibility alone, and it makes me anxious and unheard."* This shifts the tone from accusation to vulnerability, making space for understanding.

**Correct.** Propose a practical solution that brings you together. *"Could we set a reminder or agree on a time to handle it? That way, we can sort it out as a team, and I won't feel so pressured."*

Using relationship mapping and the **Magic Three** to understand emotions and needs turns arguments into opportunities for connection. This approach solves the problem and improves our partnership through collaboration and mutual respect.

## Communicating with Family Members

*"Wherever I look, I see signs of the commandment to honour one's parents and nowhere of a commandment that calls for the respect of a child."*

Alice Miller
*For Your Own Good*, 1997

Family relationships often carry the weight of history. Old roles and unspoken expectations linger – perhaps you are the peacekeeper, the fixer, or the one constantly under scrutiny. Clear communication can be challenging under these circumstances, especially when tensions escalate.

Imagine a scenario: during a family gathering, a relative asks a deeply personal question that makes your stomach tighten. You feel exposed and irritated, and the familiar urge to snap rises within you: *Why do you always have to pry into my life?* But instead of reacting, you pause. This is a moment for relationship mapping and the **Magic Three: Clarify, Communicate, and Correct**.

Relationship mapping allows you to reflect on what is happening beneath the surface. You ask yourself, *What am I feeling?* The answer is clear: discomfort and a sense of being judged. *What do I need?* To feel safe and respected in this conversation. Finally, you consider the other person: *What might they be feeling or needing?* Perhaps they are genuinely curious or trying to connect, but their approach feels intrusive.

With this understanding, you turn to the **Magic Three** to guide your response.

### Clarify

Focus on your need rather than criticising their behaviour. Instead of saying, *"You're always too nosy,"* reframe it as, *"I'd prefer to keep some parts of my life private."* This sets a boundary without escalating tension.

## Communicate

Share how the situation makes you feel. For example, *"When I'm asked about personal things unexpectedly, I feel caught off guard and uncomfortable. I want our conversations to feel relaxed and positive."* By expressing your emotions, you invite understanding and reduce defensiveness.

## Correct

Offer a solution that respects both sides. You might say, *"Can we focus on topics we both enjoy discussing? That way, our time together stays enjoyable for us both."* This keeps the conversation collaborative and forward-looking.

Clarity and empathy emerge when you use relationship mapping alongside the **Magic Three** to address the situation. Family dynamics may not shift overnight, but these small moments of awareness and intention can create lasting change.

# Communicating with Colleagues

*"Respect is how you treat everyone, not just those you want to impress."*

Sir Richard Branson (1950– )<br>British entrepreneur and author

Workplace challenges can feel particularly loaded because so much of our sense of self is tied to what we do. Our jobs are not just about earning a living; they shape our identity, provide structure to our days, and often fulfil a need for purpose and achievement. When tensions arise with colleagues, it can feel personal, even when it is not intended that way, because these interactions touch on our feelings of competence, respect, and belonging.

When faced with these challenges, it is natural to feel a mix of emotions – frustration, hesitation, or even self-doubt. These moments matter because the workplace is not just where we work; it is where we spend a significant part of our lives. Navigating these situations thoughtfully can help you protect your sense of self, strengthen your professional relationships, and create an environment where both you and your team can thrive.

## Strategies for Communicating with Colleagues Using the Magic Three

Imagine you are working on a project, and deadlines are slipping. The pressure is building, and you feel tempted to say, *"You're holding everyone up."* But you pause, knowing that approach might only lead to defensiveness. Instead, you decide to use the **Magic Three: Clarify, Communicate, and Correct** to keep the conversation productive.

You start by **clarifying** the situation. During a quiet moment, you say, *"I've noticed we've missed a few deadlines recently. Can we chat about what might be causing the delays?"* This keeps the focus on the project rather than pointing fingers, making it easier for your colleague to open up.

Next, you **communicate** the impact. You explain, *"When deadlines are missed, it can add extra stress to everyone and slow down the project. I really want to help us all stay on track."* By keeping your tone collaborative, you highlight the shared challenges without making it personal.

Finally, you **correct** by suggesting a way forward. *"What do you think about creating a system together – like weekly check-ins or reminders – to help us meet our deadlines? I think it could make things easier for all of us."* Offering a solution makes it clear you are looking for a partnership, not placing blame.

With this approach, you turn a potentially difficult conversation into an opportunity for teamwork, showing understanding while working toward a shared goal.

## Communicating with Children

*"Children are like wet cement. Whatever falls on them makes an impression"*

Haim G.Ginott (1922–1973)
Israeli psychologist, psychotherapist and author

### Teaching Through Patience, Repetition, and Connection

Children are always learning from you. Every word, tone, and gesture leaves an impression. Jess Lair's work reminds us that children are not blank slates to mould, but individuals with their own unique identities to uncover and nurture. His philosophy challenges us to guide, rather than control, allowing children the freedom to grow while feeling safe, respected, and understood.

Lair emphasised that parenting is not about perfection – it is about showing up consistently with patience and empathy. Children need time and repetition to absorb lessons, and they thrive when we approach them with respect for their individuality.

This means stepping back, listening, and creating space for them to explore who they are while guiding them through their emotions and choices. Tools like relationship mapping and the **Magic Three** can help you approach these moments with clarity and connection, building the kind of trust that allows children to flourish.

### Using the Magic Three: A Simple Narrative

Imagine your child has left their toys scattered across the floor again. Frustration rises – you've asked them so many times before. But instead of snapping, you pause. *What is happening here? What are they feeling? What do I need to communicate?*

This is a moment to reflect, a moment to teach.

You begin with **clarify**. Calmly, you say, *"The toys are all over the floor, and it's hard to walk around. Let's talk about tidying them up."* This keeps the focus on the situation, not the child, making it easier for them to engage without feeling defensive.

Next, you **communicate** the impact. *"When the toys are left out, it can make the room feel messy, and someone might trip. I feel happy and calm when things are tidy – it helps us all enjoy the space more."* Sharing how their actions affect others helps your child understand the connection between their choices and the feelings of those around them, building empathy.

Finally, you **correct** by offering a solution. For younger children, you might say, *"Let's make tidying up a game – how fast do you think we can do it?"* For older children, involve them in the solution: *"How do you think we can keep the toys organised so it's easier to find them next time?"* This approach not only resolves the immediate problem but also empowers your child to take responsibility in a way that feels collaborative and respectful.

## Patience and Repetition: The Keys to Growth

Lair believed that children learn best through patience and consistent modelling. The lessons you teach – whether about tidying, sharing, or navigating emotions – often require repeating, sometimes many times, before they stick. This process is not a sign of failure but of growth in action. Children thrive when they are guided with kindness and given the space to practise, stumble, and try again.

Over time, small, intentional moments help your child unfold into their full potential, secure in the knowledge that they are understood and supported.

## Navigating Co-Parenting Challenges

*"Co-parenting is not about being friends with your co-parent.
It is about being good partners in your shared responsibility for your children."*

Karen Bonnell
*The Co-Parenting Handbook*, 2017

## Co-Parenting: A Journey of Compassion and Strength

Co-parenting after separation is not just a logistical challenge; it is an emotional one. Balancing feelings of frustration, grief, or resentment while trying to work with your co-parent can feel overwhelming. The differences that might have been manageable during the relationship often become sources of conflict post-separation. Despite the challenges, there is an opportunity to shift the focus from conflict to collaboration, creating a partnership that prioritises your child's well-being.

In *The Co-Parenting Handbook* (2017), Karen Bonnell reminds us, *"Co-parenting is not about being friends[,] [but] about being good partners in your shared responsibility for your children."* Resentments and unresolved emotions can make this responsibility feel heavy. When these feelings arise, it helps to pause and ask, *What does my child need from me right now?* Focusing on your child's needs instead of your own issues will bring you clarity, strength, and peace of mind, enabling you to choose actions that put their happiness and safety first.

Doing the right thing, even when it feels difficult, is one of the most impactful choices you can make as a parent. It is not about ignoring your feelings but about ensuring your child is not burdened by them. Choosing respect during tense moments, staying calm, and focusing on shared goals models resilience and emotional intelligence, lessons your child will carry forward. Let's take a look at this in action.

## Sophie and Nathan:
## Finding Strength in Doing the Right Thing

Sophie and Nathan came to me for help because their co-parenting struggles were affecting both their relationship and their nine-year-old daughter, Lily. Sophie's structured, organised approach often clashed with Nathan's relaxed parenting style, leading to constant arguments about Lily's school routine. When Lily became anxious and started avoiding school, it hit them – her distress was a response to the tension between them, not something she could control. They saw the problem was not Lily but how their conflict was impacting her.

During one session, Sophie admitted feeling burdened: *"I am always the one carrying the weight of parenting."* Nathan countered with his own frustration: *"Nothing I do ever feels good enough."* Their focus on their differences was driving them apart and creating stress for Lily.

To help them reframe their thinking, I introduced the concept of relationship mapping, encouraging them to reflect on their feelings and needs, as well as Lily's. Sophie realised her frustration stemmed from feeling unsupported, while Nathan recognised his defensiveness was rooted in a desire to feel included. By shifting the focus from their grievances to their shared goal – Lily's happiness – they began to see a path forward.

Using the **Magic Three: Clarify, Communicate, and Correct**, they approached their next conversation differently. Sophie started by clarifying: *"We both want what's best for Lily, and I know how much you care about her."* This simple acknowledgment set a collaborative tone. She then communicated her concern: *"When Lily's schedule changes, I've noticed she gets anxious. I want her to feel more secure."* Finally, she proposed a solution: *"Would you be open to using a shared calendar? It might help us stay on the same page and give Lily a consistent routine."*

Nathan, feeling heard rather than criticised, agreed to try the calendar. Over time, the tension between them eased, and Lily thrived in the new-found stability. Sophie later reflected, *"Once I stopped focusing on what Nathan was doing wrong and started focusing on how we could work together, everything changed – for Lily and for us."*

## Compassionate Strategies for Co-Parenting

1. **Focus on Shared Goals:** Keep your child's needs at the centre of every decision. Ask yourself, *What does my child need from me right now, and how can we achieve this together?*

2. **Recognise When Resentment Is Taking Over:** Resentment is natural, but when it dominates, it can cloud judgement. Pausing to reflect on whether your actions are driven by frustration or by what is best for your child can create a meaningful shift.

3. **Do the Right Thing, Even When It Feels Hard:** Staying calm during arguments, showing respect, or prioritising your child's needs over your own frustrations creates stability and models healthy behaviours for your child.

4. **Set Boundaries for Communication:** Establish specific times to discuss co-parenting matters to avoid spontaneous conflicts and emotional exhaustion.

5. **Create Predictable Routines:** Consistency is key to helping children feel secure. Work with your co-parent to establish stable schedules and shared rules that benefit your child.

6. **Use Neutral Tools:** Co-parenting apps or shared calendars can help focus on logistics rather than emotions, reducing unnecessary conflict.

7. **Model Respect:** Demonstrating kindness and respect, even in challenging moments, teaches your child how to navigate conflict with grace and resilience.

8. **Seek Support When Needed:** Involving a mediator or coach can help address persistent issues and provide tools to adapt as your child grows and family dynamics evolve.

## Reflection Point

Co-parenting is a dynamic process that requires patience, compassion, and a willingness to adapt. Reflect on your co-parenting dynamic: What challenges feel most difficult right now?

Are there small changes, such as using a shared tool or reframing a conversation, that could ease tension? How might focusing on what is right for your child, rather than what feels right in the moment, shift the tone of your next discussion?

As Dr Isolina Ricci writes, *"Your child's needs are the focus of co-parenting, not your personal grievances."* Building a co-parenting partnership that benefits your child and reduces stress for everyone is possible with preparation, calmness and a lot of patience whilst you work things out.

> *"Understanding that we're all good inside is what allows you to distinguish a person (your child) from a behaviour (rudeness, hitting, saying, 'I hate you'). Differentiating who someone is from what they do is key to creating interventions that preserve your relationship while also leading to impactful change."*
>
> Dr Becky Kennedy
> American psychologist and author of *Good Inside*, 2022

---

### Strategies for Different Relationships: Key Takeaways

**Tailored Communication:** Speak to each person differently; adapting your communication style builds stronger relationships.

**Relationship Mapping:** Visualising relational dynamics offers clarity and helps identify patterns that need addressing.

**Navigating Co-Parenting:** Successful co-parenting relies on collaboration and mutual respect to provide children with stability and encourage effective communication.

**Tools for Growth:** Using reflection prompts and situational examples empowers individuals to navigate relationship complexities with confidence.

## Eve's Courage

I noticed the change slowly. At first, my friend and I talked regularly – calls filled with laughter and conversations that made life's challenges feel lighter. Then, the calls became less frequent. When I thought about reaching out, I hesitated. Maybe she was busy. Maybe she did not want to talk. A small voice in my head whispered, *What if I have done something wrong?* Instead of calling, I stayed silent, letting the doubt grow.

Weeks turned into months, and the silence between us felt heavier. Each short text or delayed reply added to my unease. I told myself it was just life – people drift apart. But deep down, I could not shake the feeling that something was wrong. I wanted to reach out, but fear held me back. *What if she is upset with me? What if asking makes it worse?*

One evening, I could not take it anymore. With my heart pounding, I picked up the phone and called her. Before I could even speak, she said, *"I am so sorry I haven't called in so long."* Her words were warm but carried a hint of hesitation.

I took a deep breath and said, *"I've missed you, and when I felt like I should have picked up the phone to you, I didn't. I wish I had."*

There was a pause before she replied, *"I've missed you too. I thought you were too busy for me."*

Her answer caught me off guard. She was not upset, and I had not done anything wrong. She had been going through her own struggles and thought I had drifted away. My silence had mirrored hers, and without realising it, we had both let the distance grow.

That conversation was not perfect. I stumbled over my words, and the awkward pauses. It was an honest conversation, and the relief I felt by the end of the call was deep, like a physical lightness. It was more than just catching up; we rekindled our friendship and reaffirmed our importance to each other.

In my role as a coaching therapist, I help people learn to manage tough conversations. Yet, the old urge to retreat when I feel uncertain remains. It is still tempting to tell myself a story that isn't true – that I have done something wrong, or that silence means rejection. What has changed is that I am learning to pause and challenge that instinct. I'm finding the courage to stay curious, ask questions, and uncover the truth instead of assuming the worst.

So now, when silence builds a wall, I tear it down. I use the same tools I share with clients – clarity, empathy, and curiosity – in my own relationships. I take my courage in my hands and speak up when I feel adrift and listening closely when others need to share. I now see conversations I used to dodge as chances to mend and improve relationships.

Words, no matter how messy, have the power to bring us closer. The hardest conversations often lead to the deepest healing. Speaking openly opens the door to trust, connection, and deeper understanding. And in the end, is that not what we all seek? To feel seen, valued, and never alone?

I wonder, what story are you telling yourself about the silence? Are you brave enough to ask instead of assuming? Taking that first step might feel scary, but even imperfect words can build a bridge. Trust in the power of connection – it is always worth the risk.

*"The roots of silence go deep, tied to fear, doubt, and conditioning, but it is only in breaking these roots that we allow space for truth to grow."*

Eve Stanway

# REACHING THE SHORE: GROWTH THROUGH DIALOGUE

Dear reader, you have come a long way on your journey. Take a moment to acknowledge the courage it has taken to face challenging conversations, to recognise your own needs, and to invite honesty into your relationships. These conversations ask us to be vulnerable and open to change, and you have shown a readiness to embrace that. Here, we explore what happens next, after the words have been spoken and the conversation has left its mark.

Relationships are not fixed; they are constantly evolving connections. Each genuine conversation brings the possibility of growth, deepening, or sometimes parting ways. The American author and poet Flavia Weedn captures it so beautifully in her book, *Forever*: *"Some people come into our lives and quickly go. Others stay, leaving footprints on our hearts."* Human connection is both beautiful and impermanent, and by accepting this, we allow ourselves to navigate transitions with resilience and compassion.

I will guide you through the changes that may follow a difficult conversation. Whether a relationship deepens, transforms, or shifts away, this section encourages you to approach each connection as part of your path forward. By aligning your communication with your true values, you will see your relationships reflect more of who you are and what you stand for. These final chapters support you as you step into your authentic self, allowing for the growth of both yourself and those around you.

## Poem: The Journey Continues

*Each word carries us forward,*
*a quiet step toward a world*
*we dare to shape.*

*With hearts willing to open,*
*we uncover the path —*
*not always easy, but real.*

*In truth, we find our compass,*
*in love, our steady ground.*

As you move forward, remember that each conversation, each choice to speak and listen with care, brings you closer to the connections you truly seek. You have the strength, clarity, and wisdom to shape a world of empathy, understanding, and genuine connection. Thank you for walking this path with such courage and openness.

# Part 10

# NAVIGATING RELATIONSHIP CHANGES: CHANGING TIDES – ADAPTING TO NEW HORIZONS

> *"Change is the undercurrent of every relationship; resisting it keeps us anchored to the past, while embracing it allows for growth."*
>
> Eve Stanway

## Introduction: Embracing Change in Relationships

Relationships are dynamic, constantly evolving alongside our own growth. Just as we change, so do our connections with others. Honest conversations can bring clarity to previously unspoken aspects of our relationships, creating opportunities for deeper understanding. At times, these moments of insight draw us closer, building trust and strengthening our bond. Other times, they may reveal a need for space or even signal that moving forward separately is the healthiest path for both people.

Navigating these changes can feel challenging. It requires openness to our own capacity for growth and a willingness to accept where others are on their journeys. This chapter explores how relationships can transform after difficult conversations, how to recognise when a relationship is deepening or nearing its natural end, and how to practise healthy detachment. As you read, you will find guidance on how to approach these transitions with clarity and compassion, allowing each relationship to find its true place in your life.

My childhood was a constant whirlwind of moves, new faces, and ever-changing surroundings. I became a quiet observer, carefully watching and learning the expectations of those around me so I could fit in seamlessly. While this honed my skills as a therapist, always attuned to others, it also left me with a deep drive to succeed at blending in. In a world where every relationship, friendship, and connection was inevitably cut short by yet another move, the idea of intentionally ending a relationship – no matter how difficult, uncomfortable, or unsuitable – simply never crossed my mind.

## Recognising the Impact of Honest Conversations

When we bring our true needs, boundaries, and vulnerabilities to the surface, we create space for growth. This level of openness invites mutual respect and deeper connection but can also disrupt familiar patterns, sometimes leading to discomfort or resistance. Honest conversations challenge us to re-evaluate relationships, uncovering what each person brings to the connection and whether both are willing to support each other's growth.

For example, if you share with a partner that you need more emotional support, the outcome can vary. This openness might inspire your partner to become more attentive, deepening your bond. Alternatively, it could reveal that they are unable or unwilling to meet this need, which can clarify the relationship's limitations. Recognising these shifts helps us approach conversations with an open mind, understanding that honest dialogue may reveal alignment – or areas of incompatibility.

*"A word after a word after a word is power."*

Margaret Atwood (1939– )
Canadian author, poet and literary critic

## Practising Healthy Detachment

Healthy detachment means allowing relationships the freedom to evolve without clinging to a specific outcome. It is not about suppressing emotions or distancing yourself but about seeing each relationship as it truly is, without trying to control it. Detachment helps us recognise a relationship's strengths and limitations, giving it space to either grow or fade naturally.

For instance, if you share with a friend that you feel unsupported when they frequently cancel plans, healthy detachment means releasing any expectation of how they should respond. Perhaps they make an effort to respect your time, or maybe they are unable to make that change. Practising detachment allows you to accept either outcome with respect for both yourself and the other person.

## Recognising When Relationships Need to End

Not every relationship is meant to last a lifetime. Some connections naturally reach a point where they no longer serve both people's growth. Learning to let go of relationships that no longer align with our values or needs is an important act of self-care. Accepting an ending does not diminish the positive experiences or memories shared but instead acknowledges that some relationships are seasonal, resonating with us at certain points in our lives.

Signs that a relationship may be reaching its end often include persistent misalignment of values, resistance to growth, or an absence of mutual respect. For example, if a friendship has started to feel more draining than uplifting, or if your values are increasingly at odds, it may be time to consider whether the relationship still supports your well-being.

## Navigating the Decision to End a Relationship

Deciding to end a relationship requires courage and compassion. This choice is not about assigning blame but about recognising that the relationship, as it currently stands, may no longer support both individuals' journeys. Reflecting on what the relationship has brought into your life, even as it concludes, can encourage a sense of closure and facilitate healing.

You might want to write a heartfelt letter of closure, expressing gratitude for the relationship and reflecting on what it taught you. This can be a personal and healing way to honour the connection and help you move forward with compassion and understanding for yourself. There is no need for it to be seen by anyone else. Writing it allows you to mark the end of this chapter with understanding and respect.

> *"In times of relational change, resilience means seeing the shifts not as losses, but as invitations to redefine and strengthen our connections."*
>
> Eve Stanway

## When Relationships Strengthen Through Change

Nurturing a relationship as it evolves can be a beautiful process, like watching the seasons change; however, a relationship undergoing change can feel like walking into an unfamiliar landscape – uncertain but full of possibility. It starts with noticing the small, tender moments – those quiet gestures that show effort and care. These moments can feel like the first warmth of sunlight breaking through the clouds, a reminder that even during hard times, progress is being made.

When you share your thoughts and listen deeply to the other person, you create space for trust to grow. In *Difficult Conversations*, Stone, Patton and Heen (2010) say, *"The single most powerful way to build trust is to actively listen to the other person's perspective."* Speaking openly and aligning your words with your actions shows that you value not only the relationship but also the person standing beside you.

There will be times when your perspectives feel worlds apart, like standing on opposite sides of a river. Differences do not have to divide you. As Gottman reminds us in *The Seven Principles for Making Marriage Work* (1999), *"Acknowledging and respecting each other's deepest, most important hopes and dreams is key to a lasting relationship."* When you embrace these differences with curiosity and care, they become a strength, offering new ways to grow together. Unity is not about always agreeing – it is about finding peace and respect in your diversity.

Shared goals can act as a guiding light during times of change. Whether it is spending more time together or finding better ways to communicate, these goals give your relationship purpose and direction. They remind you that you are on this journey together, side by side.

Change is not always easy – it can feel like navigating a winding path through a dense forest. But with patience and kindness, you can walk that path together. Compassion softens the hard edges of growth, reminding you both that it is okay to take small steps and rest when needed.

When relationships embrace change, they grow stronger and more authentic. By staying open, trusting each other's intentions, and focusing on the care that binds you, you create something lasting – a bond that weathers storms and celebrates the sunshine that follows.

## Embracing Evolving Relationships

Open, growing relationships build connections where both people can be their genuine selves. These relationships, like sturdy anchors, offer resilience, providing a bedrock of support when times get tough. Celebrating successes, communicating openly, pursuing shared objectives, and showing empathy create enduring relationships that evolve meaningfully over time.

> *"The only way to make sense out of change is to plunge into it, move with it, and join the dance."*
>
> Alan Watts (1915–1973)
> English writer and Zen philosopher

## Embracing Acceptance and Moving Forward

As you navigate changes in relationships, consider how acceptance can guide you through these transitions. Accepting that some relationships deepen while others reach a natural end allows you to experience each connection as it is, without trying to control it. Acceptance means seeing each relationship as a meaningful part of your journey, one that contributes to your personal growth.

When you accept a relationship's natural direction, whether it is strengthening or gently fading, you create inner peace. Relationships that end still carry value, leaving you with lessons about your own needs, values, and boundaries. By allowing relationships to evolve authentically, you make space for resilience and clarity.

## Moving Forward with Gratitude

Moving forward after a relationship shift can be an opportunity to practise gratitude. Even relationships that end leave us with valuable memories, insights, and personal growth. Gratitude allows you to appreciate what the relationship offered, recognising its full impact on your life.

Change in relationships can be bittersweet, but it often brings profound opportunities for growth. Taking time to reflect on a relationship that has recently shifted can help you see the value it brought to your life. Think of three things you appreciated about this connection – moments that shaped you, lessons that strengthened you, or ways it helped you grow. These insights can guide you in future relationships, allowing you to approach them with greater clarity and intention.

When you embrace acceptance and gratitude, even for relationships that evolve or end, you open yourself to peace and understanding. Each connection, whether brief or enduring, plays a role in shaping who you are. By honouring what it offered, you move forward with resilience, carrying the lessons that bring you closer to your genuine self.

*"Life is a series of natural and spontaneous changes.
Do not resist them; that only creates sorrow. Let reality be reality."*

Lao Tzu
6th-century Ancient Chinese philosopher and writer

> **Navigating Relationship Challenges:**
> **Key Takeaways**
>
> **Honest Conversations Shift Dynamics:** Speaking with clarity and vulnerability transforms relationships, even when the outcomes are unexpected.
>
> **Healthy Detachment:** Learning to detach with love enables individuals to accept change without resentment or blame.
>
> **Embracing Endings:** Recognising when relationships have run their course allows for growth and acceptance rather than lingering pain.
>
> **Visualising Growth:** Imagining how relationships evolve post-conversation helps individuals reframe loss as an opportunity for transformation.

## Eve's Learning

Over time, I began to see relationships through a different lens, like stepping back from a painting to notice the hidden patterns. There were connections I had to walk away from – some weighed down by unresolved conflicts, others frayed by unmet needs, and a few where staying meant silencing who I truly was. Letting go felt like standing on the edge of a cliff, wondering if stepping forward would bring freedom or loss. Life whispering it is time to move on.

Growing up, I lived like a leaf caught in the wind, moving from place to place so much. Other than the cabin on *Anneliese* when I was growing up, where I shared my bed with the sails, I never had my own room. Friendships ended with a new location, a new school, new people. So, I learned to detach before the pain of loss could settle, keeping me safe but distant. At other times, I clung tightly, overextending myself to keep relationships alive, even when they drained me. It was a constant tug-of-war, holding on too tightly or letting go too soon.

Then I saw my children raised in a stable home, with their daily walk to school. There and back along the same paths. They could move through friendships with an ease I had never known, forming connections, letting them go, and opening their hearts again. One day, they might be disappointed, their sadness like a cloud hanging low. Yet, the next day, a new friendship would appear like sunlight breaking through, and their spirits lifted as if they had always known the tides of connection would ebb and flow. Watching them, I began to understand freedom and choice, that relationships are not failures when they end; they are lessons, leaving behind the gifts we need for the next chapter.

For the first time, I realised I did not have to over-perform or cling to relationships that left me feeling unseen. I did not have to carry the weight of holding something together when it was no longer serving either of us. Letting go could be an act of love – for them and for myself. And the beauty of it all was this: no relationship is ever wasted. Even those that bring pain leave behind treasures – moments of joy, lessons learned, and the quiet knowledge of who we are becoming.

Letting go can feel like standing in the rain, cold and uncertain. As the storm passes, there is clarity in the air. Not a defeat; it is a clearing, a way of making space for something new. Every relationship, whether fleeting or lasting, teaches us what we need, what we value, and how to connect.

Looking back, I see my life like a river, shaped by every bend and tributary. Some connections lasted only moments, others a lifetime, but all left their mark. These relationships taught me to compost hurt into wisdom, to see endings as part of the flow. Each one added something to the story of my life, helping me embrace the truth: even when things go wrong, they are never without meaning.

> *"The world is full of ambiguous signs and instructions,*
> *of oblique confessions and misleading signals.*
> *What matters is not just what is said,*
> *but how it is heard."*
>
> A.S. Byatt
> *The Biographer's Tale*, 2000

## Poem: Knowing

*I know what I know.*
*In moments of doubt,*
*A river flows deep within my soul,*
*Etched in my DNA,*
*Speaking the language of survival,*
*The dialect of change.*

*Ever adaptable,*
*Each beat echoes:*
*I can. Da-dump.*
*I can. Da-dump.*
*I can. Da-dump.*

*In the quiet, I pause and see:*
*The steps I have taken,*
*The doors I have walked through,*
*The hills I have climbed,*
*The grass beneath my feet,*
*The sun's warmth on my skin,*
*The light on my brow,*
*The life within me.*

# Part 11

# ANCHORING YOUR TRUE NORTH: LIVING WITH INTEGRITY

*"Our values are the foundations that keep us steady
amid the shifting sands of life;
they guide our words, our choices,
and the way we hold space for others."*

Eve Stanway

## Introduction: Sailing True

When my marriage ended in 2018, something shifted inside me. For the first time, I had to stop and look at how I had been living. For years, I had tried to fit in, meet expectations, and follow a script that was not mine. I spent so much energy on being strong, doing what was "right," and helping others that I felt like I was living someone else's vision of my life.

After everything changed, I noticed the quiet absence of what I wanted. It was almost as if I had been walking down a path that did not belong to me. Slowly, I started to hear my voice beneath the noise of everything I thought I should be doing. There was no dramatic revelation, but in small moments, I finally grasped that living honestly meant making choices that reflected what mattered to me, even if they were demanding.

It was not instant. It took time to figure out what was mine to own – what I truly valued. Even now, the process continues. With each step, the decisions feel more aligned with who I am – not perfect, not always clear, but always true.

Through these pages, we have seen that our values are a compass that guides us, shaping the decisions we make and how we see ourselves. Sometimes, it is easy to forget in the whirlwind of everyday life. Choices get made on autopilot, conversations happen without thinking, and before we know it, we have stepped away from what we know is essential.

When I started to pay attention again – when I let myself pause and noticed what really matters – it made all the difference. Not in grand gestures but rather in the quiet moments of reflection. It is less about having a perfect answer and more about noticing when things feel right. When we reconnect with what we truly value, the way forward becomes clearer, and the noise quiets.

Yet, in the hustle of everyday life, one can easily lose touch with what matters. We can make decisions or have conversations that do not align with who we are or what we value. Often, it is only when we pause and reflect that we realise how far we have drifted from our sense of purpose.

Our values – those quiet yet powerful beliefs that shape us – are meant to guide us, influencing how we act, what we choose, and how we interact with the world. When we reconnect with them, we bring clarity and integrity to our choices.

Exploring understanding and living by your values can transform communication. By recognising what is most important to you, you can bring greater meaning to your interactions and every aspect of your life.

## Why Core Values Matter in Communication

Our core values are the steady constants in our lives, shaping how we navigate challenges, make decisions, and connect with others. When we align our communication with these values, we feel a sense of clarity and purpose. Conversely, when we stray from them, unease often follows – a signal that we are out of alignment with what truly matters.

During my studies in philosophy at the University of Essex, I explored the works of Jean-Paul Sartre and Simone de Beauvoir, two thinkers who examined the profound ways our values shape our lives. Sartre's assertion that *"Man is nothing else but what he makes of himself"* (*Existentialism is a Humanism*, 1946) highlights the importance of intentional choices. He argued that values only gain meaning when expressed through action, and communication is one of the most powerful ways to demonstrate what we stand for.

De Beauvoir's work complements this idea by exploring how our values emerge and evolve through relationships. She wrote, *"It is in the knowledge of the genuine conditions of our lives that we must draw our strength to live and our reason for acting"* (*The Ethics of Ambiguity*, 1947). Her words remind us that reflecting on what truly matters to us provides the foundation for meaningful connection and the courage to engage, even when conversations are challenging.

In everyday life, it can be easy to lose sight of our values. Pressures, distractions, and fear of conflict can pull us away from what feels right. I have experienced this myself – moments where I avoided expressing my thoughts or made decisions to keep the peace, only to feel unsettled afterward. These moments are not failures; they are reminders to pause, reflect, and reconnect with the principles that guide us.

Core values provide a framework for navigating communication with clarity and purpose. When we centre our words and actions around these principles, difficult conversations become opportunities for deeper understanding and mutual respect. Values such as honesty, freedom, curiosity, and understanding offer clarity and focus, especially in moments of uncertainty.

Identifying your core values begins with reflection. Think about the moments in your life when you felt most aligned with yourself and when you felt out of sync. These experiences often reveal what is most important to you. For me, values such as honesty, curiosity, and understanding are touchstones that guide how I interact with others and approach life's challenges.

If you are unsure where to start, the workbook on my website (www.evestanway.co.uk/shoreline) includes an exercise to help you explore and define your values. Once you identify what matters most, it becomes easier to approach communication with clarity and confidence.

Sartre and de Beauvoir's work illustrates that values are not abstract concepts but lived principles that shape how we engage with the world. When your words and actions align with your values, you build trust, cultivate deep connections, and experience a stronger sense of self and belonging. It is through aligning our words and actions with our values that we discover the strength to face life's complexities with purpose and integrity.

*"You are what you do, not what you say you'll do."*

Carl Jung (1875–1961)
Swiss psychiatrist and author, founder of analytical psychology

## Practising Values-Based Communication: A New Perspective

Values-based communication is more than just the words you choose – it is the way you live, the way you express yourself, and the way you shape relationships with authenticity. It is about ensuring that your words, tone, and actions reflect the principles that matter most to you – whether that is freedom, honesty, or integrity. When you align your communication with your values, conversations become less about convincing and more about connecting.

Imagine stepping into a conversation where your voice does not waver, your message is clear, and you feel deeply aligned with your truth. Practising values-based communication means honouring both your needs and the needs of others, fostering understanding rather than conflict. It is about self-awareness – knowing what you stand for, recognising your boundaries, and having the courage to express them.

Values are not abstract ideas; they are the foundation of how you interact with the world. If freedom is a core value, it might mean giving yourself and others the space to speak without fear of judgement. If honesty is important, it means speaking your truth with both clarity and kindness. If authenticity matters to you, it requires the bravery to show up as your real self, even when it feels uncomfortable.

As Victor Hugo once wrote, *"Change your opinions, keep to your principles; change your leaves, keep intact your roots."* (Les Misérables, 1862).

## How Values Shape Action

Consider Mia, a graphic designer whose days were filled with an endless string of "yeses". Yes to extra work. Yes to late nights. Yes to every request her colleagues sent her way. On the surface, she was agreeable and dependable, but beneath that, she was exhausted, drained, and increasingly resentful.

For years, Mia had avoided confrontation, telling herself it was easier to go along with things than to risk disappointing others. But as the stress piled up, she felt disconnected from herself, as though her own needs no longer mattered.

During our sessions, Mia took a step back and reflected on her core values. She realised that freedom, honesty, and creativity were at the heart of what made her thrive. Yet by constantly saying yes to everything, she was saying no to herself.

Equipped with this realisation, she approached her manager with a new perspective. Instead of simply refusing tasks, she framed the conversation around a shared goal – producing high-quality work. She expressed her concerns clearly, explaining that in order to do her best creative work, she needed to set realistic expectations.

The result? Not only did her manager understand, but he respected her for speaking up. By setting boundaries in alignment with her values, Mia did not just protect her energy – she reclaimed her passion for her work.

## Applying This to Your Own Life

We have all had moments where we said yes when we desperately wanted to say no. Often, the fear of letting others down or appearing uncommitted keeps us from speaking our truth. But when you honour your values, something shifts. Decisions become clearer, confidence grows, and self-respect strengthens.

Letting go of obligations that do not serve you is not failure; it is a declaration of what you stand for.

Values-based communication allows you to move through the world with greater clarity, ensuring your words and actions reflect the person you truly want to be. It is not about striving for perfection – it is about showing up with honesty, presence, and intention in every conversation.

## Reflections for You

- When have you agreed to something that went against your true feelings?
- Do your daily choices align with the values that matter most to you?
- How might communicating with more authenticity bring greater clarity and connection into your relationships?

By embracing values-based communication, you create a life where your words, actions, and relationships mirror the person you are at your core. The more you align with your values, the stronger your voice becomes.

> *"Embracing your values is an act of self-respect; it is standing firm in who you are and allowing that truth to shape your relationships."*
>
> Eve Stanway

## Poem: The Compass of My Soul

The poem reflects the journey of aligning with one's values, capturing the spirit of freedom, understanding, curiosity, honesty, and authenticity.

> *Each word I speak, each step I take,*
> *A path unfolds, unmasked, awake.*
> *No longer bound by the need to please,*
> *I turn toward truth, toward inner peace.*
>
> *To live by values takes steady care,*
> *A courage to speak, a strength to share.*
> *Breaking through beliefs not my own,*
> *I find the reins I once disowned.*
>
> *In living this way, whole and brave,*
> *I light a path I once forgave.*
> *For when we stand as who we are,*
> *We guide others home, a steadfast star.*

Take a moment to reflect on *The Compass of My Soul*. Let the words settle in your mind, like ripples on a quiet pond. Which lines resonate deeply with you? Perhaps it is the courage to speak or the strength to share that stirs something within. Or maybe the idea of turning toward truth and inner peace feels like a call to action in your own life.

Think about your journey. Can you recall moments when you felt truly aligned with yourself, following your inner compass? What did that feel like – was it freeing, grounding, or even quietly powerful? Alternatively, are there times when you have said yes when your heart longed to say no, or moments where choices pulled you away from your values?

Consider the beliefs or expectations you might be holding onto. Which of these could you gently release to live more authentically, more fully aligned with who you truly are? It could be the pressure to please others, a fear of disappointment, or an old habit of self-doubt.

You deserve a life where your voice is heard, and your path feels truly your own. Trusting your inner compass can bring a sense of freedom and peace that grows with every step. Take time to write your reflections, treating yourself with kindness. Remember, even the smallest steps can lead to meaningful change.

> *"You have power over your mind – not outside events. Realise this, and you will find strength."*
>
> Marcus Aurelius (121–180)
> Roman Emperor and Stoic philosopher

## Future Conversations Aligned with Values

### Preparing for Values-Based Conversations

Preparing for a values-based conversation starts with clarity. Ask yourself, *What matters most to me in this moment?* Whether it is honesty, kindness, or respect, identifying your core value sets the tone for how you show up. This value becomes your guide, ensuring your words and actions align with what you believe.

Next, think about your intention. How do you want to approach the conversation? If honesty is your focus, prepare to speak openly but thoughtfully. If kindness is your value, consider how your tone and phrasing can reflect care and understanding. By setting an intention, you empower yourself to communicate purposefully and consistently.

Staying grounded in your value keeps you focused on what you can control – your own words, actions, and presence. This means releasing the need to predict or manage the other person's response. Instead, focus on how you want to express yourself, knowing that staying true to your values will bring clarity and strength to the conversation.

Values-based conversations create opportunities for deeper connection and mutual understanding. When you approach them with intention and integrity, you lay the foundation for solutions that honour both yourself and the relationship. This is not about fixing everything at once – it is about showing up as your authentic self and trusting that each step forward matters.

> *"Be yourself – not your idea of what you think somebody else's idea of yourself should be."*
>
> Henry David Thoreau (1817–1862)
> American naturalist, philosopher and author

## The Journey to Living Your Values

Living according to your values is not a task you complete – it is a continuous process of reflection and growth. Think of it as a linear journey made up of key moments and decisions, each one moving you closer to a life aligned with what truly matters. Your values act as stepping stones, guiding you through life's complexities and shaping your choices.

The journey begins by recognising your core values – those principles that define who you are and what you stand for. It continues as you make intentional choices to align your actions with those values. Along the way, relationships may evolve, some deepening as they resonate with your principles, while others shift to reflect the person you are becoming.

Living your values often means stepping outside your comfort zone, embracing change, and allowing growth to unfold naturally. Each step forward strengthens your ability to navigate challenges with clarity and confidence. Though the journey may not always feel linear – progress often comes in cycles – each choice grounded in your values builds resilience and purpose.

Take a moment to reflect on the values that matter most to you. With every decision guided by these principles, you create a life that feels meaningful and true to who you are.

> ### Anchoring Your True North: Key Takeaways
>
> **Values-Based Communication:** Aligning words and actions with core values ensures consistency and authenticity in relationships.
>
> **Discovering Your Compass:** Taking the time to identify what truly matters – those things that resonate deep within – brings a sense of focus and calm, infusing challenging moments with the strength to persevere.
>
> **Future Conversations:** Preparing for ongoing growth helps individuals face future challenges with grace and self-assurance.
>
> **Living Authentically:** Embracing vulnerability and integrity creates freedom to build deeper, more meaningful connections.

## Eve's True North

Looking back, I have come to understand that living according to my values is not something to achieve once and tick off a list. It is a journey – an ever-unfolding process that requires patience, reflection, and self-awareness. There are moments when I slip into old patterns or let life's distractions pull me away, but every time I return to what truly matters, it feels like coming home. With each return, I feel more grounded, clearer, and more connected to my sense of direction.

Living authentically does not mean everything will suddenly fall into place. There will always be moments of doubt, times when it feels hard to stay true to yourself. Yet, these moments are not setbacks – they are opportunities. They invite you to pause, check in with your values, and recalibrate. It is not about achieving perfection; it is about staying connected to what feels right for you and aligning your choices with what matters most.

I have learned, both through my own experiences and from witnessing my clients' journeys, that our values are always with us. They are the living core of who we are, steady and constant, even in life's chaos. Like a quiet flame, they guide us back to ourselves when we feel lost. And the unease we experience when we stray from them is not failure – it is a signal, a reminder that we are out of alignment with what we know to be true.

This journey – my own, my clients', and perhaps yours – is not about searching for answers outside ourselves. The clarity, strength, and direction we seek are already within us. Our values are not rigid rules but gentle guides, evolving as we grow and adapt to life. The more we take time to listen to them, the more peace and purpose we find in our daily choices.

Writing this book has been a powerful reminder of these truths for me, and I hope it is for you as well. The answers you need, the strength you long for, and the clarity you seek – they have always been within you. You do not need to have it all figured out at once. What matters is returning to yourself, moment by moment, and trusting in your ability to live with courage and integrity. You already have everything you need to live fully, authentically, and in alignment with who you truly are.

Embrace this truth, and let it guide you forward.

> *"The ocean has its silent caves,*
> *Deep, quiet, and alone;*
> *Though there be fury on the waves,*
> *Beneath them there is none."*

Nathaniel Hawthorne (1804–1864)
American author and poet

# Conclusion

## REFLECTING ON THE JOURNEY: LOGBOOK REFLECTIONS – CHARTING GROWTH AND WISDOM

*"In facing the unknown within and between us,
we learn that each conversation holds a map –
a guide to the uncharted lands of understanding."*

Eve Stanway

### Poem: The Voyage Within

*Set sail, letting waters draw us deep,
our anchor lifted, heart as compass.
In tides of doubt and unknown shores,
we chart a course that is ours alone, yet carried together.
Words drift like currents, holding and releasing,
whispers of calm, or fierce, wild winds.
Each truth voiced, each silence honoured,
our compass steady in courage found and reclaimed.
From sheltered harbour to the wide open sea,
we become what we dared, what we believed.
A journey shared, the path unfolding,
where steady voices bring us closer, unafraid, unwavering.*

## Eve's Final Moment of Reflection

Here at the shoreline, where the earth meets the infinite sea, we find ourselves standing at the edge of what was and what can be. The waves whisper truths older than memory itself: that we are always in motion, carried by the tides of our fears, our longings, and our courage. It is here, in this liminal space, that our voices rise.

When I began this journey with you, I thought of the silver spoons I cast into the deep as a child – a quiet act of rebellion, a moment of release into the unknown. Those spoons disappeared into the waves, but they left ripples that stretched far beyond what my young eyes could see. This book, too, is a ripple, a call to unearth the silences we carry and transform them into bridges of understanding.

Through these pages, we have journeyed together into the raw, uncharted waters of difficult conversations. We have stood in the discomfort of vulnerability, traced the origins of our silences, and uncovered the courage it takes to speak and to truly listen. The stories – mine, yours, and those I have shared – are fragments of something greater: the collective strength it takes to navigate relationships, to hold boundaries, and to honour our truths.

And now, as we stand at the threshold of this final reflection, I want to leave you with the most enduring lesson the shoreline has taught me. Life, like the sea, is not static. It moves, shifts, and reshapes with every breath. Finding your voice is not about perfection; it is about presence. It is about stepping into the uncertainty, speaking even when your voice trembles, and trusting that connection, though messy and imperfect, is always worth the risk.

So, as you walk forward from here, let these lessons anchor you. When the seas of life grow stormy, remember the tools you have gained: the clarity to know your truth, the courage to communicate it, and the resilience to correct the course when needed. Let your boundaries become your compass and your compassion the wind that fills your sails.

Above all, never forget that your voice matters. Your words carry power. They have the capacity to heal, to connect, and to transform.

Whether whispered in fear, spoken with resolve, or shouted with joy, your voice is a gift the world desperately needs.

This book may end here, but your journey does not. Stand tall at your own shoreline, with the sand beneath your feet and the horizon before you. Take a step into the water. Let your words ripple outward. Speak, not to be perfect, but to be heard.

And remember, you are not alone. Somewhere, someone is waiting for the truth only you can share, the conversation only you can begin.

So, let us part here with a promise: to be braver, clearer, and more connected in our lives. To carry forward the power of our voices and the beauty of our imperfections. To meet the world with the strength of knowing we are enough.

As the tide rises and falls, so too will you. And with every wave, you will find yourself again.

Your voice is the lighthouse, the lifeline, and the bridge. Let it guide you home.

*"The hardest conversations are often with ourselves, yet in those moments, we uncover the bridges that carry us forward, piece by piece."*

Eve Stanway

## Next Steps: Continuing the Practice

As you move forward, here are some simple ways to keep growing and strengthening your communication skills:

1.  **Journal for Reflection**

    After tough conversations, take a moment to jot down your thoughts. What went well? What felt challenging? Journalling helps you understand yourself better, get clear on your boundaries, and make sure you stay true to your values. Over time, it will become easier to navigate conversations with clarity and confidence.

2.  **Listen Actively**

    Active listening is key to meaningful conversations. Practice listening fully without planning your response. Show you are engaged by nodding, making eye contact, and asking questions. When people feel heard, they are more likely to open up, and that creates deeper connections.

3.  **Use the Magic Three**

    Keep the **Magic Three: Clarify, Communicate, and Correct** in mind. Whether you are setting boundaries with a colleague or sharing your needs with a family member, this simple tool helps guide your conversations. With practice, it will become easier to express yourself clearly and handle misunderstandings with ease.

4.  **Build Your Support System**

    Honest communication thrives when you have support. Surround yourself with people who value open dialogue; friends, mentors, or a community. Having others to share with helps you grow and gives you space to practise.

5.  **Set Small Goals**

    Choose one or two things you'd like to work on each month, such as setting boundaries with a family member or listening better at work. Small goals help you stay focused and track your progress. With each step, you'll feel more confident in your communication.

6. **Celebrate Your Progress**

    Every step forward is a win. Celebrate the moments when you set a boundary, stayed calm, or listened with empathy. Communication is a journey, and every small success moves you closer to the authentic conversations you strive for.

To support you, plenty of resources, ideas, prompts, and community are waiting for you on my website. Over time, I will be developing more tools, sharing insights, blogs, workbooks, and additional books on the art of difficult conversations. Sign up for my newsletter to stay updated and continue your journey with me. (www.evestanway.co.uk/shoreline)

Communication is a living practice, and it is okay when words come easily or when silence feels like the better choice. Both are part of your journey. Each small step, each moment of pause, is a meaningful part of your path. With patience and compassion, you will find the language that resonates with your heart, turning your words into bridges that lead to true understanding.

Remember, your voice matters. When you speak with integrity and empathy, you are contributing to a world of deeper connection, even in the most challenging moments.

Thank you for allowing me to walk beside you. May your conversations continue to be brave, honest, and filled with the discovery of who you are.

With warmth and encouragement,

*Eve*

For further guidance, resources, and community, visit: www.evestanway.co.uk

# APPENDICES

The appendices are your toolkit – practical resources designed to support you as you navigate the journey of difficult conversations, set boundaries, and find your voice. These materials offer actionable steps, reflective prompts, and practical guides to help you deepen your understanding and apply the lessons from *Conversations at the Shoreline* to your daily life.

Think of these appendices as a trusted companion. Whether you are preparing for a challenging dialogue, reflecting on your progress, or seeking clarity on key concepts, they are here to guide you. Two key sections included here are:

**Glossary of Terms:** This section clarifies key concepts and introduces the language of intentional communication. It serves as a quick reference to reinforce your understanding and provide the vocabulary needed to navigate conversations with confidence.

**References:** This curated list of books, articles, and online resources aligns with the principles explored in this book. It offers opportunities to expand your knowledge on emotional regulation, relationship dynamics, and communication strategies.

Many additional tools and resources, including downloadable guides, workbooks, and reflective exercises, are available on my website, www.evestanway.co.uk. These digital materials are designed to complement your learning, offering ongoing support as you continue your journey toward more meaningful and effective conversations.

# GLOSSARY OF TERMS

### Using the Glossary

The glossary is a resource to support your journey in understanding and navigating difficult conversations.

### Active Listening

Active listening is the practice of fully engaging in a conversation, focusing on the speaker, acknowledging their words, and responding in ways that show understanding. It involves both verbal and non-verbal cues to help the speaker feel truly heard.

**Example:** Nodding, maintaining eye contact, and asking follow-up questions such as, *"Can you tell me more about that?"* are ways to demonstrate active listening.

### Adverse Childhood Experiences (ACE)

A term referring to potentially traumatic events that occur in childhood (0–17 years), such as abuse, neglect, or household dysfunction (e.g., domestic violence, substance abuse, or parental separation). ACEs can significantly impact a child's development, influencing their mental and physical health into adulthood. Studies show that higher ACE scores are linked to increased risks of anxiety, depression, chronic illness, and difficulties in forming healthy relationships.

**Example:** A client with high ACEs might struggle with trust or emotional regulation in adulthood, often without realising these challenges stem from early experiences.

**Relevance:** Understanding ACEs can help identify patterns and triggers in communication and relationships, creating opportunities for healing and growth.

## Anxiety

A natural emotional response to perceived threats or stress, characterised by feelings of worry, fear, or unease. While anxiety can be situational and adaptive, helping us respond to challenges, it can also become chronic or overwhelming, interfering with daily life and well-being. It may manifest physically (e.g., a racing heart, tension, or nausea), emotionally (e.g., dread or irritability), and cognitively (e.g., overthinking or difficulty concentrating).

**Range of Experiences:**

- **Everyday Anxiety:** Nervousness before a presentation or worry about a specific event.

- **Chronic Anxiety:** Persistent, generalised worry or fear without a clear cause.

- **Situational Anxiety:** Stress tied to a particular environment or trigger, such as social situations.

- **Clinical Anxiety Disorders:** Diagnosed conditions like Generalised Anxiety Disorder (GAD), Panic Disorder, or Social Anxiety Disorder, requiring professional intervention.

**Relevance:** Anxiety often plays a significant role in avoiding difficult conversations. It can amplify fears of judgement, rejection, or conflict, creating barriers to expression. Recognising anxiety as both a natural response and a manageable condition is the first step in navigating emotional waters and reclaiming your voice.

**Tools for Support:** This book provides strategies, such as the **Magic Three Framework** and grounding techniques like the 'anchor word,' to help manage anxiety and approach conversations with greater confidence and clarity.

## Authenticity

Authenticity is expressing oneself openly and honestly, staying true to one's values and beliefs. In communication, authenticity builds trust and connection by showing a willingness to be genuine and vulnerable.

**Example:** Sharing that you feel overwhelmed instead of saying, *"I am fine,"* is an act of authenticity, allowing others to understand your true state.

## Boundaries

Boundaries are personal limits that define acceptable behaviour to protect emotional, mental, and physical well-being. They help maintain self-respect and encourage relationships to thrive on mutual respect and understanding.

**Example:** Setting a boundary with a friend who often drops by unexpectedly might involve saying, *"I need notice before visits to ensure I am available and prepared."*

## Clarify, Communicate, and Correct (The Magic Three)

A three-step framework for expressing needs, setting boundaries, and addressing misunderstandings.

- **Clarify:** Understand your needs and limits before expressing them.
- **Communicate:** Clearly and respectfully convey your boundaries or concerns.
- **Correct:** Gently restate boundaries when needed to ensure they are upheld.

**Example:** If a colleague frequently interrupts you, you might clarify that you need uninterrupted time, communicate this boundary, and, if it continues, remind them of it calmly.

## Conflict Resolution

Conflict resolution involves addressing and resolving disagreements constructively, with a focus on mutual respect and understanding. It requires listening, empathy, and a willingness to understand the other person's perspective.

**Example:** In a work setting, a conflict resolution strategy could involve acknowledging a colleague's concerns and proposing a compromise that respects both parties' needs.

## Depression

A multifaceted condition that affects mood, thoughts, and behaviour, often resulting in persistent feelings of sadness, hopelessness, or disinterest. Depression exists on a spectrum, ranging from temporary low moods to clinical conditions such as Major Depressive Disorder. It may also manifest physically, with symptoms like fatigue, changes in sleep or appetite, and difficulty concentrating.

**Range of Experiences:**

- **Situational Depression:** Feelings of sadness or despair tied to specific life events, such as grief, loss, or major changes.

- **Chronic Low Mood:** Persistent but less severe feelings of sadness or dissatisfaction that can endure over time.

- **Clinical Depression:** A diagnosed condition requiring professional intervention, characterised by ongoing, pervasive symptoms that interfere with daily life.

**Relevance:** Depression often makes difficult conversations seem insurmountable. It can amplify feelings of inadequacy or fear, silencing the voice and discouraging expression. Many people with depression experience a sense of isolation, even when surrounded by others, which deepens the emotional barriers to connection.

**Tools for Support:** This book offers strategies to gently break through the silence that depression creates. Techniques like the **Magic Three Framework** and reflective exercises will help you reconnect with your inner voice and build the confidence to express yourself, one small conversation at a time.

## Emotional Bandwidth

The capacity to process and manage emotions in a given moment or situation. Limited emotional bandwidth can result in difficulty engaging in meaningful conversations or coping with stress.

**Example:** After a long day at work, someone may feel they lack the emotional bandwidth to discuss a sensitive topic with their partner.

**Relevance:** Being mindful of your emotional bandwidth and that of others can help determine the right timing for difficult conversations.

## Emotional Data

Emotional data refers to the valuable insights our emotions provide about our experiences, desires, and boundaries. Emotions serve as indicators, guiding our actions and helping us respond authentically to situations.

**Example:** Feeling resentment toward a friend who frequently cancels plans might indicate a need for reliability, signalling the importance of setting a boundary.

## Emotional Numbing

Emotional numbing is a state of detachment from emotions, often as a protective response to prolonged stress or suppressed feelings. It can reduce emotional pain but also limits joy and connection.

**Example:** Someone who avoids difficult conversations may feel indifferent in situations that usually evoke emotion, making it hard to connect deeply with others.

## Emotional Overload

The state of feeling overwhelmed by intense or prolonged emotions, often leading to difficulty processing or responding effectively. Emotional overload can manifest as physical tension, inability to focus, or emotional outbursts.

**Example:** During a heated argument, feeling emotionally overwhelmed might result in shutting down or reacting impulsively.

**Relevance:** Recognising emotional overload can help you step back, regulate your emotions, and approach the conversation when you feel more balanced.

## Empathy

Empathy is the ability to understand and share another person's feelings. It builds trust and shows care by validating the other person's emotions and experiences.

**Example:** When a friend expresses frustration, responding with, *"I can see why that would be challenging,"* shows empathy and support.

## Empathic Listening

A deeper form of active listening that involves truly putting yourself in the other person's shoes to understand their feelings and perspective. Empathic listening requires both verbal and non-verbal engagement, such as nodding, reflecting emotions, and using validating language.

**Example:** Saying, *"I can sense how frustrating this must be for you,"* demonstrates empathic listening.

**Relevance:** Empathic listening is a powerful tool for de-escalating conflict and building rapport during difficult conversations.

## Healthy Masks

Healthy masks are adaptive behaviours used in social or professional situations to navigate various environments while staying true to one's values. They allow for flexibility without compromising authenticity.

**Example:** Using a "professional mask" in a formal meeting allows someone to stay focused on solutions, even if they feel nervous or uncertain.

## Imposter Syndrome

A persistent feeling of self-doubt and fear of being exposed as a fraud, even when achievements clearly reflect competence. Those with imposter syndrome may attribute success to luck or external factors, struggling to believe they deserve recognition. You might say, *"I feel like I am faking it, and it is only a matter of time before everyone realises I am not as capable as they think. Even when I get praise or achieve something significant, it feels like it does not count because it wasn't truly earned."*

**Example:** In conversations, imposter syndrome can make expressing needs or setting boundaries feel daunting, as if doing so might reveal inadequacy. Recognising these thoughts is the first step toward reframing them with compassion and confidence.

## Internal Conversations

Internal conversations are reflective dialogues we have with ourselves, often involving self-assessment, processing emotions, or preparing for interactions. They help clarify values and goals, providing a foundation for external conversations.

**Example:** Before discussing a boundary with a partner, an internal conversation might help clarify why this boundary matters and how to best express it.

## Internal Triggers

Internal triggers are specific words, actions, or memories that evoke strong emotional responses, often due to past experience. Identifying triggers helps us prepare for and manage reactions thoughtfully.

**Example:** A reminder of a past disagreement might trigger defensiveness, helping someone pause before reacting impulsively.

## Mirroring

Mirroring is the subtle yet powerful act of reflecting another person's emotional state, body language, or tone during a conversation. Rapport, connection, and understanding are often naturally built through this process, which can be conscious or unconscious.

Mirroring serves as a valuable tool in emotional regulation, contributing to balanced conversations. In tense situations, a calm response, rather than mirroring the other person's upset, is more likely to de-escalate the conflict. If someone becomes frustrated or raises their voice, slowing your speech, maintaining steady breathing, and responding in a measured tone can encourage them to regulate their emotions in response.

**Example:** During a tense exchange, your colleague raises their voice and gestures sharply, frustration evident in their body language. Rather than mirroring their agitation, you make a conscious effort to slow your speech, maintain steady eye contact, and speak in a calm, measured tone. Over time, your colleague instinctively follows suit, their voice softening as they subconsciously adjust to the steadier rhythm of the conversation. This shift allows the discussion to return to a more constructive and solution-focused space.

## Non-Verbal Communication

Non-verbal communication includes body language, facial expressions, gestures, and other cues that convey emotions and intentions beyond words. It can add depth to communication by revealing feelings that words may not capture.

**Example:** Crossing arms or avoiding eye contact during a discussion might signal discomfort or defensiveness.

## Repression

An unconscious defence mechanism where distressing memories, thoughts, or emotions are automatically pushed out of conscious awareness, often as a way to protect oneself from psychological discomfort or trauma. Repressed feelings or experiences may resurface indirectly, such as through dreams, behaviours, or physical symptoms, without the individual realising their origin.

**Example:** Someone who experienced a traumatic accident in childhood has no memory of the event as an adult. However, they feel intense fear and unease when riding in cars, without understanding why these feelings arise.

## Rupture and Repair

Rupture and repair refer to the process of addressing and mending relational disconnections. "Rupture" involves a conflict or misunderstanding, while "repair" is the act of acknowledging and healing the relationship through open communication.

**Example:** If a friend feels hurt by something said in a disagreement, repair might involve an apology, clarification, and an honest discussion about intentions.

## Self-Affirmation

Self-affirmation is the practice of recognising and reinforcing one's own worth and strengths. In challenging situations, self-affirmations can bolster confidence and reduce anxiety.

**Example:** Before a high-stakes conversation, reminding yourself, *"I have the right to communicate my needs clearly,"* can reinforce self-worth.

## Self-Esteem

Self-esteem refers to the confidence and satisfaction we have in our abilities, accomplishments, and overall sense of competence. Unlike self-worth, self-esteem is conditional, shaped by external factors, such as success, recognition, and feedback.

**Relevance:** Healthy self-esteem supports a positive outlook and enhances our ability to take on challenges, while low self-esteem can lead to self-doubt and avoidance of opportunities.

**Example:** A person with healthy self-esteem might feel proud of completing a challenging project and use that confidence to tackle future tasks, reinforcing a positive self-image.

## Self-Reflection

Self-reflection is examining one's thoughts, emotions, and actions to gain clarity and insight. It promotes self-awareness, helping us identify growth areas and deepen our understanding of our boundaries and values.

**Example:** After a difficult conversation, self-reflection might reveal areas to improve responses or deepen understanding of personal triggers.

## Self-Worth

Self-worth is the intrinsic value we assign to ourselves, independent of external achievements, approval, or circumstances. It is the deep understanding that we are valuable and deserving of love and respect simply because we exist. Self-worth is unconditional and the foundation of self-esteem.

**Relevance:** Self-worth serves as the foundation for how we treat ourselves and set boundaries in relationships. It influences our ability to advocate for our needs and maintain healthy interactions.

**Example:** A person with strong self-worth can walk away from a toxic relationship, recognising that their well-being is more important than external validation.

## Stonewalling

A communication behaviour where a person withdraws or shuts down during a conversation, often to avoid conflict or manage overwhelming emotions. This can include refusing to engage, giving minimal responses, or physically leaving the discussion. While sometimes unintentional, stonewalling can increase tension and prevent resolution.

**Why It Happens:** Stonewalling is often a defensive response to stress, rooted in feeling emotionally overwhelmed or unable to cope with the conversation. It may also stem from learned behaviours, such as avoiding confrontation to feel safe.

**Impact:** Stonewalling creates barriers to connection and understanding, leaving the other person feeling dismissed, frustrated, or abandoned. Over time, it can weaken trust and intimacy in relationships.

**Relevance:** In difficult conversations, stonewalling is a common challenge to effective communication. Recognising when it happens and understanding its emotional triggers can help both parties move forward more constructively.

**Tools for Support:** The **Magic Three Framework** offers strategies to approach conversations with empathy and patience, breaking through the barriers stonewalling creates and building healthier communication dynamics.

## Suppression

The conscious act of pushing away thoughts, feelings, or desires that are uncomfortable, unwanted, or inappropriate, with the intention of not addressing them in the moment. Unlike repression, suppression involves a deliberate choice to set emotions aside, often temporarily, while remaining aware of their existence.

**Example:** During an important presentation, a person notices feelings of nervousness and decides to set those emotions aside to focus on delivering their message confidently. They are fully aware of their nerves but choose not to dwell on them.

## Triggers

Triggers are situations, words, or behaviours that evoke strong emotional reactions tied to past experience or unresolved issues. Recognising triggers allows us to approach conversations with greater awareness, reducing reactive responses.

**Example:** If being interrupted triggers frustration, recognising it as a trigger helps prepare you to calmly address it when it occurs.

## Validation

Validation is acknowledging and accepting another person's feelings or experiences. It shows that their perspective is heard and valued, even without agreement.

**Example:** Saying, *"I understand that this situation is difficult for you,"* validates the other person's feelings.

## Values Alignment

Values alignment ensures that one's choices and actions reflect core personal values, promoting integrity and authenticity in relationships.

**Example:** If honesty is a core value, aligning with it may involve setting boundaries that encourage transparent communication.

## Vulnerability

To be vulnerable is to be willing to expose your genuine feelings, thoughts, and experiences, despite the potential for judgement or rejection. It builds real relationships based on trust.

**Example:** Sharing feelings of insecurity with a friend instead of masking them, shows vulnerability and encourages mutual understanding.

# REFERENCES

## References in the Text

**Page 8**

Brené Brown, *Daring Greatly: How the Courage to Be Vulnerable Transforms the Way We Live, Love, Parent, and Lead* (Avery, 2012)

**Page 9**

Pete Walker, *The Tao of Fully Feeling: Harvesting the Healing Power of Emotions* (New Harbinger Publications, 2013). Walker highlights the power of processing emotions as a pathway to self-awareness and growth. His practical tools help readers break patterns of avoidance and build emotional resilience.

**Pg 10**

Daniel Goleman, *Emotional Intelligence: Why It Can Matter More Than IQ* (Bloomsbury, 1996)

**Page 13**

Esther Perel, *The State of Affairs: Rethinking Infidelity* (HarperCollins 2017)

**Page 21**

Thomas Moore, *The Eloquence of Silence* (New World Library, 2024). Moore reflects on silence as a space for deep reflection and transformation, viewing it as a powerful element in relationships and inner life.

**Page 25**

Gabor Maté, *The Myth of Normal: Illness, Health & Healing in a Toxic Culture* (Vermilion, 2022). In this profound work, Maté explores the modern world's impact on health and stress. He examines how societal norms contribute to emotional disconnection and offers guidance for reclaiming authentic health.

**Page 26**

Bruno Bettelheim, *The Uses of Enchantment: The Meaning and Importance of Fairy Tales* (Knopf, 1976)

**Pg 27**

Katherine May, *Wintering: The Power of Rest and Retreat in Difficult Times* (Penguin, 2020). May explores the necessity of rest and retreat during life's challenges, offering a thoughtful guide to navigating emotional winters.

Bessel van der Kolk, *The Body Keeps the Score* (Viking, 2014). A groundbreaking exploration of how trauma affects the body and mind, emphasising the importance of healing through awareness and self-care. This book is essential for understanding the deep connection between emotional and physical health.

**Page 35**

Douglas Stone, Bruce Patton, Sheila Heen, *Difficult Conversations: How to Discuss What Matters Most* (Penguin, 1999).

**Page 46**

Alice Miller, *The Drama of the Gifted Child* (Basic Books, 1981). Miller explores the emotional impact of childhood experiences and offers insights for breaking free from limiting family narratives.

## Page 47

Tanya Byron, *Your Child, Your Way* (Michael Joseph, 2007). Byron offers practical, compassionate advice for parenting with confidence and adaptability, focusing on the unique needs of each child.

## Page 50

Maya Angelou, *I Know Why the Caged Bird Sings* (Random House, 1981)

## Page 51

John Bradshaw, *Homecoming* (Little, Brown, 1991). Bradshaw's guide helps people reconnect with their inner child, heal past trauma, and create more emotionally balanced families.

## Page 53

Robert Collier, *The Secret of the Ages: The Master Code to Abundance and Achievement* (Robert Collier Publications, 1926)

## Page 55

Stephen Daldry, Director of *The Hours* (2002). Screenplay by David Hare, based on the novel by Michael Cunningham. Paramount Pictures, Miramax Films.

Gabor Maté, *When the Body Says No: The Cost of Hidden Stress* (Vintage, 2003). Maté delves into how unaddressed emotional stress can manifest in physical illness. His compassionate approach encourages readers to explore the link between emotions and well-being.

## Page 71

Susan David, *Emotional agility: Get Unstuck, Embrace Change and Thrive in Work and Life* (Avery, 2016)

## Page 72

Marshall B. Rosenberg, *Nonviolent Communication: A Language of Life* (Puddle Dancer Press, 2015). Rosenberg provides a framework for empathetic and effective communication, with tools for resolving conflict peacefully.

**Page 91**

Stephen R. Covey, *The 7 Habits of Highly Effective People* (Simon & Schuster, 2020) In this influential book, Covey highlights *Habit 5: Seek First to Understand, Then to Be Understood*, as a cornerstone for empathetic listening and meaningful communication.

**Page 93**

Kerry Hudson, *Lowborn: Growing Up, Getting Away and Returning to Britain's Poorest Towns* (Chatto & Windus, 2019)

**Page 94**

Felitti, V.J., Anda, R.F., Nordenberg, D., Williamson, D.F., Spitz, A.M., Edwards, V., Koss, M.P., and Marks, J.S. (1998). Relationship of childhood abuse and household dysfunction to many of the leading causes of death in adults: The Adverse Childhood Experiences (ACE) Study. *American Journal of Preventive Medicine*, 14(4), pp. 245-258.

**Page 97**

Carl Jung, *Psychological Aspects of the Personality*. In Read, H., Fordham, M. and Adler, G. (eds.), *Collected Works of C.G. Jung: Volume 7*. (Princeton University Press, 1953)

Brené Brown, *The Gifts of Imperfection* (Hazelden Publishing, 2022). Brown encourages readers to embrace vulnerability and self-compassion as strengths, challenging the perfectionism that can stifle growth.

**Page 99**

Carl Rogers, *On Becoming a Person: A Therapist's View of Psychotherapy* (Houghton Mifflin, 1961)

**Page 105**

Ed Tronick, *The Neurobehavioral and Social-Emotional Development of Infants and Children* (Norton, 2007)

## Page 106

Daniel Siegel and Tina Payne Bryson, *The Power of Showing Up: How Parental Presence Shapes Who Our Kids Become and How Their Brains Get Wired* (Ballantine Books, 2020)

## Page 119

Julia Cameron, *The Artist's Way* (Souvenir Press, 2020). A guide to unlocking creativity through journalling and self-reflection, Cameron's exercises encourage personal exploration and growth.

## Page 148

Steve Peters, *The Chimp Paradox: The Mind Management Programme to Help You Achieve Success, Confidence, and Happiness* (Vermilion, 2012)

## Page 151

Viktor Frankl, *Man's Search for Meaning* (Rider, 2004)

## Page 175

John Gottman and Nan Silver, *The Seven Principles for Making Marriage Work* (Three Rivers Press, 1999). This classic guide provides research-based strategies for creating healthier relationships and managing conflict with emotional insight.

## Page 216

Lewis Carroll, *Alice's Adventures in Wonderland* (Macmillan, 1865)

Shahida Arabi, *The Highly Sensitive Person's Guide to Dealing with Toxic People: How to Reclaim Your Power from Narcissists and Other Manipulators* (New Harbinger Publications 2020)

## Page 221

Nicole LePera, *How to do the work: Recognize your patterns, heal from your past, and create yourself* (Harper Wave, 2021)

**Page 229**

Karen Bonnell, *The Co-Parenting Handbook: Raising Well-Adjusted and Resilient Kids from Little Ones to Young Adults Through Divorce or Separation* (Sasquatch Books, 2017)

**Page 232**

Isolina Ricci, *Mom's House, Dad's House: Making Two Homes for Your Child* (Simon & Schuster, 2006)

**Page 235**

Flavia Weedn, *Forever* (Blue Mountain Arts, 1994). Weedn reflects on love, loss, and the enduring impact of relationships, capturing the beauty and complexity of human connection.

**Page 249**

Jean-Paul Sartre, *Existentialism is a Humanism*. Translated by C. Macomber (Yale University Press 2007) (Original work in French 1946)

Simone De Beauvoir, *The Ethics of Ambiguity*. Translated by B. Frechtman (Citadel Press, 1976) (Original work in French 1947)

# Further Reading

Tara Brach, *Radical Acceptance: Awakening the Love That Heals Fear and Shame* (Rider, 2003)

Brach introduces mindfulness and self-compassion as transformative tools for managing anxiety and addressing fear or shame with kindness.

Dr Sue Johnson, *Hold Me Tight: Seven Conversations for a Lifetime of Love* (Little, Brown, 2008)

Johnson offers techniques for building emotional closeness and resolving conflicts, rooted in the science of attachment.

# References

Amir Levine and Rachel Heller, *Attached: The New Science of Adult Attachment* (TarcherPerigee, 2010)

This book explains how attachment styles influence relationships and provides practical advice for improving relational dynamics.

Esther Perel, *Mating in Captivity: Unlocking Erotic Intelligence* (Harper, 2006)

Perel explores intimacy and desire in long-term relationships, offering thought-provoking insights on connection and communication.

Nedra Glover Tawwab, *Set Boundaries, Find Peace: A Guide to Reclaiming Yourself* (Piatkus, 2021)

Tawwab's actionable strategies for setting boundaries offer tools for reducing stress and creating healthier, more balanced relationships.

Don Miguel Ruiz, *The Four Agreements: A Practical Guide to Personal Freedom* (Amber-Allen Publishing, 2018)

Ruiz introduces four principles for personal freedom, including being impeccable with your word and avoiding assumptions, which resonate with themes of self-respect and intentional communication.

Max Ehrmann, *Desiderata* (Crown, 1972)

Ehrmann's timeless prose poem inspires readers to live with grace and equanimity, offering guidance for balanced and thoughtful living.

Tara Westover, *Educated* (Random House, 2018)

A moving memoir about resilience and self-discovery, Westover recounts her journey from an isolated, strict upbringing to earning a PhD. Her story highlights the power of education, self-awareness, and reclaiming one's voice.

Pete Walker, *Complex PTSD: From Surviving to Thriving. A Guide and Map for Recovering from Childhood Trauma* (CreateSpace Independent Publishing Platform, 2013)

Jess Lair, *I Ain't Much Baby: But I'm All I've Got* (Hawthorn Books, 1972)

This work delves into themes of self-discovery and personal growth, offering insights that resonate with the broader philosophy of respecting individuality, including in the context of children.

Lair's philosophy often focused on treating people, particularly children, with respect and empathy, encouraging a nurturing environment where individuals could grow and flourish. His famous quote, *"Children are not things to be moulded, but are people to be unfolded,"* underscores his belief in recognising the inherent individuality of children and allowing their personalities and talents to develop naturally, rather than imposing rigid expectations on them.

Through his books and lectures, Lair influenced not only parents but also educators and professionals who sought a more compassionate approach to human development and interaction.

## Websites

**greatergood.berkeley.edu**

Greater Good Science Center (University of California, Berkeley)

A hub for articles, videos, and podcasts on empathy, mindfulness, resilience, and emotional intelligence. These resources complement the themes of self-awareness and emotional growth explored in *Conversations at the Shoreline*.

**psychologytoday.com**

Psychology Today features accessible articles on boundaries, communication skills, and relationship dynamics. Practical tips and evidence-based insights make this a go-to resource for personal development.

## mindful.org

Mindful.org provides resources on mindfulness and stress management. Their articles on grounding exercises and breathing techniques align with the emotional regulation strategies highlighted in this book.

## gottman.com/blog

Based on John Gottman's research, this blog offers insights into managing conflict, building trust, and understanding emotional needs. A valuable resource for deepening your understanding of relationship dynamics.

## ted.com

TED Talks offer powerful presentations on communication, vulnerability, and emotional intelligence. Talks by Brené Brown, Susan David, and Esther Perel provide inspiration and actionable advice for improving relationships.

# Podcasts

## Unlocking Us with Brené Brown

Brené Brown dives into themes of courage, vulnerability, and empathy. Featuring expert interviews and personal reflections, this podcast offers practical advice for navigating relationships and building emotional resilience.

## Where Should We Begin? with Esther Perel

Therapist Esther Perel takes listeners into live counselling sessions, offering insights into communication, relationships, and conflict resolution. This podcast provides real-life applications of the techniques discussed in *Conversations at the Shoreline*.

### On Being with Krista Tippett

Krista Tippett's podcast explores the essence of being human, with episodes on mindfulness, kindness, and active listening. A thought-provoking resource for anyone seeking to deepen their emotional awareness and communication skills.

### The Science of Happiness (Greater Good Science Center)

Produced by the Greater Good Science Center, this podcast offers science-backed strategies for enhancing happiness and resilience. Each episode features practical tips that align with the book's emotional regulation techniques.

## Books & People Mentioned in Passing

Louisa M Alcott, *Little Women* (Robert Brothers, 1869)

*Bruce Lee: Artist of Life*, edited by John Little (Black Belt Communications, 2001)

Ayn Rand, *Atlas Shrugged* (Random House, 1957)

Isabel Allende, *The Sum of Our Days* (HarperCollins, 2007)

Rollo May, *The Courage to Create* (W. W. Norton & Company, 1975)

Martin Luther King, Jr., *A Testament of Hope* (HarperCollins, 1986)

François de La Rochefoucauld, *Maxims* (1655)

Oscar Wilde, *The Soul of Man Under Socialism* (1891)

Alan Lakein (1932–2024), American author and time management professional

Henri Nouwen, *Out of Solitude* (Ave Maria Press, 1994)

Katherine Mannix, *Listen: How to find the words for tender conversations* (William Collins, 2021)

T.S. Eliot, *Little Giddings: Four Quartets* (Faber and Faber, 1942)

# References

Dan Millman, *Way of the Peaceful Warrior* (1999)

Rudyard Kipling, *If*, in *Rewards and Fairies* (Doubleday, 1910)

Josiah Gilbert Holland (1819–1881), American novelist, biographer and mentor

Mary Flannery O'Connor, *A Good Man is Hard to Find*, in *Modern Writing 1* (1953)

Elizabeth Gilbert, *Committed: A Skeptic Makes Peace with Marriage* (Bloomsbury, 2010)

Elizabeth Gilbert, *Big Magic: Creative Living Beyond Fear* (Bloomsbury, 2016)

Sir Richard Branson, *Screw It, Let's Do It: Lessons in Life and Business* (Virgin Books, 2006)

Dr Becky Kennedy, *Good Inside* (Harper Wave, 2022)

Margaret Atwood, *Selected Poems II: 1976-1986* (1987)

Alan Watts (1915–1973), English writer and Zen philosopher

A.S. Byatt, *Possession: A Romance* (1990)

Carl Jung, *Modern Man in Search of a Soul* (1933)

Marcus Aurelius, *Meditations* (Penguin Classics, 2006)

Henry Thoreau, *Walden* (1854)

Lord Byron, *Don Juan* (1823)

Victor Hugo, *Les Misérables*. Translated by N. Denny (Penguin Classics, 1982) (Original work in French pub 1862)

Libby Purves, *How Not to Be a Perfect Mother* (William Heinemann Ltd, 1986)

Haim G. Ginott, *Between Parent and Child* (Macmillan, 1965)

Becky Kennedy, *Good Inside: A Guide to Becoming the Parent You Want to Be* (Harper Wave, 2002)

A.S. Byatt, *The Biographer's Tale* (Chatto & Windus, 2000)

Robert Jordan, *The Fires of Heaven* (Tor Books, 1993)

John Dewey, *How We Think* (DC Heath, 1933)

Nathaniel Hawthorn, *The Ocean* (The Salem Gazette, 1825)

# POSTSCRIPT

## Continue Your Journey: The Conversations at the Shoreline Course

Let me introduce you to my six-module course designed to seamlessly guide readers toward deeper learning and application of the book's concepts.

Navigating difficult conversations is not just about knowing what to say – it is about feeling confident enough to say it. This book has given you the tools to explore and transform the way you communicate, but real change comes from practice. That is why I have created **Conversations at the Shoreline: A Six-Module Guided Course** – an immersive learning experience designed to help you put these skills into action.

This course expands on the core principles of the book, offering practical exercises, guided reflections, and real-world strategies to help you master the art of difficult conversations. Whether you are seeking clarity in relationships, setting boundaries, or finding your voice after years of silence, this programme will support you every step of the way.

## What You Will Learn

Over six modules, you will gain the skills to navigate difficult conversations with confidence, clarity, and purpose.

### Module 1: Understanding Your Voice

- Recognise the impact of past experiences on your communication style
- Identify the fears and limiting beliefs that keep you silent
- Develop a deeper awareness of your emotional triggers

### Module 2: The Foundations of Difficult Conversations

- Understand why some conversations feel harder than others
- Learn the **Magic Three Framework: Clarify, Communicate, and Correct**
- Develop techniques to manage anxiety and emotional overwhelm

### Module 3: Setting Boundaries with Strength and Compassion

- Learn how to express your needs without guilt or apology
- Develop responses for when others resist or push back
- Practice scripts and strategies for real-world boundary setting

### Module 4: Navigating High-Stakes Conversations

- How to stay calm and present in difficult moments
- Managing accusations, deflections, and emotional shutdowns
- How to repair conversations that go wrong

### Module 5: Speaking So You Are Heard

- The psychology of effective communication – why some words land, and others do not
- Recognising defensive responses and how to work with them

- How to frame conversations to encourage understanding and trust

**Module 6: Moving Forward with Confidence**

- Creating a long-term strategy for handling difficult conversations
- Recognising when a conversation is not worth having
- How to maintain healthy communication habits for life

## How It Works

Each module includes:

- ✓ **Video lessons** breaking down key concepts
- ✓ **Downloadable workbooks** with exercises and guided reflections
- ✓ **Real-life case studies** to apply techniques in context
- ✓ **Live Q&A sessions** where you can ask questions and receive personalised guidance

You will have lifetime access to all materials, allowing you to move at your own pace and revisit any lessons whenever needed.

## Join the Course Today

If you are ready to take your learning deeper and transform the way you communicate, sign up now to access the full course. Visit www.evestanway.co.uk/shoreline-course or scan the QR code below to get started.

**Exclusive Offer:** As a reader of *Conversations at the Shoreline*, you receive an exclusive discount on enrolment. Use the code SHORELINE25 at checkout.

**Because every conversation has the power to change the course of your life. Let's navigate them together.**

# ACKNOWLEDGEMENTS

*"The universe buries strange jewels deep within us all, and then stands back to see if we can find them."*

Elizabeth Gilbert
American author and journalist

Writing this book has been a journey of courage – one that I could not have undertaken alone. While writing may be a solitary act, the strength to persist, to push through doubt, and to shape raw thoughts into something meaningful has come from the unwavering support of so many people. Each of you has, in some way, helped bring this book to life, and I am deeply grateful.

To my children, Michael and Lucy – this book belongs to you as much as it does to me. Your patience and steadfast belief in me have carried me through long nights and early mornings. You have tolerated my distractions, forgiven my absences, and given me the strength to keep going. You are my favourite human beings.

To my clients – you are at the heart of this book. Your courage in navigating life's most difficult conversations has deepened my understanding of what it means to speak, to listen, and to be truly heard. Thank you for trusting me with your stories and reminding me, time and again, of the power of honest communication.

To my friends, who have held me up, cheered me on, and kept me sane – Andrea Kampta, for your unwavering encouragement and those unforgettable glasses of Prosecco in the hot tub as we unravelled ideas for this book. Estelle Ross, whose strength and determination lifted me each time I stumbled. Tracy Connellan, for your daily check-ins, boundless motivation, and much-needed pub debriefs filled with laughter. You three have been my compass, reminding me where true support lies.

To Dominic Lavington, for the beautiful pen and the loving but firm instruction to *"Just get on with it, you can do this."*

To Steve Maunder, Sarab Rihal, Miguel McKenzie, Rose Millard, Caroline Westcote-White and all the Larkswood Mums (Sue, Katie, Polly and Angie), for keeping me going when I most needed it. Celebrating the wins and comforting the losses.

To those who have encouraged me along the way – JB, GL, SY, JM, JH, FC, MH, JR, AC, SD, TB, JC, SW, WM, LE, and so many more – your voices have shaped this work in ways you may never fully realise.

To my publishing team at Book Brilliance Publishing – Brenda Dempsey, Olivia Eisinger, and Zara Thatcher – thank you for believing in this book and in me. Your expertise, patience, and unwavering support have helped refine this work into something I hope will truly serve those who need it.

To my friends and consummate professionals: Mitch Herber of Catalyst Design, for your superb work in crafting my brand logo; Matt Risley of EppTech, for bringing my website to life; Elliott Frisby and the team at Monkeynut Audiobooks & Sound, for your professionalism in producing the videos for my courses and the audio version of this book.

To Nicola Rowley and Anna Foxx at NJRPR – your insight and expertise in PR and media have made all the difference. Thank you for your dedication, your guidance, and for ensuring the messages in this book reach those who need it most.

To my beautiful team – Stacey Keen from Keen2Assist, my patient, kind, and extraordinary PA, whose wisdom, steady presence, and unwavering support have been invaluable. Sarah Brand of OpsWiz, my operational manager, for keeping everything on track and stepping in when the technical details threatened to overwhelm me. And to Estelle, once again, for your meticulous beta reading and your invaluable contributions to the modules and workbooks that complement this book and my courses. Your insight has been essential in shaping these resources into something truly meaningful.

To my beta readers, Suzanne Heywood, Gillian Layhe, and Walter Nowlan – your sharp eyes, thoughtful feedback, and attention to detail have strengthened this book in ways I could not have done alone. Thank you for your generosity, patience, and care.

And finally, to you – the reader. This book is for you. Whether you are learning to set boundaries, finding the courage to speak, or navigating the hardest of conversations, know that you are not alone. Even when your voice trembles and your knees shake, speaking your truth is an act of bravery. I salute you.

**Thank you.**

*Eve*

# ABOUT EVE

## Book Eve as a Speaker

### Transforming Conversations, Strengthening Connections

Eve Stanway is an internationally recognised therapist, coach, and speaker, specialising in communication, emotional intelligence, and relationship dynamics. With over 25 years of experience in psychotherapy and coaching, she has helped individuals, families, and professionals navigate life's most difficult conversations.

Eve's expertise has been featured in *Grazia*, *The Metro*, *Top Sante/Platinum*, and other major publications. She is a sought-after keynote speaker, podcast guest, and media commentator, known for her insightful, engaging, and deeply practical approach to communication and human connection.

## Speaking Topics

Eve speaks on a range of subjects related to emotional resilience, communication, and relationships. Below are her key topics:

1. **The Power of Difficult Conversations**

- Why we avoid difficult conversations – and how to have them anyway

- Tools to communicate with confidence, clarity, and emotional intelligence

- How open dialogue strengthens relationships, even in moments of conflict

2. **Adverse Childhood Experiences: Supporting Children Through Family Turmoil**

- The lifelong impact of childhood adversity and emotional suppression

- How parents can minimise stress and uncertainty during separation or family conflict

- Ways to build children's resilience, security, and emotional intelligence.

3. **Supporting Fathers Through Separation: Reducing Conflict & Strengthening Parenting**

- Why fathers are often overlooked in conversations about family breakdowns

- How men can remain present, emotionally available, and supportive parents post-separation

- Strategies to co-parent effectively and reduce long-term conflict for the sake of children

4. **Boundaries in Relationships: Holding Space Without Losing Yourself**

- How to set and hold boundaries with confidence, clarity, and compassion
- The difference between boundaries, control, and ultimatums
- Strategies for responding when others resist or push back against your boundaries

5. **Emotional Intelligence & Resilience in Leadership**

- Why emotional intelligence is the key to strong leadership and professional success
- How to navigate high-pressure conversations with emotional control
- The neuroscience of stress, communication, and decision-making

6. **The Psychology of Silence: Why We Struggle to Speak Up**

- How early experiences shape our ability to express emotions and needs
- The physiological impact of suppressing emotions – and how to break free
- How to find your voice and communicate your needs without fear or guilt

## Booking and Enquiries

Eve is available for:

- ✓ Keynote speeches at conferences and summits
- ✓ Panel discussions and expert commentary
- ✓ Corporate training and workshops on communication, leadership, and emotional intelligence

- ✓ Podcast interviews and media appearances
- ✓ TV and radio commentary on relationships, resilience, and human behaviour

To enquire about booking Eve for a speaking engagement, podcast, interview, or expert commentary, please email: eve@evestanway.co.uk

## Media Pack and Showreel

For Eve's speaker profile, media appearances, testimonials, and video clips, download her Media Pack and Showreel, available at www.evestanway.co.uk

## Why Book Eve?

- ✓ Expertise: Over 25 years of professional experience in communication, relationships, and psychology.
- ✓ Engaging Delivery: Thought-provoking, relatable, and emotionally compelling presentations.
- ✓ Customised Talks: Every event is tailored to the audience's specific needs and challenges.
- ✓ Media-Trained: Skilled in delivering clear, insightful, and impactful commentary across TV, radio, and podcasts.

Secure your date today – visit www.evestanway.co.uk or email eve@evestanway.co.uk

# About Eve

Nicky Bamber Photography

eve@evestanway.co.uk

www.evestanway.co.uk

www.linkedin.com/in/evestanway

www.facebook.com/evestanway

www.instagram.com/evestanway

www.youtube.com/@Evestanway